The Consequences of Nuclear Proliferation: Lessons from South Asia

BCSIA Studies in International Security
Published by The MIT Press

Michael E. Brown, Sean M. Lynn-Jones, and Steven E. Miller, series editors
Karen Motley, executive editor
Belfer Center for Science and International Affairs (BCSIA)
John F. Kennedy School of Government, Harvard University

Allison, Graham T., Owen R. Coté, Jr., Richard A. Falkenrath, and Steven E. Miller, *Avoiding Nuclear Anarchy: Containing the Threat of Loose Russian Nuclear Weapons and Fissile Material* (1996)

Allison, Graham T., and Kalypso Nicolaïdis, eds., *The Greek Paradox: Promise vs. Performance* (1996)

Arbatov, Alexei, Abram Chayes, Antonia Handler Chayes, and Lara Olson, eds., *Managing Conflict in the Former Soviet Union: Russian and American Perspectives* (1997)

Blackwill, Robert D., and Michael Stürmer, eds., *Allies Divided: Transatlantic Policies for the Greater Middle East* (1997)

Brown, Michael E., ed., *The International Dimensions of Social Conflict* (1996)

Brown, Michael E., and Šumit Ganguly, eds., *Government Policies and Ethnic Relations in Asia and the Pacific* (1997)

Elman, Miriam Fendius, ed., *Paths to Peace: Is Democracy the Answer?* (1997)

Falkenrath, Richard A., *Shaping Europe's Military Order: The Origins and Consequences of the CFE Treaty* (1994)

Feldman, Shai, *Nuclear Weapons and Arms Control in the Middle East* (1996)

Forsberg, Randall, ed., *The Arms Production Dilemma: Contraction and Restraint in the World Combat Aircraft Industry* (1994)

Hagerty, Devin T., *The Consequences of Nuclear Proliferation: Lessons from South Asia* (1998)

Kokoshin, Andrei A., *Soviet Strategic Thought, 1917–91* (1998)

Shields, John M., and William C. Potter, eds., *Dismantling the Cold War: U.S. and NIS Perspectives on the Nunn-Lugar Cooperative Threat Reduction Program* (1997)

The Consequences of Nuclear Proliferation: Lessons from South Asia

Devin T. Hagerty

BCSIA Studies in International Security

The MIT Press
Cambridge, Massachusetts
London, England

Library of Congress Cataloging-in-Publication Data

Hagerty, Devin T.
The consequences of nuclear proliferation: lessons from South Asia / Devin T. Hagerty.
p.   cm.—(BCSIA studies in international security)
Includes bibliographical references and index.
ISBN 0-262-58161-2 (pbk.: alk. paper)
1. Nuclear weapons—Government policy—India—History. 2. Nuclear weapons—
Government policy—Pakistan—History. 3. India—Foreign relations—Pakistan.
4. Pakistan—Foreign relations—India. I. Title. II. Series.
UA840.H26   1998
355.02′17′0954—dc21   98-3463
                                                                                                                        CIP

10 9 8 7 6 5 4 3 2 1
Printed in the United States of America

For Herb Hagerty

Contents

List of Maps   ix

List of Tables   xi

Author's Note   **xvi**

Acknowledgments   xvii

Introduction   1

Chapter 1   Debating the Consequences of Nuclear Proliferation   9

Chapter 2   Opaque Proliferation, Existential Deterrence, and Nuclear Weapon Stability   39

Chapter 3   The India-Pakistan Security Rivalry   63

Chapter 4   Nuclear Weapons and the 1986–87 Brasstacks Crisis   91

Chapter 5   The Legacy of Brasstacks: South Asian Proliferation Dynamics, 1987–90   117

Chapter 6   Nuclear Weapons and the 1990 Kashmir Crisis   133

Chapter 7   Lessons and Implications   171

Index   197

About the Belfer Center for Science and International Affairs   206

List of Maps

The Subcontinent   xiii

India-Pakistan Border Areas
and the 1986–87 Brasstacks Crisis   xiv

India-Pakistan Border Areas
and the 1990 Kashmir Crisis   xv

List of Tables

Preventive War Scenarios   35

The Relationship Between Proliferation and Deterrence Types   51

The Consequences of Nuclear Proliferation: Theory and   183
South Asian Evidence

The Impact of Opacity   189

The Subcontinent

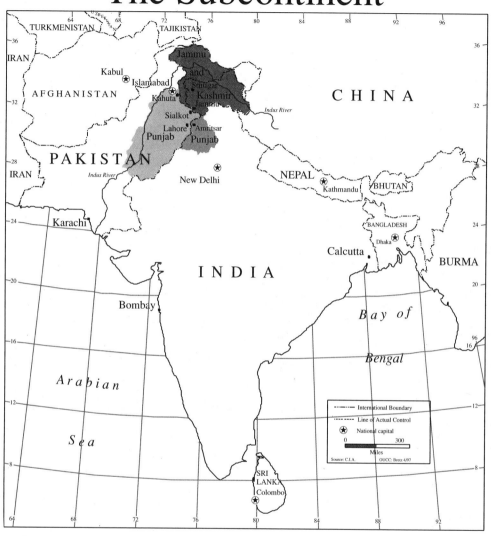

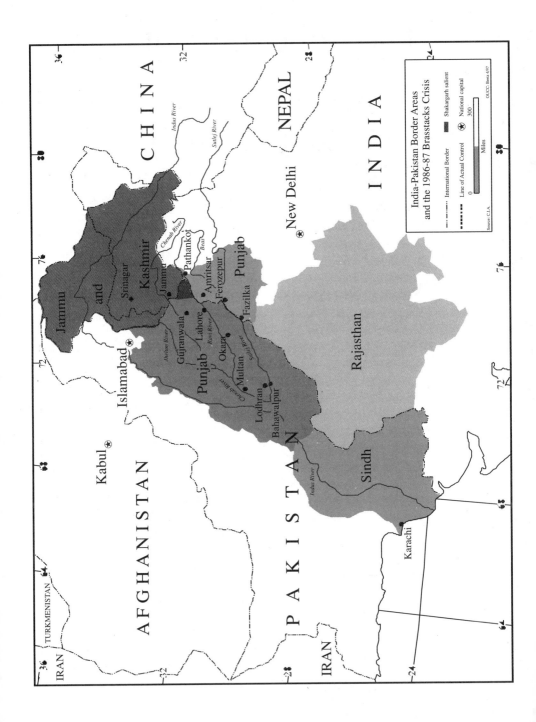

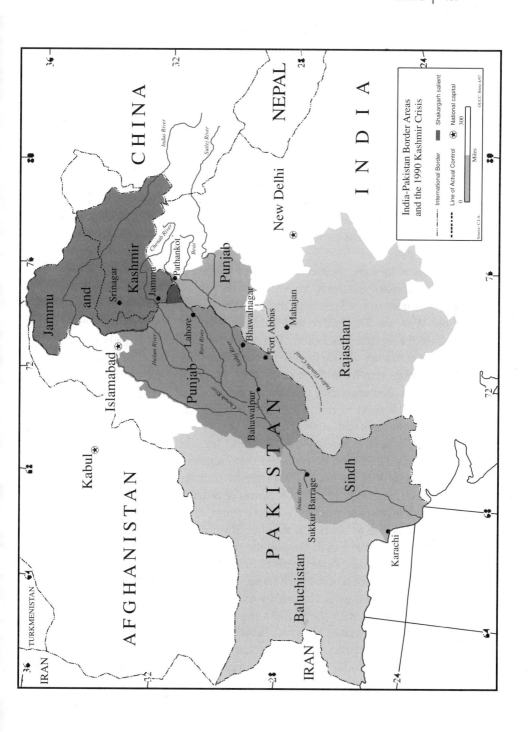

India-Pakistan Border Areas
and the 1990 Kashmir Crisis

Author's Note

I wrote this book prior to the Indian and Pakistani nuclear tests of mid-1998. Although the book's main empirical focus is the period between late 1986 and mid-1990, it seems advisable to suggest briefly how the momentous events of 1998 influence certain of my conclusions.

My general argument—that Indian and Pakistani nuclear weapon capabilities deter war in South Asia—remains intact. Despite the fact that the rest of the world now knows more about those capabilities, in a sense we are simply catching up with Indian and Pakistani perceptions. New Delhi and Islamabad have long believed each other to be nuclear weapon–capable; their recent tests have confirmed these mutual perceptions, rather than created new ones. At this point in time, I have no reason to believe that nuclear deterrence in South Asia is any less robust than it was when I completed the book; indeed, it may be more so.

A secondary conclusion concerns the persistence of the opaque pattern of nuclear proliferation. My analysis suggests that the incentives for countries to nuclearize in this fashion are still strong in the post–Cold War era. The Indian and Pakistani nuclear tests would seem to cast doubt on that conclusion. But recall that India had already tested a nuclear device in 1974, and the prototypical opaque proliferant—Israel—may also have done so in 1979. We know now that Pakistan, too, has a demonstrable nuclear explosive capability. Although this suggests the need to refine the concept of opacity, it does not change my view that it is still a useful one.

A third issue concerns the prospects for nuclear arms control in South Asia. Here I can do no better than to refer readers directly to the last paragraph of the book. Although the Indian and Pakistani nuclear tests have generated predictable howls of outrage in the capitals of the so-called legitimate nuclear weapon states, these governments have only themselves to blame for the sluggish progress of denuclearization since the Cold War's end. Despite the passage of nearly a decade since the Berlin Wall came down, each of these countries continues to rely on nuclear deterrence to safeguard its security. This is so despite the enormous amount of intellectual energy that has been expended in an effort to come to grips with the world's post–Cold War nuclear dangers. If leaders in Washington, Moscow, Beijing, Paris, and London had taken seriously the numerous studies that arms controllers have written over the last decade, India and Pakistan might not have felt compelled to demonstrate their own nuclear prowess. The powers that be should revisit these studies: Shrill rhetoric is no substitute for honest analysis.

Acknowledgments

Many people and organizations helped me in writing this book. Four scholars deserve special thanks for contributions too numerous to list here. Two are mentors, Avery Goldstein of the University of Pennsylvania and Steve Cohen of the University of Illinois at Urbana-Champaign. The other two are good friends from Penn, Jim Hentz and Rey Koslowski. I am also grateful to Sean Lynn-Jones for his incisive editorial comments, and to Hubert Bloemer of Ohio University for creating the maps. For support of all kinds, from moral to financial, thanks also to Craig Baxter, Calli Berg, Jim Blight, Dan Deudney, Ben Frankel, Šumit Ganguly, Neil Joeck, Hank Kennedy, janet Lang, Pete Lavoy, Jack Nagel, and Ollie Williams.

As for organizations, one has been particularly helpful. The Program in Arms Control, Disarmament, and International Security (ACDIS) at the University of Illinois provided me with a stimulating intellectual home from August 1995 to June 1997. Steve Cohen, Merrily Shaw, and Mary Anderson tend to make ACDIS researchers feel as if they have stumbled onto the holy grail. There is, quite simply, no better place in the United States to write a book on South Asian security issues. While I was at ACDIS, my research was supported by the U.S. Department of Energy, Argonne National Laboratory sub-contract no. 941452401. For additional research support, I am also grateful to the John M. Olin Institute for Strategic Studies at Harvard University's Center for International Affairs, the Jennings Randolph Program for International Peace at the United States Institute of Peace, and the American Institute of Pakistan Studies.

Special mention should also be made of several data sources that were especially useful in my empirical examination of South Asian nuclear issues. In writing Chapter 4, I relied heavily on *Brasstacks and Beyond: Perception and Management of Crisis in South Asia*, an ACDIS/ Illinois monograph. This was the product of an ambitious oral history project comprising interviews with senior policymakers and military officers in India, Pakistan, and the United States. In writing Chapter 6, I profited from the Henry L. Stimson Center's *Conflict Prevention and Confidence-Building Measures in South Asia: The 1990 Crisis*. This was a long transcript of discussions between Indian, Pakistani, and U.S. leaders who had been involved in the crisis. Both of these works were invaluable sources of information on sensitive topics.

I would also like to note the work of Sandy Spector at the Carnegie Endowment for International Peace in Washington, D.C. Without his series on trends in nuclear proliferation, filling in the periods before, between, and after the case studies would have required much more work on my part. Spector and his associates have given scholars both a valuable source of information and a useful guide to other materials. The National Security Archive's *Nuclear Nonproliferation, 1949–1990*, a set of declassified U.S. government documents, was useful, too. Unless otherwise noted, all U.S. executive branch documents cited in the notes were found at the archive. I am also grateful to the U.S., Indian, and Pakistani decision-makers who consented to being interviewed. Those who preferred to remain anonymous know who they are, and those who did not are cited in the notes.

Throughout this project, I have been blessed with the love and support of family. To Herb and Ann Hagerty, David and Cynthia Patriquin, and Shirley Hagerty: thanks for being there when I needed you, which was often. Most of all, I would like to thank my wife, Wendy Patriquin, for her seemingly infinite reserve of good-natured patience and understanding. If you have ever been someone's copilot during his maiden flight, you probably have some idea of what spouses go through with first-time book writers.

Devin T. Hagerty
Champaign, Illinois, June 1997

Introduction

Heat not a furnace for your foe so hot
That it do singe yourself . . .
—The Duke of Norfolk, *King Henry VIII*

This study examines the consequences of nuclear proliferation in South Asia. It does so by assessing the impact of maturing nuclear weapon capabilities on Indo-Pakistani relations from the early 1980s to the present, especially during crises in 1986–87 and 1990. In turn, by providing a window into Indian and Pakistani behavior in the "shadow of mutual destruction,"[1] these crises enhance our more general understanding of the influence that nuclear weapons have on world politics.

Theoretical Issues in the Study of Proliferation's Effects

My empirical analysis of South Asia's nuclear dynamics is conceptually framed by several important controversies in the study of nuclear proliferation. First, it is embedded in a lively debate over the effects of proliferation. The orthodox position in this debate, which I call the *logic of nonproliferation*, considers the spread of nuclear weapons to be extremely dangerous: more weapons in more hands increase the likelihood of future nuclear explosions, whether intended or not. In contrast, the *logic of nuclear deterrence* suggests that proliferation is stabilizing: nuclear weapons have deterred war between their possessors

---

1. This term is borrowed from Robert Jervis, *The Meaning of the Nuclear Revolution: Statecraft and the Prospect of Armageddon* (Ithaca, N.Y.: Cornell University Press, 1989), p. 79.

and will continue to do so.[2] My goal is not to resolve this debate, but rather to further it by adding to our cumulative understanding of how nuclear weapons have transformed international relations. For too long, arguments over proliferation's consequences were stalled in a quicksand of irresolvable deductive squabbles; when scholars did make reference to real-world nuclear dynamics, they drew almost exclusively from the experience of the U.S.-Soviet arms race, thereby neglecting the distinctive historical, political, cultural, and geographical circumstances that shape nuclear behavior in other contexts. Of late, this gap has been partially filled by several analyses of Middle Eastern nuclear dynamics.[3] This study extends that trend to another so-called conflict-prone region, South Asia.

OPAQUE PROLIFERATION

At another level, my empirical research is theoretically situated in the analysis of *opaque proliferation*.[4] Opaque proliferants publicly deny developing nuclear weapons while secretly doing just that. This behavior has characterized every emerging nuclear power since China's nuclear explosive test in 1964, and the subsequent evolution of the nonproliferation norm in international politics. The Nuclear Non-Proliferation Treaty (NPT) and related components of the non-proliferation regime have not prevented the spread of nuclear weapons; instead, they have pushed it underground. This transformation in the prevailing mode of acquiring nuclear weapons has profound implications for nuclear dynamics in the relevant regions—the Middle East, South Asia, and the Korean peninsula. In particular, the nature of nuclear deterrence is fundamentally different in the opaque and transparent proliferation universes. Benjamin Frankel writes: "The theory of nuclear deterrence in its various manifestations

---

2. For concise overviews of these competing arguments, see Scott D. Sagan and Kenneth N. Waltz, *The Spread of Nuclear Weapons: A Debate* (New York: W.W. Norton, 1995); and Peter R. Lavoy's "The Strategic Consequences of Nuclear Proliferation: A Review Essay," *Security Studies*, Vol. 4, No. 4 (Summer 1995), pp. 695–753.

3. See Shlomo Aronson with Oded Brosh, *The Politics and Strategy of Nuclear Weapons in the Middle East: Opacity, Theory, and Reality, 1960–1991* (Albany: State University of New York Press, 1992); Yair Evron, *Israel's Nuclear Dilemma* (Ithaca, N.Y.: Cornell University Press, 1994); and Shai Feldman, *Nuclear Weapons and Arms Control in the Middle East* (Cambridge, Mass.: MIT Press, 1997).

4. For a preliminary exploration of this concept, see Benjamin Frankel, ed., "Opaque Nuclear Proliferation: Methodological and Policy Implications," special issue, *Journal of Strategic Studies*, Vol. 13, No. 3 (September 1990).

is ultimately the waving of a big and visible nuclear stick at a potential aggressor." But, as Frankel and Avner Cohen note, "there is little in the literature to tell us how a country should plan to use its nuclear weapons to deter its adversaries while denying the possession of these weapons."[5]

EXISTENTIAL DETERRENCE

This study's core theoretical contribution is that the logical nature of nuclear deterrence under conditions of opacity is *existential deterrence*, a concept invented by the late McGeorge Bundy. Bundy observed that nuclear weapons deter aggression by virtue of the simple fact that they exist, and not because of "strategic theories or declaratory policies or even international commitments." Existential deterrence "rests on uncertainty about what *could happen*, not in what has been asserted."[6] Opaque proliferants deny having nuclear weapons, declare no public nuclear doctrines, and know relatively little about each other's force postures; consequently, nuclear deterrence between them is based primarily on the perceived existence of the technology itself, not on relative capabilities or announced intentions. The chapters on South Asia's nuclear dynamics illustrate the practical mechanics of this theoretical nexus between opaque proliferation and existential deterrence.

Nuclear Danger at the End of the Twentieth Century

Theory should help us understand the world we live in. What real-world stakes suggest that a theoretically driven study of the South Asian nuclear arms competition is a useful contribution at this point in time? Nuclear proliferation will be the stiffest international security challenge of the twenty-first century.[7] While other issues are important, only nuclear weapons have the potential to alter the very essence of world politics within a matter of minutes. As an influential

---

5. Benjamin Frankel, "Notes on the Nuclear Underworld," *National Interest*, No. 9 (Fall 1987), p. 123; and Avner Cohen and Benjamin Frankel, "Opaque Nuclear Proliferation," in Frankel, "Opaque Nuclear Proliferation," pp. 31–32.

6. McGeorge Bundy, "Existential Deterrence and its Consequences," in Douglas MacLean, ed., *The Security Gamble: Deterrence Dilemmas in the Nuclear Age* (Totowa, N.J.: Rowman and Allanheld, 1984), pp. 8–9.

7. For an official U.S. perspective, see Office of the Secretary of Defense, *Proliferation: Threat and Response* (Washington, D.C.: U.S. Government Printing Office, 1996).

U.S. analysis puts it, nuclear warheads still constitute the "most massive single threat to humanity . . . it could be dangerously wrong to suppose that the end of the cold war means an end of nuclear danger, and it would be a grave error for our people or our government to let nuclear fear be replaced by nuclear complacency. Indeed it is not at all clear that the overall level of nuclear danger has gone down."[8]

RECENT ARMS CONTROL STRIDES

Nuclear arms controllers can, of course, reflect with considerable satisfaction on the accomplishments of the last decade. As we approach the twenty-first century, the United States and Russia are making deep reductions in their nuclear arsenals. The non-Russian former Soviet republics have renounced nuclear weapons entirely. Erstwhile holdouts France and China have signed the NPT, which in 1995 was extended indefinitely. Argentina and Brazil have recoiled from the nuclear threshold, and South Africa has terminated its nuclear program. Iraq's nuclear ambitions have been squelched for the time being, while Pyongyang may have bartered North Korea's away. A Comprehensive Test Ban Treaty (CTBT) was concluded in 1996 and is now open for signature. Momentum is also building for a worldwide cessation of fissile material production.

REMAINING CHALLENGES

Notwithstanding these gains, crucial challenges remain. Moscow and Washington still view each other warily, with both governments instinctively hedging their bets after four decades of arms racing. They will continue to reduce their strategic nuclear arsenals in fits and starts. Little has yet been done to broaden the process of negotiating reductions in nuclear arsenals to include the other three acknowledged nuclear powers, Britain, France, and China. Nuclear dangers also persist in the Middle East and the Korean peninsula, where ideologically militant, terrorism-sponsoring states are striving for the bomb. Perhaps most worrisome, the disintegration of the Soviet Union has yielded a variety of new dangers, particularly an enhanced risk of the accidental or unauthorized use of nuclear weapons—often termed "loose nukes."

---

8. McGeorge Bundy, William J. Crowe, Jr., and Sidney D. Drell, *Reducing Nuclear Danger: The Road Away from the Brink* (New York: Council on Foreign Relations Press, 1993), pp. 1–2.

NUCLEAR DANGER IN SOUTH ASIA

Some informed observers believe that "bad blood between India and Pakistan make South Asia the likeliest place for a[n atomic] bomb to be detonated in anger."[9] In the words of James Woolsey, then U.S. director of central intelligence, "the arms race between India and Pakistan poses perhaps the most probable prospect for future use of weapons of mass destruction, including nuclear weapons."[10] For these proliferation pessimists, the history of three Indo-Pakistani wars, the festering Kashmir conflict, the small, crude Indian and Pakistani nuclear capabilities, and the Pakistan Army's paramount influence on Islamabad's nuclear decision-making are a recipe for nuclear disaster.

As with the theoretical debate over proliferation's consequences, a few analysts beg to differ. These deterrence optimists argue that Indian and Pakistani nuclear capabilities help to stabilize South Asia by making war less likely. According to this logic, it is not happenstance that India and Pakistan fought three wars between 1947 and 1971, but none from 1972 to 1997. In the immediate aftermath of the 1971 Bangladesh war, New Delhi decided to carry out a nuclear explosive test, and Islamabad began to pursue its own military nuclear option. Optimists reason that, since then, India and Pakistan have increasingly perceived one another to be full-fledged nuclear weapon states; and, like other nuclear powers, they are deterred from war by their mutual fear of devastation.

Again, my aim is not to test the logic of nonproliferation and the logic of nuclear deterrence in South Asia; we know that the region has been spared a nuclear calamity, and thus that the worst fears of the proliferation pessimists have gone unrealized. It is my contention, however, that the subcontinental nuclear experience sheds substantial light on a previously obscured subject: the impact of maturing nuclear weapon capabilities on relations between two bitter regional antagonists. India has been nuclear weapon–capable since its 1974 explosive test and has steadily refined its weaponization options. Pakistan was not a nuclear weapon state in 1986 but was one by 1990. In the meantime, the period from 1986 to 1990 saw two Indo-Pakistani crises. Conventional wisdom holds that the transition

---

9. "A Test Ban for All," *The Economist* (editorial), July 6, 1996, pp. 20–22.

10. House Committee on Foreign Affairs, Subcommittee on International Security, International Organizations and Human Rights, *U.S. Security Policy Vis-à-Vis Rogue Regimes*, 103rd Cong., 1st sess., July 28, 1993.

to nuclear weapons is extremely dangerous, posing high risks of crisis instability, nuclear accidents, and other horrific outcomes. This study shows that, to the contrary, evolving nuclear weapon capabilities can have soothing or neutral effects, even during this allegedly destabilizing phase of the proliferation process.

Although scholars have done a great deal of research on why certain states acquire nuclear weapons, why other states do not, and the various policy options for preventing proliferation, we have surprisingly little empirical work on the actual consequences of proliferation once countries begin moving down the nuclear path. If governments are to develop effective policies addressing regional nuclear dangers, it would behoove them first to understand the dynamics of nuclearization in the various regions of concern.

WHY SHOULD WE CARE?
The possibility of a regional conflict escalating to a global conflagration vanished with the end of the Cold War. Why, then, should the rest of the world care if India and Pakistan fight a nuclear war? The main reason is a humanitarian one. Indians and Pakistanis constitute about 20 percent of the world's population. Many are clustered in heavily populated cities well within the reach of the adversary's nuclear-capable bombers. In the event of even a limited exchange of rudimentary fission weapons, millions of people would perish. The human suffering from such a catastrophe would be magnified considerably by the dearth of societal recovery capabilities—hospitals, doctors, emergency personnel, etc.—in both countries. Under these conditions, it is no exaggeration to say that the survivors might wish they had been lucky enough to die. A second reason for concern is the continued maintenance of the nuclear taboo that has developed in world politics since the United States dropped atomic bombs on Hiroshima and Nagasaki in August 1945. For more than five decades now, the military use of nuclear weapons has been steadily delegitimized. The end of the Cold War has given this process material form, with the ongoing drawdown of U.S. and former Soviet nuclear forces. The use of nuclear weapons by India or Pakistan would shatter this nuclear taboo, with potentially grave consequences.

Organization of the Book

This study is organized in the following way. In the first chapter, I survey and analyze the debate between the logic of nonproliferation and the logic of nuclear deterrence. These composite perspectives yield competing sets of expectations about the dynamics of nuclear proliferation, which in turn provide a conceptual framework for the empirical research on South Asia. My analysis suggests that while nuclear capabilities should deter war between India and Pakistan, the dangers of loose nukes are a distinct, and more worrisome, matter. In the second chapter, I flesh out the concepts of opaque proliferation and existential deterrence, and then develop a theory of existential nuclear deterrence between opaque proliferants. I argue that deterrence in this situation is achieved via tacit bargaining between the proliferants themselves and inadvertent *transparency-building* by the nonproliferation community.

The third chapter is a historical overview of Indo-Pakistani security dynamics. It is intended not to break new ground, but to provide sufficient context for the non-specialist reader to appreciate the subsequent empirical chapters. The fourth chapter is a case study of the 1986–87 Brasstacks crisis. I conclude that nuclear weapon capabilities had little influence on the outcome of the crisis, which was resolved peacefully because no compelling political objective drove either side to a decision for war. Given the conventional wisdom that crises erupting during the transition to nuclear weapons should be hazardous, the fact that the Brasstacks crisis did not evolve into a nuclear crisis is significant. I discuss its implications at the end of the fourth chapter.

The fifth chapter is an examination of South Asian nuclear dynamics between 1987 and 1990. The main legacy of the Brasstacks crisis was that it spurred both India and Pakistan into vigorous efforts to improve and refine their nuclear capabilities. In doing so, they were paradoxically aided and abetted by the nonproliferation community, which, in trying to inhibit South Asia's nuclear programs, actually gave them publicity and thus credibility. By 1990, India and Pakistan perceived each other as actual—not aspiring—nuclear weapon states. The sixth chapter is a case study of the 1990 Kashmir crisis. Here I argue that existential nuclear deterrence was the most important cause of peace on the subcontinent.

In the seventh chapter, I elaborate on the analytical conclusions reached in each of the case studies. Most important, I argue that the Indo-Pakistani experience with nuclear weapons more closely matches the expectations of the logic of nuclear deterrence than the logic of nonproliferation. I then examine the implications of this conclusion for proliferation scholarship, nuclear deterrence theory, and security studies in general. The concluding sections of the book analyze the prospects for subcontinental strategic stability and nuclear arms control.

Chapter 1

Debating the Consequences of Nuclear Proliferation

In this chapter I examine the debate over the effects of nuclear proliferation. I do so by analyzing two competing logics: the logic of nonproliferation, which is a composite of various arguments about why proliferation is dangerous; and the logic of nuclear deterrence, which suggests instead that proliferation has less harmful or even beneficial effects on international relations. For each element of these contrasting bodies of thought, I first explicate the logic of nonproliferation—the conventional wisdom regarding nuclear spread—and then critique that reasoning with insights drawn from the logic of nuclear deterrence. Together, these perspectives provide a conceptual framework for the subsequent empirical study of South Asia's nuclear dynamics.

The theoretical debate over proliferation's effects is inconclusive for two main reasons. First, consideration of this issue tends to be conjectural, with analysts at any given point in time trying to predict the effects of future proliferation based on historically reasonable, but still speculative, assumptions about new proliferants' expected force postures. These political and technical assumptions are not necessarily useful in a world of opaque proliferation, which is a point I will develop thoroughly in the second chapter.

Second, both logic and history point to an analytical divide between the strategic[1] consequences of proliferation and non-strategic concerns like the accidental or unauthorized use of nuclear weapons. My analysis of the strategic impact of proliferation suggests

---

1. By this I mean the interdependence of decision-making between two nuclear powers.

that it stabilizes adversarial relationships by deterring conflict. In contrast, the threat of loose nukes suggests that proliferation can be dangerous. Even within the realm of strategy itself, much of what separates the two logics boils down to individual analysts' gut feelings about the robustness of nuclear deterrence. This is a matter of instinct which cannot be resolved by logic alone.

These conclusions argue strongly for a theoretically driven, historically informed, case-by-case approach to the phenomenon of nuclear proliferation. Decades of blanket generalization about the characteristics of a more proliferated world have not served us well. The post-1945 nuclear taboo and the absence of nuclear weapon accidents belie the dire warnings of many experts. Nuclear proliferation has not been an unmitigated disaster for the world; treating it as such inhibits understanding and sound policy.

Several other points should be made at the outset. The analytical perspective of this chapter is generic, in the sense that the phenomena under study are the *inherent* consequences of nuclear proliferation, not the impact of any particular nation's acquisition of nuclear weapons on any other nation's interests. A detached analyst may view the inherent effects of proliferation on international relations as relatively benign, while at the same time holding, as a U.S. citizen, that it is not in the best interests of the United States for Iran or North Korea to deploy nuclear weapons. It should also be noted that few analysts embrace either the logic of nonproliferation or the logic of nuclear deterrence in its entirety. Most accept certain parts of each logic in their individual conceptualization of the consequences of nuclear proliferation. Thus, the logics presented here are composites, intended to frame the debate in an analytically fruitful manner.

The utility of examining the consequences of nuclear proliferation may appear questionable. It might be argued that, however unlikely a future nuclear disaster, the devastation that would result merits whatever efforts necessary to slow the spread of nuclear weapons. Why not just acknowledge the dangers of nuclear proliferation and then focus on what can be done to prevent it? The answer is that this has been the nonproliferation community's stance for more than three decades, and it has been viewed as illegitimate by several aspiring nuclear powers. Americans in particular have been hard-pressed to explain why nuclear weapons are good for them but not for others. Countries like India and Pakistan understandably reject such arguments as ethnocentric. Nonproliferation advocates therefore have the most incentive to sharpen their reasoning about the consequences of proliferation; otherwise, their policies will continue to be perceived as hypocritical.

The Logic of Nonproliferation

Many prominent international relations scholars believe that nuclear weapons contributed to peace between the superpowers during the Cold War.[2] They argue that mutual, assured second-strike capabilities created a situation in which the United States and the Soviet Union convinced each other that the costs of aggression would far outweigh any conceivable benefits. Contrary to the apparently pacifying effect of U.S. and Soviet nuclear weapons, however, their wider spread is generally considered to be dangerous.[3] As Joseph Nye wrote in 1985: "Paradoxically, under many circumstances the introduction of a single bomb in some non-nuclear states may be more likely to lead to nuclear use than the addition of a thousand more warheads to the U.S. and Soviet stockpiles."[4] This conventional wisdom reflects an instinctive aversion to nuclear weapons stemming from their massive destructive power. Lewis Dunn has argued, for example, that "a proliferated world is likely to be a nasty and dangerous place, entailing threats to the security and domestic well-being of virtually all nations and posing a serious possibility of a longer-term decay of global political order."[5]

THE LOGIC OF NONPROLIFERATION'S INTELLECTUAL LINEAGE

Proliferation studies have passed through several distinct phases. Most writing on nuclear weapons in the 1940s and 1950s analyzed the implications of "the bomb" for world politics in general and for

---

2. For variations on this theme, see John Lewis Gaddis, "The Long Peace: Elements of Stability in the Postwar International System," *International Security*, Vol. 10, No. 4 (Spring 1986), pp. 99–142; Robert Jervis, *The Meaning of the Nuclear Revolution: Statecraft and the Prospect of Armageddon* (Ithaca, N.Y.: Cornell University Press, 1989); and Kenneth N. Waltz, "Nuclear Myths and Political Realities," *American Political Science Review*, Vol. 84, No. 3 (September 1990), pp. 731–745.

3. For a critical review of recent scholarship in this vein, see David J. Karl, "Proliferation Pessimism and Emerging Nuclear Powers," *International Security*, Vol. 21, No. 3 (Winter 1996/97), pp. 87–119.

4. Joseph S. Nye, Jr., "NPT: The Logic of Inequality," *Foreign Policy*, No. 59 (Summer 1985), p. 128.

5. Lewis A. Dunn, "Nuclear Proliferation and World Politics," *Annals of the American Academy of Political and Social Science*, No. 430 (March 1977), p. 97.

the tense U.S.-Soviet relationship in particular.[6] Sustained thinking about the wider spread of nuclear weapons—eventually dubbed nuclear proliferation—was only stimulated by the progress of the British, French, and Chinese nuclear programs in the late 1950s and early 1960s.[7] The possibility of nuclear weapons finding their way into the arsenals of innumerable states was originally referred to in the scholarly literature as the "nth country problem." The main concern about "nth countries" was the threat they posed to the stability of the "central," or U.S.-Soviet, balance.[8] As Richard Rosecrance wrote, the wider diffusion of nuclear weapons was alarming insofar as it raised the possibility of a superpower nuclear exchange.[9] Henry Kissinger's opinion that the "major instability produced by the spread of nuclear weapons is not so much in the increase of the risk of general war as in the relations of nth countries to each other"[10] was a dissenting view in the 1960s, although the arguments he developed about the instabilities of small nuclear forces would become the logic of nonproliferation's central foundation by the 1970s. Most analysts in the 1960s agreed with Albert Wohlstetter's contention that "from the standpoint of world stability, wide nuclear diffusion would be gravely disruptive. It would increase the likelihood of the use of nuclear weapons both by accident and by deliberation."[11]

6. See Bernard Brodie, ed., *The Absolute Weapon: Atomic Power and World Order* (New York: Harcourt, Brace, 1946); and Brodie, *Strategy in the Missile Age* (Princeton, N.J.: Princeton University Press, 1959).

7. Nuclear proliferation has technically referred to the spread of nuclear weapons to any previously nonnuclear nation. In reality, though, most of the arguments comprising the logic of nonproliferation have focused on the alleged dangers posed by the spread of nuclear weapons to Third World countries, especially since China's 1964 nuclear test.

8. For early discussions of the impact of nuclear proliferation on the central balance, see Arthur Lee Burns, *Power Politics and the Growing Nuclear Club*, Policy Memorandum No. 20 (Princeton, N.J.: Center of International Studies, Princeton University, 1959); and Alastair Buchan, "Introduction," and Stanley Hoffmann, "Nuclear Proliferation and World Politics," in Buchan, ed., *A World of Nuclear Powers?* (Englewood Cliffs, N.J.: Prentice-Hall, 1966), pp. 7, 101.

9. R.N. Rosecrance, "Introduction," in Rosecrance, ed., *The Dispersion of Nuclear Weapons: Strategy and Politics* (New York: Columbia University Press, 1964), pp. 22–23.

10. Henry A. Kissinger, *The Necessity for Choice: Prospects of American Foreign Policy* (New York: Harper and Brothers, 1960), p. 244.

11. Albert Wohlstetter, "Nuclear Sharing: NATO and the N + 1 Country," in Rosecrance, *Dispersion of Nuclear Weapons*, p. 204.

The focus of proliferation studies shifted in the 1970s and 1980s from the central balance to the Third World. India's 1974 nuclear test raised fears that numerous countries in areas of chronic instability were well on the road to deploying nuclear weapons. In a book typical of the period, Wohlstetter suggested the possibility of "an exponential rate of growth in the future in contrast with the low, linear rate of the spread of nuclear weapons since 1945."[12] As a consequence of this perceived trend, the possibility of regional nuclear conflict henceforth became a serious concern in and of itself; proliferation specialists began to concentrate on the differences that Kissinger had alluded to earlier between the nuclear forces of industrialized and developing countries.

These analysts formulated two types of argument. The first type acknowledged the stability of superpower nuclear deterrence, but argued that "many of the political, technical, and situational roots of stable nuclear deterrence between the United States and the Soviet Union may be absent in South Asia, the Middle East or other regions to which nuclear weapons are spreading. *There is a high risk of nuclear weapons being used.*" More specifically, the "heightened stakes and lessened room for maneuver in conflict-prone regions, the volatile leadership and political instability of many of the next nuclear powers, and the technical deficiencies of many new nuclear forces all threaten the first decades' nuclear peace."[13] A smaller group of scholars argued that the influence of nuclear deterrence between the United States and the Soviet Union was itself exaggerated, and therefore that nuclear deterrent balances involving other countries were even less likely to form. As William Potter wrote near the end of the Cold War: "To the extent that a deterrence relationship characterizes U.S.-Soviet relations, it is probably more delicate than stable and

---

12. Albert Wohlstetter, "Life in a Nuclear Armed Crowd," in Wohlstetter et al., *Swords from Plowshares: The Military Potential of Civilian Nuclear Energy* (Chicago: University of Chicago Press, 1979), p. 127. Common is this perception at any given time that the world is on the brink of widespread nuclear diffusion. In 1977, for example, David Gompert wrote: "Not having nuclear weapons in 1990 might prove analogous to not having military aircraft in 1935." See his "Strategic Deterioration: Prospects, Dimensions, and Responses in a Fourth Nuclear Regime," in Gompert et al., *Nuclear Weapons and World Politics: Alternatives for the Future* (New York: McGraw-Hill, 1977), p. 222.

13. Lewis A. Dunn, *Containing Nuclear Proliferation,* Adelphi Paper No. 263 (London: International Institute for Strategic Studies [IISS], 1991), p. 4 (emphasis added); and Dunn, *Controlling the Bomb* (New Haven, Conn.: Yale University Press, 1982), p. 75. These issues will be discussed extensively below.

represents a theoretical goal not yet violated rather than a description of the actual relationship."[14] For Steven Miller, "the proposition that nuclear weapons promote peace and stability is properly regarded not as a fact but as an interpretation, largely based on the evidence of a single case."[15]

The Logic of Nuclear Deterrence

The logic of nuclear deterrence contradicts the logic of nonproliferation in important ways. Arguments under this rubric can be divided into two distinct groups: those that advocate the selective spread of nuclear weapons and those that do not go this far but nonetheless downplay the negative consequences of nuclear proliferation. Although few, if any, analysts have adopted an unrestrained pro-proliferation position, some have suggested that the diffusion of nuclear weapons to certain states could balance against other nuclear powers and act as a force for stability. William Bader wrote in 1968 that to "maintain the flexibility necessary to correct an arms imbalance in one region by providing nuclear weapons cooperation to one or more of the antagonists may be as stabilizing to the global system as denying all arms cooperation—nuclear and conventional—in another."[16] That same year, Walter Wentz advocated "stabilizing the present world political system in part by the discrete diffusion of atomic arms." According to Wentz, the credibility problems inherent in U.S. extended deterrence could be solved by creating an "indigenous nuclear deterrent" in certain regions: "what is appropriate is the selective and conditional distribution of controlled atomic weapons to those states threatened by the Republic of China [sic] and the Soviet Union and currently protected by the nuclear shield of the United States." Wentz thought India and Japan were good candidates for selective proliferation.[17] Surprisingly, given the subsequent legitimation of the global nonproliferation norm, these were not just

---

14. William C. Potter, "On Nuclear Proliferation," in Edward A. Kolodziej and Patrick M. Morgan, eds., *Security and Arms Control*, Vol. 2, *A Guide to International Policymaking* (New York: Greenwood, 1989), p. 321.

15. Steven E. Miller, "The Case Against a Ukrainian Nuclear Deterrent," *Foreign Affairs*, Vol. 72, No. 3 (Summer 1993), p. 69.

16. William B. Bader, *The United States and the Spread of Nuclear Weapons* (New York: Pegasus, 1968), p. 106.

17. Walter B. Wentz, *Nuclear Proliferation* (Washington, D.C.: Public Affairs Press, 1968), pp. 11, 178–179, 182–185.

voices in the wilderness. Glenn Seaborg describes high-level deliberations within the Johnson administration over the feasibility of Wentz's idea.[18]

The more common heterodox position disputes the logic of nonproliferation but stops short of advocating the purposeful diffusion of nuclear technology. Associated primarily with Kenneth Waltz, this perspective draws on nuclear deterrence theory to argue that the impact of proliferation will be less menacing than typically believed. As Waltz writes, predictions based on the logic of nonproliferation "point less to likelihoods and more to dangers we can all imagine. They identify some possibilities among many, and identifying more of the possibilities would not enable one to say how they are likely to unfold in a world made different by the slow spread of nuclear weapons." Waltz says flatly: "Nuclear weapons have reduced the chances of war between the United States and the Soviet Union and between the Soviet Union and China. One may expect them to have similar results elsewhere."[19] This logic stresses that nuclear weapons promote deterrent, not offensive, strategies and thus decrease the probability of war. Bruce Bueno de Mesquita and William Riker argue that the "presence of an explicit or underlying nuclear threat constrains conflict by reducing its likelihood of escalating into war."[20]

---

18. In a November 1964 meeting, roughly five weeks after China's first nuclear explosion, Secretary of State Dean Rusk "said he thought a basic question was whether we really should have a nonproliferation policy prescribing that no countries beyond the present five might acquire nuclear weapons. Were we clear that this should be a major objective of U.S. policy? For example, might we not want to be in a position where India or Japan would be able to respond with nuclear weapons to a Chinese threat?" Secretary of Defense Robert McNamara responded that Rusk's idea merited further study; but both McNamara and President Johnson's special assistant for national security affairs, McGeorge Bundy, agreed that this should be kept strictly confidential, so as not to undermine stated U.S. policy. Glenn T. Seaborg, *Stemming the Tide: Arms Control in the Johnson Years* (Lexington, Mass.: Lexington Books, 1987), pp. 135–136.

19. Kenneth N. Waltz, *The Spread of Nuclear Weapons: More May Be Better*, Adelphi Paper No. 171 (London: IISS, 1981), p. 1; and Waltz, "What Will the Spread of Nuclear Weapons Do to the World?" in John Kerry King, ed., *International Political Effects of the Spread of Nuclear Weapons* (Washington, D.C.: U.S. Government Printing Office, 1979), p. 165.

20. Bruce Bueno de Mesquita and William H. Riker, "An Assessment of the Merits of Selective Nuclear Proliferation," *Journal of Conflict Resolution*, Vol. 26, No. 2 (June 1982), pp. 290–291. Also see John J. Weltman, "Nuclear Devolution and World Order," *World Politics*, Vol. 32, No. 2 (January 1980), p. 190; and Steven J. Rosen, "A Stable System of Mutual Nuclear Deterrence in the Middle East," *American Political Science Review*, Vol. 71, No. 4 (December 1977), pp. 1367–1383.

For the logic of nuclear deterrence, the chief impact of nuclear weapons is to induce caution. Waltz writes: "In a conventional world one is uncertain about winning or losing. In a nuclear world, one is uncertain about surviving or being annihilated." Since the destructive power of even small nuclear weapons is immense, their possessors can have little doubt about the devastating consequences that would ensue from a nuclear exchange. By removing any uncertainty about the outcome of such an exchange, nuclear weapons inhibit conflict. As Waltz argues, miscalculation causes wars, and "nuclear weapons make military miscalculations difficult and politically pertinent prediction easy."[21]

Analyzing the Two Logics

The logic of nonproliferation rests on five main arguments: that the risks of nuclear use increase with the number of nuclear decision centers; that nuclear competitions in the developing world will be prone to severe instabilities because of the deep antagonisms and high stakes involved in new proliferants' international political conflicts; that the command and control arrangements governing Third World nuclear forces will be inadequate and therefore vulnerable to preemptive attacks, nuclear accidents, and unauthorized nuclear use; that some future proliferants are less likely than their predecessors to be deterred by nuclear weapons; and that emerging nuclear powers will be especially prone to preventive wars.

QUANTITATIVE ARGUMENTS
The most intuitive arguments against the spread of nuclear weapons are based on sheer numbers. The early characterization of nuclear proliferation as the "*n*th country problem" effectively captured the simple but compelling notion that nuclear spread means "more fingers on more triggers and, probably, a greater risk that a trigger might be pulled with incalculable consequences."[22] Some policymakers and scholars have tried to move beyond this basic argument into a more rigorous specification of the correlation between the number of nuclear decision centers and the likelihood of nuclear explosions. A 1964 comment by U.S. Secretary of Defense Robert

---

21. Waltz, *More May Be Better*, pp. 5–7.

22. Hans M. Blix, "Forward," in Joseph F. Pilat and Robert E. Pendley, eds., *Beyond 1995: The Future of the NPT Regime* (New York: Plenum Press, 1990), p. ix.

McNamara is representative of this argument: "You can imagine the danger that the world would face if 10, 20, or 30 nations possessed nuclear weapons instead of the four that possess them today. . . . The danger to other nations increases geometrically with the increase in the number of nations possessing these warheads."[23] Bruce Russett argues that the probability of nuclear war "is a function not of the number of nuclear-armed states, but of the number of pairs of nuclear-armed states. If there are only two nuclear-armed states in the world, there is only one pair of states that can fight a nuclear war. If there are 20 nuclear-armed states, then there are 190 pairs of states between which nuclear war is possible."[24]

QUANTITATIVE ARGUMENTS AND THE LOGIC OF NUCLEAR DETERRENCE. The logic of nuclear deterrence posits a different relationship between the number of nuclear powers and the likelihood of nuclear war. One deductive argument suggests that early proliferation increases the probability of nuclear war, but that this risk declines after a certain point. Bueno de Mesquita and Riker maintain that the "number of potential bilateral nuclear conflicts" increases until half of the countries in a "hypothetical geopolitical system" acquire nuclear weapons. Then the number of such conflicts declines as nuclear deterrence characterizes more pairs of states. This number goes to "zero when all countries have sufficient capabilities to deter their relevant adversaries."[25]

ANALYSIS. Quantitative arguments are the most problematic gener-alizations in the debate over the consequences of nuclear proliferation. While many scholars would likely agree with the general presumption that increases in the total number of nuclear decision centers raise the probability of a nuclear explosion, attempts to specify this relation-ship in an ostensibly more rigorous manner are contradicted by both logic and history. Five points are salient here. First, the "more fingers on more triggers" case neglects to address whose fingers we are talking

23. Quoted in Bader, *United States and the Spread of Nuclear Weapons*, p. 11.

24. Bruce Russett, "Away from Nuclear Mythology," in Dagobert L. Brito, Michael D. Intriligator, and Adele E. Wick, eds., *Strategies for Managing Nuclear Proliferation* (Lexington, Mass.: Lexington Books, 1983), p. 153. Russett's formula is $n(n-1)/2$, where n = the number of nuclear weapon states.

25. Bueno de Mesquita and Riker, "Selective Nuclear Proliferation," pp. 287–288. For similar arguments, see two pieces by Michael D. Intriligator and Dagobert L. Brito: "Nuclear Proliferation and Stability," *Journal of Peace Science*, Vol. 3, No. 2 (Fall 1978), pp. 176–178; and "Nuclear Proliferation and the Probability of Nuclear War," *Public Choice*, Vol. 37 (1981), pp. 247–259.

about, a detail that certainly matters. Would most people not prefer a world with five nuclear powers— Japan, Canada, Singapore, New Zealand, and Costa Rica—to one with only three—Libya, Iraq, and North Korea? The fact that some countries' records of international adventurism are more alarming than others' suggests that conclusions about the consequences of nuclear proliferation based on numbers alone are spurious.

Second, Russett's position that what matters is not the number of nuclear weapon states, but the number of nuclear pairs makes a similar mistake. The addition of a nuclear pair composed of Brazil and Iran, for example, would not seem to affect the probability of war at all. All possible nuclear dyads are not necessarily important ones. Third, and related to the last point, if Argentina and Iraq already possess nuclear weapons, might not the addition of Brazil and Iran to the nuclear club have potentially stabilizing rather than destabilizing consequences? Correcting nuclear asymmetries may decrease the chances of war. As Hedley Bull says, quantitative arguments ignore "differences in the political nature of the decision-makers and the strategic situation in which they find themselves: the acquisition of nuclear weapons by a country that does not threaten others but is itself threatened by a nuclear weapon state may make war less likely, not more."[26]

Fourth, along these same lines, if we use Russett's formula, $n(n-1)/2$, the addition of France (the fourth nuclear power) to the ranks of nuclear weapon states increased the number of nuclear pairs from three to six. Does this mean that France's deployment of nuclear weapons doubled the likelihood of nuclear war? This is a difficult argument to sustain. For a more contemporary example, think of a world in which Iran becomes the ninth nuclear weapon state. This would increase the number of nuclear pairs from twenty-eight to thirty-six (29 percent). Does this make nuclear war 29 percent more likely? Specifying the consequences of proliferation with this kind of precision defies the nature of international behavior, indeed all social behavior. Individual situations and circumstances matter. Finally, all of these arguments are undermined by the fact that the only time nuclear weapons have ever been used was in 1945, when only one country possessed them.

For many of the same reasons, quantitative arguments claiming that nuclear proliferation *increases* stability are equally tenuous.

---

26. Hedley Bull, "Rethinking Nonproliferation," *International Affairs*, Vol. 51, No. 2 (April 1975), pp. 177–178.

Logically, which states proliferate is important here, too, as is whether they create symmetries or asymmetries. In addition, as usually presented, quantitative arguments about nuclear proliferation being stabilizing are fatally tautological. For instance, Bueno de Mesquita and Riker first assume in constructing their model of nuclear proliferation that "in a conflict between two nuclear powers, the conflict is unlikely to become nuclear by reason of fear of retaliation." They later infer from the model that "given the logic of deterrence, the probability of a rationally calculated use of nuclear weapons is higher when there are pairwise asymmetries in the possession of such weapons than when there is symmetry."[27] Here, the assumption is the conclusion.

In sum, then, quantitative arguments are weak. More may be better or worse; how much better or worse depends not on quantitative measurements, but on the qualitative characteristics of individual nuclear competitions. What really matters is not how many nations have nuclear weapons, but rather which nations have them, and the nature of the political dynamics among those countries. Quantitative attempts to specify the impact of increases in nuclear weapon states are not only fruitless, but they distract analysts from the more important political issues surrounding the consequences of further proliferation and what the world might do to affect them.

GEOPOLITICAL ARGUMENTS

The logic of nonproliferation's second pillar is the belief that future nuclearizing regions may be qualitatively different from the central balance, and that their unique geopolitical conditions will make the acquisition of nuclear weapons destabilizing. One prominent line of reasoning is that the stakes are higher in conflict-prone regions like the Middle East and South Asia, relative to those of the superpower competition. According to this argument, a Third World country's territorial integrity, independence, and national survival may ride on the outcome of conflicts with adversaries. Because they "perceive the stakes to be so high, some of these countries' leaders may be ready to risk nuclear confrontation, if not even to *accept a surprisingly high level of nuclear damage,* in pursuit of their objectives."[28] Others believe that nuclear weapons would likely be dangerous in the developing world because of the endemic political instability that characterizes relations

---

27. Bueno de Mesquita and Riker, "Selective Nuclear Proliferation," pp. 283, 288.
28. Dunn, *Controlling the Bomb,* p. 70 (emphasis added).

between regional adversaries. From this perspective, not only would the stakes be higher, but the opportunities for conflict to erupt and escalate to the nuclear level would be more frequent. Common is Steve Fetter's view that states "such as India and Pakistan, North and South Korea, and Israel and various Arab states, have deep religious, ideological, or cultural animosities, often combined with active border disputes, that weaken deterrence."[29] Another impetus to nuclear instability is said to be the potentially disastrous timing of proliferation. Many analysts feel that new nuclear powers may have so little time to assimilate nuclear weapons into their military forces and doctrines before conflict erupts that nuclear learning will be impossible. David Gompert warns that future proliferants may "assemble their nuclear weapons in the heat of conflict," with disastrous consequences.[30]

GEOPOLITICAL ARGUMENTS AND THE LOGIC OF NUCLEAR DETERRENCE. The logic of nuclear deterrence denies that future nuclear competitions will be more prone to nuclear use than was the U.S.-Soviet balance. Waltz criticizes the notion that the antagonisms and political stakes involved in regional conflicts are greater than in those between the established nuclear weapon states: "bitterness among some potential nuclear states, so it is said, exceeds that experienced by the old ones. Playing down the bitterness sometimes felt by the United States, the Soviet Union, and China requires a creative reading of history." For Waltz, severe animosities and political conflicts will not make nuclear use any more likely in future nuclear balances than in previous ones, because nuclear deterrence will prevail: "new nuclear states will confront the possibilities and feel the constraints that present nuclear states have experienced. New nuclear states will be more mindful of dangers than some of the old ones have been."[31] From this perspective, nuclear weapons have to date induced caution in their possessors and can be expected to continue doing so. Waltz agrees, however, with one element of the logic of nonproliferation: that the timing of nuclear spread in regions of chronic political turmoil may lead to instability. His entire analysis is predicated on the gradual diffusion of nuclear weapons, and he notes that more rapid proliferation may negate

---

29. Steve Fetter, "Ballistic Missiles and Weapons of Mass Destruction: What is the Threat? What Should Be Done?" *International Security*, Vol. 16, No. 1 (Summer 1991), p. 30.

30. Gompert, "Strategic Deterioration," p. 233.

31. Waltz, *More May Be Better*, p. 11; and Waltz, "Spread of Nuclear Weapons," p. 11.

some of his conclusions. John Weltman concedes that "hostilities involving nuclear weapons may occur prior to the lapse of enough time for a mutually stable weapons posture to develop."[32]

ANALYSIS. In the area of geopolitics, the logic of nuclear deterrence is more compelling than the logic of nonproliferation. Despite the dire predictions of most proliferation experts, there is no geopolitical reason to expect nuclear behavior to be markedly different in regional security environments than that exhibited by the established nuclear weapon states. Several points are relevant here. First, Waltz is surely correct to say that playing down the antagonisms and stakes involved in political conflicts between the first five nuclear powers constitutes historical revisionism of the first order. It is easy for contemporary analysts to forget the profound animosities between the United States and the Soviet Union during the various crises over Berlin and Cuba, or between the Soviet Union and China during the 1960s. The political stakes in the Korean peninsula, South Asia, and the Middle East today do not exceed those that faced the United States, the Soviet Union, and China at the height of the Cold War.

In a related point, the notion of developing countries whose national survival is threatened by adversaries is popular but exaggerated. Even the bitterest regional rivalries have not yielded wars in which one side threatens to erase the other from the map. None of the three Indo-Pakistani wars threatened the survival of either country, including the Bangladesh war of 1971, in which New Delhi helped to liberate East Pakistan. Similarly, at no time did the Iran-Iraq war, the most devastating conventional conflict since World War II, threaten either country with extinction. Land battles were confined to border areas, and deeper strikes with ballistic missiles were militarily ineffective. North Korea nearly succeeded in overrunning all of South Korea in 1950, but this initial thrust of the Korean War is viewed most appropriately as a civil conflict: the division of Korea was intended to be temporary, and Pyongyang's aggression was aimed at unifying what had, until recently, been one country with an ethnically homogenous population.

The logic of nonproliferation's warnings about regional geopolitical environments bear the burden of a profound contradiction: on

---

32. John J. Weltman, "Managing Nuclear Multipolarity," *International Security*, Vol. 6, No. 3 (Winter 1981/82), p. 192. These convergent expectations are particularly salient for the South Asia cases described in Chapters 4 and 6 where a period of three and one-half years saw two crises between nuclearizing—and possibly weaponizing—Third World states.

one hand, it is said that bitter enemies are divided by deep religious, ethnic, and ideological disputes, and on the other, that they threaten each other's national survival. But threatening another country's survival implies taking it over and ruling it, for withdrawing would amount to restoring its sovereignty. What country would relish the prospect of administering a new territory whose population is utterly alienated from its own? This is a recipe for festering conflict. It is even less logical to expect any country to back a *nuclear-armed* adversary into a corner, forcing its leadership to contemplate a desperation blow. While one could argue that the Yom Kippur War briefly threatened Israel's national survival in 1973, it would be a foolish Arab leader who tried to push Israel into the sea in the 1990s, given the revelations about Israel's nuclear capabilities in the intervening two decades, combined with the obvious resolve of Israeli leaders to prevent such an outcome by whatever means necessary. Dunn's contention that certain conflicts might lead decision-makers to "accept a surprisingly high level of nuclear damage" is simply unfounded.

With respect to timing, the logic of nonproliferation suggests that deploying nuclear weapons in areas of chronic political instability is dangerous because the pressures of ongoing conflicts and nuclear immaturity may result in a nuclear exchange. A look at history leads to a more sanguine view. This is an issue I will discuss extensively in the context of opacity in the next chapter; suffice it to say here that Israel, India, and Pakistan have been busy with nuclear research and development during the last forty years, a period that has seen intense political conflicts in the Middle East and South Asia. During this time, the exact extent of the Israeli, Indian, and Pakistani nuclear programs has been shrouded in mystery. Arguments about the timing of proliferation misconceive its dynamics, which involve a *process* that takes decades, not a sudden, definitive *outcome* that can be pinpointed with certainty. While the notion of Third World countries hastily assembling nuclear weapons in the heat of battle is an alarming one, it ignores the fact that the nuclear development process takes many years, and that this process itself shapes behavior by moderating tendencies toward war.

The bottom line is that, with one exception, there is no situation in the world today in which an attacking nuclear power does not face the distinct possibility of having its major cities reduced to ashes, an outcome in which the costs would be far out of proportion to any conceivable political gain. India and Pakistan have the means to retaliate against each other. South Korea remains under Washington's East

Asian nuclear umbrella. The exception is Israel. Since Israel enjoys nuclear hegemony in the Middle East, its adversaries may fear a nuclear, perhaps preventive, strike; however, as I will argue below, the international taboo against a nuclear power attacking a nonnuclear state with nuclear weapons is so deeply ingrained that the political costs of such a strike would be prohibitive.

COMMAND AND CONTROL OF SMALL NUCLEAR FORCES

The logic of nonproliferation's third pillar is the belief that the command and control arrangements governing Third World nuclear arsenals will be deficient and therefore dangerously unstable. According to this viewpoint, future proliferants will lack the material resources and technological capabilities that have helped the five established nuclear powers to avoid nuclear explosions since 1945. The logic of nuclear deterrence suggests that these fears are overblown. Waltz reasons that every nuclear power must go through a period in which its nuclear forces are "crudely designed," yet each has survived this transition without mishap. Relations between several nuclear weapon states "were at their bitterest just when their nuclear forces were in early stages of development, were unbalanced, were crude and presumably hard to control." Waltz predicts that new nuclear powers will be equally capable of surmounting the dilemmas posed by unsophisticated command and control practices.[33] These competing logics consider two main dangers stemming from command and control deficiencies: the preemptive use of nuclear weapons during an international crisis, and the domestic challenge of loose nukes, i.e., nuclear accidents and the unauthorized use of nuclear weapons. These will be analyzed individually.

PREEMPTIVE PRESSURES

One widely discussed concern is that the nuclear arsenals of future proliferants may be so rudimentary as to promote crisis instability. From this standpoint, developing countries are likely to deploy a limited number of vulnerable nuclear weapons. During a crisis, what Thomas Schelling called the "reciprocal fear of surprise attack"[34] could foster a use-them-or-lose-them attitude, in which striking second is seen as the worst option and striking first only the second

---

33. Waltz, *More May Be Better*, p. 16.

34. Thomas C. Schelling, *The Strategy of Conflict* (New York: Oxford University Press, 1963), pp. 207–229.

worst choice. As Steve Fetter writes, if "one side believes that war is inevitable, it may try to preemptively destroy the other side's vulnerable but valuable weapons of mass destruction. Even if both sides prefer not to preempt, each may fear that the other side will; consequently, both may decide to launch at the first (perhaps false) indication of an attack."[35] Lewis Dunn agrees: "fear that escalation to nuclear conflict no longer could be avoided might lead a country to get in the first blow, so as partly to disarm the opponent and to minimize damage." These imperatives are said to be exacerbated by the limited command, control, communications, and intelligence (C^3I) capabilities regional proliferants can be expected to muster. Inadequate C^3I may promote miscalculation of an adversary's actions or intentions and lead to unnecessarily hasty decision-making. Launch-on-warning procedures might be adopted to reduce the weapons' vulnerability, tempting leaders into hair-trigger reactions during crises.[36]

In a twist on this argument, Bruce Blair claims that the superpowers were themselves more vulnerable to crisis instability than is commonly believed, and that aspiring proliferants' lesser technological capabilities make them even more subject to preemptive war pressures. Blair maintains that because U.S. and Soviet leaders knew that their C^3I systems were vulnerable to disruption by even a few incoming warheads, Washington and Moscow delegated alert and launch authority to lower levels in the chain of command and shortened response times to perceived attacks. Sophisticated early warning networks created an extremely time-sensitive interaction between the two C^3I systems, generating intense escalation pressures. As Blair writes, "classic preemptive instability resulted, and the command and control systems became prone to overreaction to erroneous indications of enemy attack." He believes that emerging nuclear powers face the "same dilemmas as those faced by their predecessors during the Cold War. A similar evolution of their nuclear postures and an attendant increase in the risk of inadvertence are predictable."[37]

COMMAND, CONTROL, AND THE LOGIC OF NUCLEAR DETERRENCE. The logic of nuclear deterrence downplays the possibility of preemptive nuclear strikes in the midst of crises. Waltz argues that preemption is

35. Fetter, "Ballistic Missiles," p. 29.

36. Dunn, *Controlling the Bomb*, pp. 72, 75.

37. Bruce G. Blair, *The Logic of Accidental Nuclear War* (Washington, D.C.: Brookings, 1994), pp. 6–10, 19–20.

viable "only if the would-be attacker knows that the intended victim's warheads are few in number, knows their exact number and locations, and knows that they will not be moved or fired before they are struck. To know all of these things and to know that you know them for sure, is exceedingly difficult." Furthermore, because nuclear weapons are easy to hide and move, creating uncertainty for the attacker does not require great technological sophistication. Countries can get by with a small number of weapons and a small number of dummies, while insinuating that they have more real weapons.[38]

ANALYSIS. From the standpoint of strategy, or the interdependent interactions of two nuclear powers, the main fear is that crude command and control arrangements will generate a situation in which both sides feel compelled to use, rather than lose, their limited stock of nuclear weapons. Here, too, the logic of nuclear deterrence is more persuasive than the logic of nonproliferation. There is no historical evidence to support the fear of nuclear preemption, despite the fact that every nuclear weapon state has endured a period of command and control backwardness. Indeed, recent research indicates that preemptive wars of any kind have been rarer than conventionally believed.[39] Of course, history is no sure predictor of the future, but it is one of the two ways by which we can evaluate theoretical arguments. The other is logic, which is also on the side of nuclear deterrence. The reciprocal fear of surprise attack is only valid if the potential attacker is certain that he can destroy all of the defender's nuclear weapons in a first strike. Partial or near-total success is not good enough in the nuclear realm. Failing to destroy a few or even one of the adversary's nuclear weapons means that heavily populated areas on the attacker's own territory would be subject to nuclear devastation.

LESSONS OF THE GULF WAR. The Gulf War experience suggests the difficulties inherent in launching a successful first strike. The allied coalition had at its disposal the best weaponry and intelligence-gathering capabilities in the world. Washington and its allies enjoyed overwhelming superiority over Iraq in every aspect of the balance of forces, including absolute control of the skies. Still, although the

---

38. Waltz, *More May Be Better*, pp. 15–16. On the uncertainties involved in executing a successful preemptive strike, see also Weltman, "Managing Nuclear Multipolarity," p. 190.

39. In a survey of all wars since 1816, Dan Reiter finds that only three out of sixty-seven were preemptive in origin. See his "Exploding the Powder Keg Myth: Preemptive Wars Almost Never Happen," *International Security*, Vol. 20, No. 2 (Fall 1995), pp. 5–34.

January 1991 allied bombing-target list included only two Iraqi nuclear installations, after the war UN inspectors discovered more than twenty Iraqi nuclear weapon facilities. Moreover, roughly 1,000 hours of allied air strikes left much of the Iraqi nuclear infrastructure untouched.[40] The coalition also failed to locate and destroy most of Iraq's SCUD missiles, illustrating the great potential for deception in moving and concealing even primitive delivery systems. In sum, despite nearly perfect conditions for conducting devastating first strikes against Iraq's third-rate nuclear and missile infrastructure, the United States and its Gulf War partners failed to obliterate it. In a future Third World crisis, all that would be necessary to deter preemptive strikes is "first-strike uncertainty," or the planting of a seed of doubt in the minds of the potential attacker's leaders about whether it would be possible to destroy all of the opponent's nuclear weapons preemptively. The same technological backwardness that is said to make nuclear forces vulnerable also implies that they will be nowhere near sophisticated enough to achieve first-strike effectiveness. What political leader would risk losing a few cities and millions of people by ordering a preemptive strike whose outcome is decidedly uncertain?

Although analysts speak of future proliferants "getting in the first blow" so as to minimize the damage of an opponent's retaliatory strike, a first strike could prove to be suicidal even if it achieved near-total success. Do Indian military leaders know how many nuclear weapons Pakistan has, or could have by next week? Do they know exactly where these weapons are, or where they might be next week? How would the Pakistanis' use of dummies, concealment, and mobility affect these calculations? In discussions of preemption, the onus is on the attacker to work through these nagging questions. It is virtually impossible to imagine a realistic scenario in which an Indian military planner could convince his political leadership that a preemptive strike would *definitely* succeed in destroying *all* of Pakistan's nuclear warheads or delivery systems.

THE SUPERPOWER EXPERIENCE AS *SUI GENERIS*. Viewed from this perspective, regional balances of terror do not appear delicate; indeed, consideration of this whole issue is distorted rather than clarified by the inordinate preoccupation with huge margins of survivability and windows of vulnerability during the U.S.-Soviet

---

40. Thomas A. Keaney and Eliot A. Cohen, *Gulf War Air Power Survey: A Summary Report (GWAPS)* (Maxwell Air Force Base, Ala.: Air War College for the U.S. Air Force, 1992), p. 82, cited in Barry R. Schneider, "Nuclear Proliferation and Counter-Proliferation: Policy Issues and Debates," *Mershon International Studies Review,* Vol. 38, Supplement No. 2 (October 1994), p. 226.

nuclear competition. Although survivability in any regional nuclear balance will be lower than that of the central balance, it will hardly be negligible. The experience of the U.S.-Soviet arms race obscures the fact that first-strike uncertainty is relatively easy to achieve even with small nuclear forces. Standards of measurement regarding stability in regional security environments should be based not on the inflated "requirements" for crisis stability during the superpower arms race, but on distinctive regional conditions. This reasoning has broader significance: deriving our expectations about the strategic calculus between emerging nuclear nations solely from the U.S.-Soviet experience is not analytically productive. Contrary to ingrained strategic thought, sub-superpower nuclear weapon states may actually be less subject to preemptive instability than were the superpowers. As Blair notes, during much of the Cold War, Washington and Moscow had counterforce targeting strategies, which placed a premium on detecting and responding rapidly to signs of enemy attacks; any hesitation on the defender's part would have left it vulnerable to an attack that might have degraded its ability to command and control a counterforce response. The threat of preemptive war between the United States and the Soviet Union stemmed from the *counterforce* doctrines they followed, not from any inherent logic of nuclear strategy.

Countervalue doctrines are theoretically more crisis-stable than counterforce doctrines because they have only one essential requirement: that a small number of nuclear warheads can be delivered against the enemy even after its attempted first strike. Ensuring that an adversary cannot be certain of launching a successful first strike is relatively easy. Prompt responses are unnecessary if one is not targeting the opponent's own nuclear weapons. With a counter-city strategy, the defender can wait to see if an attack actually materializes before responding. As a former Indian army chief notes, a "very highly sophisticated, highly responsive" C^3I system that "functions in real time" is not necessary for an effective countervalue strategy.[41] U.S. nuclear planners' preoccupation with C^3I was related to expanding their range of flexible responses, a menu of options in which the second-generation proliferants have shown little interest. The assumption that regional nuclear arms competitions will mimic the

41. General Krishnaswami Sundarji, "Changing Military Equations in Asia: The Relevance of Nuclear Weapons," paper prepared for the Indo-American Seminar on Non-Proliferation and Technology Transfer, Center for the Advanced Study of India, University of Pennsylvania, October 3–6, 1993, p. 7.

dynamics of the superpower arms race is not useful. It obscures the fact that there can be more than one road to nuclear deterrence and the possibility that non-U.S. defense planners may have accepted the fundamental principles of the nuclear revolution more readily than their U.S. counterparts, who have struggled in vain to overcome these principles through "rational" planning.

THE PROBLEM OF LOOSE NUKES

The logic of nonproliferation and the logic of nuclear deterrence have narrower differences in the area of loose nukes. Analysts on both sides of this divide agree to some extent that emerging nuclear arsenals, especially in the Third World, may be prone to accidents or weapon theft and use by terrorists or other unauthorized personnel. The two logics differ in their assessment of how likely these developments are. For the logic of nonproliferation, accidents and unauthorized use are serious possibilities, even likelihoods; for the logic of nuclear deterrence, they are more remote possibilities that nonetheless merit concern because of their potentially devastating consequences.

LOOSE NUKES AND THE LOGIC OF NONPROLIFERATION. Supporters of the logic of nonproliferation frequently assume that new proliferants will be less capable of accident-proofing their weapons than the first-generation nuclear weapon states. Although new nuclear states could minimize the likelihood of accidents by refraining from assembling their nuclear weapons, this might generate fears of being caught off guard by an adversary's crippling first strike. Moreover, even if the weapons were unassembled in peacetime, their hasty assembly during a crisis could lead to an accidental detonation. Alternatively, emerging proliferants might perceive launch-on-warning strategies as the only reliable way to safeguard a few precious nuclear weapons, leading to the possibility of mechanical or human error causing an accidental nuclear exchange.[42] Another perceived danger is unauthorized nuclear use: new proliferants' weapons may not be secure against theft and use by people outside the official chain of command, including terrorists, who could use stolen weapons or materials for blackmail or nuclear strikes. Also, separatists or renegade military officers might commandeer nuclear weapons and use them in domestic power struggles.[43]

---

42. For an analysis of the trade-offs between positive and negative control of nuclear weapons, see Peter D. Feaver, "Command and Control in Emerging Nuclear Nations," *International Security*, Vol. 17, No. 3 (Winter 1992/93), pp. 163–168.

43. Dunn, *Controlling the Bomb*, pp. 71–75.

LOOSE NUKES AND THE LOGIC OF NUCLEAR DETERRENCE. The logic of nuclear deterrence has no cohesive position on the problem of loose nukes. The sources of this problem are domestic and non-strategic in nature. John Mearsheimer supports the main premises of the logic of nuclear deterrence in selected cases, but concedes that widespread proliferation increases the chances of accidents and nuclear terrorism.[44] However, Waltz writes: "What is hard to comprehend is why, in an internal struggle for power, any of the contenders should start using nuclear weapons. Who would they aim at? How would they use them as instruments for maintaining or gaining control? . . . Those who fear the worst have not shown with any plausibility how those expected events may lead to the use of nuclear weapons."[45] Robert Art argues that the fear of nuclear terrorism is overstated because the terrorists would have to identify themselves or their constituents to achieve their political objectives, but in so doing could be countered or deterred like a national government.[46]

ANALYSIS. Perhaps the most definitive assessment that can be made about the possibility of nuclear accidents and unauthorized nuclear use is that they are more likely, but not inevitable, in a more proliferated world. Some nuclear optimists undermine their own position by glossing over nuclear security questions as if they were unimportant. For their part, nuclear pessimists often exaggerate the dangers of loose nukes. Historically, despite the fact that a handful of countries have built tens of thousands of nuclear warheads over the course of five decades, the world has been spared accidental and unauthorized nuclear weapon detonations. We can take wary solace from this record. Also, lest we view our good fortune as unique to the industrialized world, it should be remembered that China has been nuclear-capable for more than three decades, and India for more than two. On the other hand, a growing body of evidence shows that Cold War nuclear security lapses were sufficiently frequent to warrant serious efforts at minimizing the possibility of regional nuclear accidents.[47] The World Trade Center and Oklahoma City bombings suggest that, contrary to Art's analysis, deterring terrorists is indeed more challenging than deterring governments.

---

44. John J. Mearsheimer, "The Case for a Ukrainian Nuclear Deterrent," *Foreign Affairs*, Vol. 72, No. 3 (Summer 1993), p. 51.

45. Waltz, *More May Be Better*, pp. 10–11.

46. Robert J. Art, "A Defensible Defense: America's Grand Strategy After the Cold War," *International Security*, Vol. 15, No. 4 (Spring 1991), p. 27.

47. See Scott D. Sagan, *The Limits of Safety: Organizations, Accidents, and Nuclear Weapons* (Princeton, N.J.: Princeton University Press, 1993).

ACCIDENTS CAN HAPPEN.   The spread of any nuclear technology means an increased potential for nuclear accidents. Indeed, the world's two most serious civilian nuclear mishaps—at Three Mile Island in Pennsylvania and Chernobyl in then-Soviet Ukraine—occurred in industrialized countries. Still, supporters of the logic of nonproliferation do not explain why a scientific security community that has mastered the research and development of nuclear weapons cannot also devise basic accident-proofing and other security measures. Future proliferants are often portrayed as being likely to exhaust their limited resources just by going nuclear; but the proliferation process takes decades, requiring millions of dollars and the specialized services of hundreds of people. Why could these resources not also be applied to command and control arrangements?

The spread of nuclear materials and expertise also increases the likelihood of nuclear weapons falling into the hands of terrorists or personnel outside the official chain of command. Particularly worrisome is nuclear leakage: Soviet-style fragmentation poses severe challenges for the prevention of nuclear terrorism.[48] Nuclear technology and underemployed scientists can cross borders and be put to use by terrorists who have plenty of money but limited nuclear know-how. Indeed, it is possible, though not likely, that the fragmentation of nuclear weapon states may be a recurring feature of the international landscape: China faces the possibility of domestic discord in the post–Deng Xiaoping era, and India is racked by a variety of separatist conflicts. We should not, though, underestimate how difficult it would be for internal combatants to use nuclear weapons effectively. No one can predict with any certainty the consequences of civil wars in nuclear weapon states. All in all, proliferation raises the likelihood of nuclear accidents and nuclear terrorism; by how much is impossible to specify in the abstract.

"UNDETERRABLE" LEADERS

A fourth pillar of the logic of nonproliferation stresses that certain political leaders may be immune to the logic of nuclear deterrence. As Kathleen Bailey writes, "ruthlessness or lack of sanity has led some Middle Eastern leaders to use chemical weapons on their own populations or to engage in terrorism. This lends credibility to the argument that some leaders might be irresponsible with a weapon of

---

48. The most comprehensive examination of the Russian loose nukes problem is Graham T. Allison et al., *Avoiding Nuclear Anarchy: Containing the Threat of Loose Russian Nuclear Weapons and Fissile Material* (Cambridge, Mass.: MIT Press, 1996).

mass destruction, if one were at hand."[49] Another view is that some leaders' political goals may be so radical as to make the costs of using nuclear weapons worth the potential benefits; in other words, "it may be fully 'rational' for leaders to initiate wars, *in certain situations,* even against nuclear adversaries."[50] James Blight and David Welch use the Cuban Missile Crisis to illustrate the plausibility of this type of deterrence failure. They argue that Cuban leader Fidel Castro "would not have been deterred from launching a nuclear attack against the United States had he possessed nuclear weapons of his own, notwithstanding the United States's massive nuclear superiority and the certainty that American nuclear forces could have devastated his country."[51] Castro urged Soviet leader Nikita Khrushchev to launch a nuclear first strike against the United States if it invaded Cuba.[52] Blight and Welch argue that "Castro 'rationally' would have chosen nuclear war to surrender, notwithstanding the high likelihood that the United States and the Soviet Union faced mutual assured destruction." They further maintain that "Castro's calculations and behavior during the crisis are especially instructive" in the debate over the consequences of proliferation, since there are "many startling parallels between Castro's Cuba and post–Kim Il Sung North Korea, Saddam Hussein's Iraq, Hafez Assad's Syria, and Moammar Qaddafi's Libya—regimes known to be actively seeking nuclear capabilities."[53]

THE LOGIC OF NUCLEAR DETERRENCE AND THE "UNDETERRABLES." The logic of nuclear deterrence denies the thesis that some leaders may be undeterrable. John Weltman, for example, sees no basis for

---

49. Kathleen C. Bailey, *Doomsday Weapons in the Hands of Many: The Arms Control Challenge of the 1990s* (Urbana: University of Illinois Press, 1991), p. 2.

50. James G. Blight and David A. Welch, "Risking 'The Destruction of Nations': Lessons of the Cuban Missile Crisis for New and Aspiring Nuclear Nations," paper prepared for a conference on Preventing Nuclear War in South Asia, Rockefeller Foundation Study and Conference Center, Bellagio, Italy, September 19–23, 1994, p. 9.

51. Ibid., pp. 42–43.

52. Castro told Khrushchev that if the "imperialists invade Cuba with the goal of occupying it, the danger that that aggressive policy poses for humanity is so great that following that event the Soviet Union must never allow the circumstances in which the imperialists could launch the first nuclear strike against it." He continued: "That would be the moment to eliminate such danger forever through an act of clear legitimate defense, however harsh and terrible the solution would be, for there is no other." James G. Blight, Bruce J. Allyn, and David A. Welch, *Cuba on the Brink: Castro, the Missile Crisis, and the Soviet Collapse* (New York: Pantheon, 1993), p. 481.

53. Blight and Welch, "Risking 'The Destruction of Nations'," pp. 43, 46.

the claim that future proliferants would lack "those patterns of behavior and modes of thought that produced prudence in the Soviet-American relationship. . . . Such an assertion would assume that the capacity for political rationality is a narrow, culturally based attribute." Weltman also cautions us not to "automatically take bizarre behavior patterns and wild rhetorical posturing at face value. Cultivation of an image of inflexibility, monomaniacal commitment, or even sheer madness may at times prove to be a useful bargaining device."[54] From this perspective, even extremist political leaders are subject to the logic of nuclear deterrence.

ANALYSIS. No one can say for certain that a crazy or extremely radical leader would never use nuclear weapons against his adversaries. Leaders have ordered shocking deeds in the past. The savagery exhibited by Hitler, Stalin, and Mao suggests that there exists a certain breed of leader whose personality, ideology, or political goals diverge so far from everyday notions of rationality that even the most heinous acts are possible. There is, though, no record of these acts being committed in the face of nuclear retaliation, a likelihood faced by each of today's oft-mentioned candidates for nuclear first use. These leaders can have no doubt that a nuclear attack on Israel, South Korea, or U.S. territory or forces would be met with a rapid and even more devastating response. Although it is possible, we should not expect to see adventurism in the face of nuclear reprisal. Blight's and Welch's account of Fidel Castro's willingness to risk a nuclear holocaust during the Cuban Missile Crisis is not convincing evidence for the plausibility of the rational use of nuclear weapons. Since Castro had no nuclear launch authority, it is impossible to say what he would have done. Indirect nuclear threats should not be conflated with an actual readiness to use nuclear weapons in the face of nuclear devastation, especially if the threatener commands no weapons himself.

THE FALLACY OF FOREKNOWLEDGE. Another flaw in the logic of nonproliferation is that it mistakenly infers irrationality from outcomes. It is often heard that Iraq's 1990 invasion of Kuwait demonstrates Saddam Hussein's irrationality: given the ultimate defeat of Iraqi forces in 1991, surely no rational leader would have taken such a gamble. This would be an appropriate characterization of Saddam Hussein only if he expected that his armed forces would be forcibly ejected from Kuwait, but ordered the invasion anyway. To the contrary, it seems clear that he expected *not* to be punished for invading

---

54. Weltman, "Nuclear Devolution," pp. 189, 190.

Kuwait. His decision to do so may have been unwise, but it was not irrational. It was made with the expectation of achieving tangible political and economic benefits at low cost, not with the expectation that Baghdad would be obliterated. Would Saddam Hussein have invaded Kuwait if that country had been armed with nuclear weapons? Inferring irrationality from outcomes ignores the fact that the more egregious, allegedly irrational acts are committed without expectation of reprisal.

PREVENTIVE WAR IMPERATIVES

The fifth pillar of the logic of nonproliferation stresses that, while unlikely, premeditated nuclear attacks are still possible in a more pro-liferated world. As Lewis Dunn says, "the first use of nuclear weapons since Nagasaki may be a carefully calculated policy deci-sion."[55] Of particular concern are periods when the spread of nuclear weapons is asymmetrical, making a preventive strike attractive to the country with the advantage. As precedents, analysts cite Israel's 1981 attack on Iraq's nuclear facility at Osirak and the fact that Washington and Moscow contemplated launching preventive nuclear strikes during the Cold War.[56] Scott Sagan attempts to but-tress this historical record with logical rigor by deducing from orga-nization theory a basis for preventive nuclear war. He reasons that "military officers are predisposed to view *preventive war,* in particular, in a much more favorable light than are civilian authorities," and that "preventive war is more likely to be chosen . . . if military leaders have a significant degree of influence over the final decision. While there have not been, obviously, any nuclear preventive wars among the new proliferants, the probability of such attacks will increase since civilian control over the military is more problematic in many" nations of proliferation concern.[57]

---

55. Dunn, *Controlling the Bomb,* p. 76.

56. For a discussion of U.S. deliberations over launching a preventive nuclear strike against the Soviet Union in the 1940s and 1950s, see Scott D. Sagan, "The Perils of Proliferation: Organization Theory, Deterrence Theory, and the Spread of Nuclear Weapons," *International Security,* Vol. 18, No. 4 (Spring 1994), pp. 77–82. On Moscow's interest in eliminating China's nascent nuclear capabilities in the 1960s, see Wohlstetter, "Life in a Nuclear Armed Crowd," p. 132. For similar U.S. sentiment and an overture to Moscow on the possibility of joint preventive action against China, see Seaborg, *Stemming the Tide,* pp. 111–117.

57. Sagan, "The Perils of Proliferation," pp. 75, 82.

PREVENTIVE WAR AND THE LOGIC OF NUCLEAR DETERRENCE. Contrary to this thinking, those persuaded by the logic of nuclear deterrence find it hard to conceive of situations where the gains to be expected from a nuclear strike would outweigh the losses involved in a nuclear response. As with preemption, since uncertainty about the efficacy of a first strike is easy to induce, deterrence should prevail in situations where two adversaries have nuclear weapons. Where there is asymmetry, that is, where one side is a nuclear power and its enemy is either a nonnuclear or nascent nuclear state, the nuclear power may contemplate a preventive strike, either conventional or nuclear. Waltz distinguishes two periods when an emerging proliferant might be subject to a preventive strike: at the earliest stages of weapon development, when it is "obviously unable to make nuclear weapons," and later, when its status is unknown. For Waltz, preventive strikes in the first period will not be effective; unless the attacking state could completely destroy the new proliferant's weapon potential in the first attack, it must be "prepared to repeat it or to occupy and control the country. To do either would be difficult and costly." Preventive strikes in the second stage are even more problematic because "if the country attacked has even a rudimentary nuclear capability, one's own severe punishment becomes possible."[58]

ANALYSIS. Here again, theory and practice suggest that the logic of nuclear deterrence is more compelling than the logic of nonproliferation. In the case of two nuclear-capable antagonists, such as India and Pakistan, it is difficult to imagine one side making a premeditated decision to attack the other with nuclear weapons, in the face of a near-certain response in kind. Pakistan might threaten to use nuclear weapons to forestall a massive conventional defeat, but the United States and its allies did this for more than four decades in Europe. Why would the Indian armed forces run the risk of testing the Pakistan Army? What Indian political gain could possibly be worth the explosion of one or several nuclear bombs in Bombay?

PREVENTIVE WAR SCENARIOS. The most likely scenario involving nuclear weapons in asymmetrical situations is one in which an established nuclear power launches a preventive strike against the nuclear facilities of an aspiring nuclear state. Table 1 depicts four possible preventive war scenarios. Two pairs of variables are germane to this problem. First, the preventive strike could be conventional or nuclear. Second, the target nation could be in Waltz's first (nonnuclear) or second (possibly nuclear) stage of weapon development.

---

58. Waltz, *More May Be Better*, p. 14.

Table 1. Preventive War Scenarios.		
	Conventional	Nuclear
Nonnuclear	Osirak, Gulf War	Nuclear Taboo
Possibly Nuclear	Extremely Unlikely	Extremely Unlikely

In the northwest corner of this matrix is the possibility of a conventional preventive attack against a target country that is in the earliest stages of the proliferation process. This is at once the most plausible and least worrisome possibility. History offers two examples of this type of attack: Israel's Osirak strike and the allied coalition's 1991 air war against Iraq.[59] Neither threatened to escalate to a nuclear exchange, because both were nonnuclear strikes against a nonnuclear country. It is unlikely that either attack would have been ordered had Iraq been judged capable of nuclear retaliation. One may support or oppose conventional preventive strikes for reasons of personal politics or national interest, but the fact remains that the strategic consequences of the strikes against Iraq were limited.

The northeast quadrant of Table 1 houses the possibility of a preventive nuclear strike against a nonnuclear state. Restraint in the use of nuclear weapons against nonnuclear nations is a firmly embedded element of the post-1945 nuclear taboo. Despite numerous wars between nuclear and nonnuclear states, nuclear weapons have never been used by the country enjoying the advantage. Nuclear preventive strikes against nonnuclear states are extremely unlikely, both because it is unnecessary to use nuclear weapons in such an attack and because of the international outcry that would engulf the attacking state. Imagine if Israel were to destroy Iran's nascent nuclear research and development facilities with nuclear weapons. The devastation and loss of life would be immense, and Israel would overnight become an international pariah. No political objective could be worth the isolation that would result. If Israel felt threatened by Iran's nuclear progress, it would likely resort to sabotage or another Osirak-style conventional raid.

In the table's southwest corner lies the possibility of a conventional attack against an adversary's late-stage nuclear facilities, which may or may not have produced deliverable nuclear weapons. In this

---

59. The Gulf War attacks on Iraq's nuclear facilities were, of course, embedded in a larger political-military context, but their purpose was clearly preventive in nature.

situation, given the inherent uncertainty about whether all of the target country's nuclear weapon potential could be destroyed, the attacking country would face the danger of suffering nuclear punishment in response. Even if the defender could not mount a nuclear response, what would prevent it from destroying the attacking country's own nuclear facilities with conventional explosives? These and other vexing questions create uncertainty so profound that it is likely to inhibit preventive attacks against possibly nuclear states.

Finally, in the southeast quadrant of Table 1 rests the possibility of a nuclear preventive strike against a late-stage nuclear proliferant. This, too, is extremely unlikely. Although Washington and Moscow contemplated such strikes in the early decades of the nuclear era, in no case were the imperatives of prevention judged sufficiently compelling to risk nuclear retaliation. For the logic of nonproliferation, the fact that these attacks were even considered is evidence of danger; for the logic of nuclear deterrence, the fact that they have never been ordered is evidence of their implausibility. Plans to launch preventive strikes are not convincing evidence that such attacks are likely: military officers plan for every imaginable contingency, but the vast majority of their plans are never implemented. More definitive evidence lies in actual decisions about which plans to follow. Political leaders have so far eschewed preventive nuclear strikes, and there is little reason to expect that this will change.

Conclusions

This chapter demonstrates that the theoretical debate over the consequences of nuclear proliferation is indeterminate. One reason for this is that a deep analytical divide between the realm of strategy and the non-strategic realm of loose nukes undermines our ability to generalize broadly about the nuclear experience. In the area of strategy, or the interdependent interactions of nation-states, my analysis suggests that new proliferants will be subject to the same constraints that shaped the behavior of the superpowers during the Cold War. Simply put, the powerful logic of nuclear deterrence will tend to discourage nuclear-armed adversaries from warring with one another.

On the other hand, loose nukes pose stiff challenges for international security. Despite the fact that every nuclear weapon state thus far has a strong record of protecting against the accidental or unauthorized use of nuclear weapons, no one can say what the future will bring. The dramatic international developments of the last decade, including the rapid fragmentation of one of the world's two nuclear superpowers, render optimism difficult. Fortunately, the Soviet Union had a commendable forty-year record of protecting its nuclear infrastructure; other nuclear weapon states might not weather domestic instability as well. The possibilities of major nuclear accidents and of the domestic or terrorist use of nuclear weapons argue for limiting their spread where feasible.

Furthermore, the inherent nature of deterrence militates against theoretical generalization. Since successful deterrence results in non-events, i.e., continued peace, it is logically impossible to prove that nuclear deterrence has worked in any given situation. As a consequence of this empirical vacuum, much of the abstract disagreement between the logic of nonproliferation and the logic of nuclear deterrence stems from individual analysts' instinctive view of the efficacy of nuclear deterrence.

Some analysts straddle the composite logics I have outlined. They take a compromise position that sees merit in the logic of nuclear deterrence, but also acknowledges the dangers that might arise from loose nukes. As Joseph Nye says: "There can be no decisive answer in the debate over the effects of proliferation. Particular outcomes may differ. Some cases may start a disastrous chain of events; other [cases] may turn out to have benign effects."[60] This sensible conclusion suggests the advisability of a theoretically driven, historically informed, case-study approach to the analysis of proliferation dynamics. This is the approach I adopt in Chapters 3 through 6, where I examine the evolution of the South Asian nuclear arms competition. In the meantime, though, one important theoretical issue remains to be addressed: the phenomenon of nuclear opacity, which has supplanted the more visible nuclear weaponization process characteristic of the five declared nuclear powers. The implications of opaque proliferation—and its logical outgrowth, existential deterrence—are the subject of Chapter 2.

---

60. Joseph S. Nye, "Maintaining a Nonproliferation Regime," *International Organization*, Vol. 35, No. 1 (Winter 1981), p. 33.

Chapter 2

Opaque Proliferation, Existential Deterrence, and Nuclear Weapon Stability

In Chapter 1, I argued that the theoretical debate over the consequences of nuclear proliferation is inconclusive. One reason for this is that consideration of the issue has typically relied on an inappropriate model of nuclear proliferation—one derived from the historical experience of the five acknowledged nuclear weapon states, especially the United States and the Soviet Union. The characteristics of this transparent proliferation universe are very different from those of the opaque pattern established by the second-generation proliferants of the past three decades: India, Israel, North Korea, Pakistan, and South Africa. This chapter moves from a consideration of the effects of proliferation in general to a more focused analysis of this more recent form of proliferation.

In the first part of the chapter, I discuss the fundamental characteristics of nuclear opacity. I then explore the international and domestic sources of opaque proliferation. Next, I examine the relationship between opaque proliferation and existential deterrence, arguing that any deterrent effect to be derived from opaque nuclear postures is logically existential in nature. Then I explore the logic of existential deterrence by presenting a model of nuclear-political behavior in proliferating regions. This model is based on two processes: tacit bargaining and inadvertent transparency-building, both of which lend credibility to existential deterrence. In the next section, I compare opaque nuclear balances with transparent ones and conclude that opaque postures are theoretically more stable. Finally, I delve more deeply into the concept of existential deterrence by asking which types of behavior it deters and which it does not. I conclude that it deters nuclear and conventional aggression, but not the unconventional military operations characteristic of guerrilla warfare.

Opaque Proliferation

Opaque proliferation is a government's covert development of nuclear weapon capabilities combined with its public denial of any intention to deploy nuclear weapons. The term was coined in 1987 by Benjamin Frankel who observed that there are now two "distinct nuclear cultures." In the overt culture of the five declared nuclear powers, "nuclear weapons, their testing, and the means to deliver them were all on display—an integral and pronounced part of the nuclear age's politics." In the covert culture embraced by subsequent proliferants, nuclear capabilities have been acquired secretly and often in violation of international norms and national laws against the spread of nuclear weapons. Most important from an analytical standpoint is that opaque proliferants deny developing nuclear weapons and profess loyalty to global nonproliferation norms.[1] The cornerstone of nuclear opacity is this tension between what the international community believes about a country's nuclear program and that country's public stance concerning nuclear weapons.[2]

OPACITY AS AN IDEAL TYPE

Avner Cohen and Frankel describe opacity as a Weberian ideal type; as with any ideal type, the experience of individual opaque proliferants may deviate in certain respects from the theoretical concept. They suggest several core features of opacity;[3] I will discuss these characteristics with reference to three opaque proliferants—India, Israel, and Pakistan.

NO NUCLEAR TESTS. The international community has traditionally viewed testing a nuclear device as tantamount to announcing that a country is building nuclear weapons. Israel and Pakistan have apparently resisted nuclear testing, although there have been persistent rumors that Israel exploded a nuclear device in collaboration with South Africa in 1979, and that Pakistan received from China

---

1. Benjamin Frankel, "Notes on the Nuclear Underworld," *National Interest*, No. 9 (Fall 1987), p. 124; and Avner Cohen and Benjamin Frankel, "Opaque Nuclear Proliferation," *Journal of Strategic Studies*, Vol. 13, No. 2 (September 1990), p. 17.

2. John Schulz likens the overt nuclear culture to the game of chess, where features are open for all to see, and the covert nuclear culture to the game of poker, where certain features are hidden. See his "Bluff and Uncertainty: Deterrence and the 'Maybe States'," *SAIS Review*, Vol. 7, No. 2 (Summer–Fall 1987), p. 184.

3. Cohen and Frankel, "Opaque Nuclear Proliferation," pp. 21–22.

bomb design information that makes testing unnecessary.[4] India's detonation of a nuclear device in 1974 violates the no-testing norm, but its subsequent policy of no further testing conforms to the model—in contrast to the five acknowledged nuclear weapon states, which continued to test their nuclear explosives for decades. Despite their restraint in nuclear testing, opaque proliferants are perceived as no less threatening to adversaries than are the transparent proliferants.[5]

DENIAL OF NUCLEAR WEAPON POSSESSION. Cohen and Frankel argue that "under opacity, proliferator states deny the possession of nuclear weapons, although they acknowledge—*some more so than others*—*their capability to build nuclear weapons quickly.* In all these cases, the operational distance between 'capability' and 'possession,' if it exists at all, is insignificant."[6] This public posture allows the opaque proliferant to derive deterrent security from its nuclear capabilities without suffering the international opprobrium that would result from a public admission of weapon possession. There are many ways of maintaining such a stance, and each opaque proliferant does so differently. Israel, for example, pledges not to be the "first nation to introduce nuclear weapons into the Middle East,"[7] a formulation that leaves ambiguous its intentions but not its capabilities. India proved itself nuclear weapon–capable by its 1974 test but has subsequently disclaimed any intention actually to build nuclear weapons, unless driven to do so by Pakistan's nuclear strides. After coyly alluding to its nuclear progress for years, the government of Pakistan finally admitted in 1992 that it is nuclear weapon–capable. Islamabad today maintains that its nuclear program has been "frozen," short of actual deployments. Each of these efforts at plausible denial is intended to conform loosely to nonproliferation norms

---

4. Leonard S. Spector, *The Undeclared Bomb* (Cambridge, Mass.: Ballinger, 1988), pp. 126–127, 294–296.

5. As Frankel points out on p. 124 of "Nuclear Underworld," the "testing of nuclear bombs is no longer necessary to attain a high degree of confidence in their operational reliability. Simulation techniques have been developed that provide information on the weapon's components and activation." Proliferation expert Leonard Spector concurs: "Reliable early generation atomic weapons . . . can be developed without testing; indeed, the type of bomb dropped on Hiroshima had never been tested." *Undeclared Bomb*, p. 8.

6. Cohen and Frankel, "Opaque Nuclear Proliferation," p. 21 (emphasis added).

7. Avner Cohen, "Nuclear Opacity and the Israeli Press: The Gulf Drift," *New Outlook* (Tel Aviv), Vol. 34, No. 5 (September–October 1991), p. 19.

while leaving adversaries with no doubt that they will face the prospect of nuclear punishment in a future war.

NO DIRECT NUCLEAR THREATS. Cohen and Frankel contrast the relatively restrained signalling behavior of opaque proliferants with that of the acknowledged nuclear weapon states, whose deterrence strategies have encompassed a variety of explicit threats that are intended to demonstrate resolve *vis-à-vis* adversaries. This is not to say that opaque proliferants do not trumpet their nuclear resolve; never alluding to one's capacity to inflict enormous damage lessens the deterrent value of nuclear capabilities. But opaque proliferants signal their resolve to enemies in a more oblique fashion. During the Gulf War, for example, Israel's prime minister, Yitzhak Shamir, "warned Iraq that Israeli retaliation to unprovoked aggression would be 'ayom venora'—'awesome and dreadful'."[8] Threats of this nature carry sufficient force to get the desired message across (it is unlikely that Saddam Hussein, who had earlier threatened to "scorch half of Israel" with chemical weapons, interpreted Shamir's statement as anything less than a promise to respond to Iraqi chemical attacks with nuclear reprisals), while being vague enough for the opaque proliferant to continue denying its possession of nuclear weapons.

NO OPEN NUCLEAR DEBATES OR PUBLIC NUCLEAR DOCTRINES. Unlike the transparent nuclear weapon states, which have a long history of debate about nuclear policy and have subsequently made public at least the outlines of the resultant doctrines, opaque proliferants condone little by way of officially sanctioned public debate or doctrine. There are, of course, important citizens in India, Israel, and Pakistan who vigorously debate the merits of openly going nuclear and of different strategic concepts. Participants in these debates typically include journalists, scholars, and retired civil servants and military officers. Such debates usually have one thing in common, though, and that is their non-official or at best quasi-official quality. Lines of argument and conclusions may reflect certain constituencies within the government or the military, but any fragments of doctrine that emerge enjoy no official sanction. To illustrate this point, many analysts believe that Israel and Pakistan loosely subscribe to similar last-resort, countervalue nuclear doctrines, but policymakers in neither country openly detail any such strategies.

NO DEPLOYED NUCLEAR WEAPONS. This is a debatable characteristic of opacity. In the first place, it may be inaccurate to portray the

---

8. Ibid., pp. 20–21.

Indian, Israeli, and Pakistani nuclear postures as existing somewhere short of actual deployment. Israel, at least, is widely thought to deploy operational nuclear weapons. And although India and Pakistan are believed to have resisted the temptation to deploy assembled nuclear weapons, this may or may not be true. Even if it is true, it may not be important: as U.S. Director of Central Intelligence James Woolsey told Congress in February 1993, "both India and Pakistan have the capability to assemble the components of nuclear weapons . . . within a very short period of time." He added that "the distinction between whether those weapons are in fact assembled or only able to be assembled within a few days is a very small distinction."[9] The essential point is that the opaque proliferant's adversary simply cannot be sure whether it has deployed nuclear weapons or not, and must therefore assume that it has.

NUCLEAR PROGRAM INSULATION. Opaque proliferants insulate their nuclear weapon programs from routine national security activities. This is an accurate depiction of the Indian, Israeli, and Pakistani nuclear weapon stances, although different communities within each polity predominate in nuclear affairs. In India, the civilian nuclear scientific community has always enjoyed a great deal of influence over nuclear decision-making; in Pakistan, a comparable role belongs to the army.

WHY OPACITY?

Why do second-generation proliferants maintain opaque instead of overt nuclear postures? It is easy to understand why a country at the beginning stages of nuclear research and development would want its program shrouded in secrecy. Such countries are typically embroiled in acute security competitions in which there may be a premium on being the first to master nuclear weapon technology. Openly advertising that one is seeking nuclear capabilities might spur the other side to do the same, thereby negating any strategic advantage. Conversely, if a country were lagging behind an adversary, the first steps toward nuclear capabilities, if taken too openly, might promote a preventive strike against its nascent nuclear facilities, like the one launched by Israel against Iraq in 1981. It is harder to understand why a nuclear weapon–capable country would continue to conceal its nuclear status. One would think that, having achieved a certain proficiency, countries would then go openly

9. Aziz Haniffa, "CIA on India's Navy and A-Plans," *India Abroad*, March 5, 1993, p. 10.

nuclear so as to receive the full benefits of deterrence. This is not the case, though; every new nuclear nation since the 1960s has chosen to maintain its opacity long after developing nuclear capabilities. The most important reason for this pattern is the steady legitimation of the global nonproliferation norm since the signing of the NPT in 1968. When China went nuclear in 1964, the only obstacle it faced was the possibility of preventive strikes or sabotage by its nuclear-armed adversaries. When Pakistan took the same course from the mid-1970s on, it too faced the possibility of absorbing a preventive strike, but also, and perhaps more daunting, Islamabad ran up against a variety of international norms and national laws intended to inhibit more countries from going nuclear. These included the NPT itself and an array of U.S. laws that threatened an aid cutoff if Pakistan persisted in its attempts to develop nuclear weapons.

DOMESTIC IMPERATIVES. While it is one important factor, international pressure is not the only determinant of opacity.[10] Cohen and Frankel argue that domestic political culture may also be an important variable. In Israel, for example, the strategic legacy of the Holocaust may have been twofold: first, it "provides Israelis with a concrete, as opposed to hypothetical, worst case scenario," which strongly promotes the development of a "weapon of last resort"; and second, "it may well be that the holocaust also brought about a certain inhibition in the way Israel handles nuclear weapons.... Opacity thus reflects an essential Israeli ambivalence about nuclear weapons."[11] Still, political culture does not seem to be important in every case. One could argue (though I would not) that Pakistan's Islamic political culture gives it a martial strategic tradition. Indeed, the misguided characterization of Pakistan's nuclear development as a quest for the "Islamic bomb" invokes this stereotype of a scripturally sanctioned martial mentality. To pursue this line of reasoning to its logical conclusion, however, Pakistan should be predisposed toward a transparent nuclear posture, one that would unambiguously demonstrate its military prowess—to its Islamic friends and non-Islamic enemies alike. The fact that Islamabad's nuclear program remains opaque suggests that Pakistan's motives for opacity are entirely international in origin: Islamabad wants to attain a measure

---

10. Shlomo Aronson, *The Politics and Strategy of Nuclear Weapons in the Middle East: Opacity, Theory, and Reality, 1960–1991* (Albany: State University of New York Press, 1992), pp. 290ff.

11. Cohen and Frankel, "Opaque Nuclear Proliferation," p. 28.

of nuclear deterrence against India without suffering the diplomatic penalties associated with open weaponization.

OTHER SOURCES OF OPACITY. Several other factors may influence the evolution of opaque rather than transparent nuclear postures. Opacity is a way to signal a country's nuclear capabilities and flex some deterrent muscle without antagonizing adversaries into like responses and spurring a destabilizing and expensive nuclear arms race. In this context, India's "peaceful nuclear explosion," followed by its refusal to deploy nuclear weapons, may have been meant to send a message of rough nuclear equivalence to China without driving Pakistan into its own pursuit of nuclear weapons. If this was in fact New Delhi's strategy, it obviously failed. In addition, opacity is much less expensive than a transparent nuclear posture, which for the first-generation nuclear weapon states involved developing redundant and diverse nuclear forces to ensure the survivability of second-strike weapons. Finally, opacity preserves the flexibility that future policymakers may need to denuclearize if security conditions change, without losing face or suffering domestic discontent owing to the popularity of an open nuclear stance.[12] Whatever the relative influence of these factors—and it differs across cases—the most compelling reason for opacity seems to be the belief that it provides deterrent security while avoiding the steep international costs of open deployments.

Opacity and Existential Deterrence

The implications of opaque proliferation for regional nuclear balances are intriguing. Second-generation proliferants pursue nuclear weapon capabilities at least in part because of the deterrent effect they expect such capabilities will have on adversaries. This imperative raises an interesting question: can opaque proliferants derive deterrence value from nuclear weapons they publicly deny having? If so, how?[13]

---

12. For a discussion of this quality of opacity, see Neil Joeck, "Tacit Bargaining and Stable Proliferation in South Asia," *Journal of Strategic Studies*, Vol. 13, No. 3 (September 1990), pp. 77–91. The South African denuclearization process provides empirical support for Joeck's theoretical insight.

13. As Cohen and Frankel note on p. 32 of "Opaque Nuclear Proliferation," deterrence has traditionally been "predicated on the visibility of nuclear weapons. . . . It is worth examining whether deterrence theory has the same validity in situations where this essential component of certainty is absent."

EXISTENTIAL DETERRENCE

The logical form of nuclear deterrence under opacity is "existential deterrence," a concept invented by McGeorge Bundy,[14] and defined by Marc Trachtenberg as a strategic interaction in which "the mere existence of nuclear forces means that, whatever we say or do, there is a certain irreducible risk that an armed conflict might escalate into a nuclear war. The fear of escalation is thus factored into political calculations: faced with this risk, states are more cautious and more prudent than they otherwise would be."[15] Bundy argued during the Cold War that any nuclear conflict between the superpowers would be fraught with "inescapable uncertainties." As he said,

no one can hope to have any clear idea of what would in fact happen 'if deterrence failed'—that is, if nuclear war began. This difficulty is not escaped by any theory, because no theory can predict with any confidence the behavior of any government, friend or foe, in such a situation. Most scenarios for nuclear warfare between the Soviet Union and the United States reflect nothing more than the state of mind of their authors.

What we are left with, according to Bundy, are unreliable "estimates of interacting behavior under conditions of quite unprecedented stress and danger, possibly in the midst of already appalling destruction." The performance of weapons, the maintenance of credible communication between enemies, the accurate reading of adversary intentions, and innumerable other variables inevitably remain question marks, despite the best efforts of strategists to model the likely course of nuclear confrontations. For Bundy,

these terrible and unavoidable uncertainties have great meaning for the theory of deterrence. They create what I will call existential deterrence. My aim in using this fancy adjective is to distinguish this kind of deterrence from the kind that is based on strategic theories or declaratory policies or even international commitments. As long as we assume that each side has very large numbers of thermonuclear weapons which *could* be used against the opponent, even after the strongest possible pre-emptive attack, existential deterrence is strong.

---

14. McGeorge Bundy, "Existential Deterrence and Its Consequences," in Douglas MacLean, ed., *The Security Gamble: Deterrence Dilemmas in the Nuclear Age* (Totowa, N.J.: Rowman and Allanheld, 1984), pp. 3–13.

15. Marc Trachtenberg, "The Influence of Nuclear Weapons in the Cuban Missile Crisis," *International Security*, Vol. 10, No. 1 (Summer 1985), p. 139. For similar assessments of the nuclear condition, see Robert Jervis, *The Meaning of the Nuclear Revolution: Statecraft and the Prospect of Armageddon* (Ithaca, N.Y.: Cornell University Press, 1989), pp. 79, 105; and Bernard Brodie, *War and Politics* (New York: Macmillan, 1973), pp. 375–432.

It rests on uncertainty about what *could happen,* not in what has been asserted.[16]

THE COLD WAR EXPERIENCE. Bundy and others have suggested that during the Cold War superpower competition, this existential quality of nuclear deterrence was more compelling for decision-makers during crises than relative nuclear superiority or inferiority. In 1969, Bundy noted the sharp differences between the complex technical calculations of nuclear planners and the simpler equations that present themselves to political leaders in times of crisis. He argued that the threat of losing even one city to an opponent's nuclear strike is a disaster any political leader would do his utmost to avoid. Implicit in Bundy's argument is the notion that decision-makers are deterred not by virtue of the fact that their nuclear forces are relatively inferior, but by the fact that the weapons exist and by the possibility that they might be used *at all.*

It is one thing for military men to maintain our deterrent force with vigilant skill, and it is quite another for anyone to assume that their necessary contingency plans have any serious interest for political leaders. The object of political men—quite rightly—is that these weapons should never be used. I have watched two Presidents working on strategic contingency plans, and what interested them most was simply to make sure that none of these awful events would occur.[17]

According to Bundy, existential deterrence was "strong in every major crisis between the superpowers since 'massive retaliation' became possible for both of them in the 1950s. As everyone closely involved recalls, such deterrence was particularly powerful during the Cuban missile crisis."[18] President John Kennedy's secretary of defense, Robert McNamara, concurs with this assessment. He relates that during the October 1962 crisis the United States was deterred from "even considering a nuclear attack by the knowledge that, although such a strike would destroy the Soviet Union, tens of their weapons would survive to be launched against the United States. These would kill millions of Americans. No responsible political leader would expose his nation to such a catastrophe."[19] Trachtenberg's research on the crisis

---

16. Bundy, "Existential Deterrence," pp. 8–9.

17. McGeorge Bundy, "To Cap the Volcano," *Foreign Affairs,* Vol. 48, No. 1 (October 1969), pp. 9–10, 12.

18. McGeorge Bundy, "The Bishops and the Bomb," *New York Review of Books,* June 16, 1983, p. 4.

19. Robert McNamara, *Blundering Into Disaster: Surviving the First Century of the Nuclear Age* (New York: Pantheon, 1986), pp. 44–45.

also supports the notion that it was the absolute possibility of a nuclear exchange, not any relative calculation of advantage, that conditioned the behavior of Kennedy and his advisers. He writes: "It was as though all the key concepts associated with the administration's formal nuclear strategy . . . in the final analysis counted for very little." As Kennedy said during the crisis, "'what difference does it make? They've got enough to blow us up now anyway'."[20]

THE RELATIONSHIP BETWEEN OPACITY AND EXISTENTIAL DETERRENCE
Under opacity, the relative role of existential deterrence is even more pronounced. Since each side in a regional nuclear arms competition like the one in South Asia can muster little hard evidence concerning the other side's forces, any deterrent effect derived from nuclear capabilities will logically be existential; that is to say, even more than with the superpowers, mutual calculations about the efficacy of nuclear deterrence are based not on the details of relative capabilities—which are shrouded in secrecy—but on the shared notion that each side is nuclear weapon–capable and thus that any outbreak of conflict might lead to a nuclear exchange. Of course, there are important differences between the central balance and regional nuclear balances. Bundy's analysis of the nuclear condition rests on three characteristics of the superpowers' nuclear forces: they were large, unambiguously survivable, and thermonuclear. In particular, the *sine qua non* of existential deterrence, as with all nuclear deterrence, is survivability. Bundy writes: "As long as each side retains survivable strength so that no leader can ever suppose that he could 'disarm' his opponent completely, nuclear war remains an overwhelmingly unattractive proposition for both sides." This deterrent power is largely immune to deployment changes "except those which might truly challenge the overall survivability of the forces on either side."[21]

The differences between the huge hydrogen bomb standoff between Washington and Moscow and the comparatively tiny atomic bomb balance between India and Pakistan are stark. Might these disparate situations have dissimilar implications for relations between the opposing sides? A closer examination reveals that the differences are not as pronounced as they seem. The main distinction

20. Trachtenberg, "Nuclear Weapons in the Cuban Missile Crisis," p. 148. Also see McGeorge Bundy's account of the crisis in his *Danger and Survival: Choices About the Bomb in the First Fifty Years* (New York: Random House, 1988), pp. 391–462.

21. Bundy, "Bishops and the Bomb," p. 6; and Bundy, "Existential Deterrence," pp. 9, 12; also see Jervis, *Nuclear Revolution*, pp. 9, 105.

between the central balance and regional balances like the one in South Asia is the fact that the United States and the Soviet Union had unambiguous, assured second-strike capabilities for most of the Cold War. To the extent that Washington and Moscow had no doubt about each other's nuclear prowess, their capabilities were "visible" and helped make mutual deterrence credible. The important question for opaque nuclear proliferants is: can deterrence be achieved with more modest capabilities?

LESSONS OF THE CUBAN MISSILE CRISIS. This question can be answered by returning to the discussion of preemptive logic in Chapter 1. The only compelling scenario for the purposeful use of nuclear weapons stems from a situation where one side in a crisis views a crippling strike to be the second worst option and passivity the worst choice. As I argued, however, first-strike uncertainty will deter preemptive attacks. The Cuban Missile Crisis illustrates the robustness of this principle. As Bundy recalls, President Kennedy had decided on a naval quarantine of Cuba, "subject only to a final discussion of the [alternative] air strike [option] with the responsible air commander." In a review of the requirements and prospects of a massive air strike against the Soviet missiles in Cuba, the U.S. Air Force "could not promise to destroy more than 90 percent of the Soviet missiles" in a first attack. Nor could the Air Force "guarantee beyond doubt that no Soviet missile would be fired in reply by a local commander." Bundy reports that "discussion was quickly over, and the president's decision [for the quarantine] became final."[22] This episode demonstrates the implausibility of an Indian or Pakistani military planner convincing the political leadership that a preemptive nuclear strike would *definitely* succeed in destroying *all* of the other side's nuclear warheads in a first strike.

Furthermore, the requirement for *large* nuclear forces in Bundy's conception is epiphenomenal. As the superpower arms race spiralled into ever larger forces on both sides, U.S. and Soviet strategists came to equate survivability with redundancy. Logically, though, large forces are required only to ensure survivability against preemption by *other* large forces. For the maintenance of first-strike uncertainty, only a very rough equivalence is needed to ensure that one side cannot simply overwhelm the other in a massive attack. Finally, the question of fusion versus fission weapons arises. Is the deterrent power of the nuclear shadow limited to thermonuclear weapons? Is

---

22. Bundy, *Danger and Survival*, pp. 401–402.

the qualitative difference between atomic and hydrogen weapons so great that the effects of existential deterrence are negated in situations where the weapons of concern are rudimentary fission devices? In the U.S.-Soviet competition, there is reason to believe that, had the two sides stopped short of developing hydrogen bombs, the effects of existential deterrence may have been greatly diminished. The United States is, and the Soviet Union was, a huge land mass with a widely dispersed population. It is conceivable that an exchange of fission devices, if terminated quickly, might not have totally devastated the two societies. This may have implied *some* increased willingness to use nuclear weapons during a crisis. For Robert Jervis, Bernard Brodie's 1946 argument that "military victory in a nuclear war was not possible" was "certainly incorrect" when he made it. "It took the hydrogen bomb to bring about the world Brodie had foreseen."[23]

It is not self-evident that this distinction between fission and fusion weapons is as meaningful in regional security environments. Because Third World countries typically have dense populations crowded into a few sprawling cities, even small fission weapons can cause enormous human suffering. For example, the northwestern subcontinent has one of the highest population densities in the world; consequently, the detonation of one or a handful of basic fission devices would suffice to kill millions of Indians and Pakistanis. In the event of a nuclear exchange, no Indian or Pakistani leader can have any illusion that the use of fission weapons would result in an "acceptable" number of deaths. Furthermore, the proximity of heavily congested areas of northern India and Pakistan means that radioactive fallout could blow back across the border to poison the aggressor's own population. In short, the distinction between fission and fusion weapons was significant in the U.S.-Soviet case, but is less so in South Asia.[24] A simple deterrence hierarchy clarifies the linkage between opaque proliferation and existential deterrence. Table 2 depicts the various relationships between proliferation type (transparent vs. opaque) and deterrence type.

---

23. Jervis, *The Meaning of the Nuclear Revolution*, p. 47.

24. McGeorge Bundy expressed to me his agreement with the substance of this argument: "I generally agree with your view of the nuclear standoff in the subcontinent. . . . as I listen to officials from nuclear-weapon states I find an implicit acceptance of existential deterrence. I don't think it guarantees against all smaller conflict, but it does afford a thickening deterrent to acts of escalation. I find this line of thought consistent with my own assessments of existential deterrence between the superpowers." Correspondence, December 30, 1993.

Table 2. The Relationship Between Proliferation and Deterrence Types.			
Proliferant	Proliferation Type	Main Adversary	Deterrence Type
Superpowers	Transparent	Each other	MAD/warfighting (existential)
Medium Powers	Transparent	Superpower	Limited (existential)
Israel	Opaque	Hostile neighbors	Nuclear hegemony (existential)
India/Pakistan	Opaque	Each other	Existential

In the superpower balance, declared nuclear capabilities contributed to a deterrence relationship framed by the debate among U.S. analysts between deterrence through "mutual assured destruction" (MAD) versus a "warfighting" posture. Here, nuclear deterrence was perceived to rest at least in part on relative capabilities. At the next level, the British, Chinese, and French nuclear deployments have historically been based on the logic of limited deterrence. Nuclear deterrence at this level is based less on calculations of a relative balance, which is always lopsided, than on the concept of first-strike uncertainty, in which the country with much greater capabilities could still not be confident of its ability to launch a perfectly successful first strike against a lesser nuclear power.[25] At the third level, in the absence of meaningful nuclear competition, at least for now, Israeli deterrence is based on its neighbors' fear of Israel's overwhelming nuclear superiority. Finally, at the fourth level, nuclear deterrence in South Asia today rests not on calculations of a relative balance, which are all but impossible for either side to make, but on the notion that nuclear capabilities exist and might be used in a future conflict.[26]

---

25. Avery Goldstein, "Deterrence and Security in a Changing World: Some Lessons from the Second-Ranking Powers," *Journal of Strategic Studies*, Vol. 15, No. 4 (December 1992), pp. 476–527.

26. As noted in the table, existential deterrence is also a factor at all other levels in the hierarchy. At higher levels it is bolstered by other forms of deterrence, like mutual assured destruction, which are based in part on doctrines and relative capabilities. In an opaque nuclear competition, existential deterrence is the only logical form of mutual deterrence, since doctrines and relative capabilities are not a factor in the deterrence calculus.

The Logic of Existential Deterrence

Existential deterrence is a structural condition affecting the behavior of all nuclear weapon states, but its power is in turn enhanced by the behavior of those states; in other words, even existential deterrence rests to some extent on the adversary's perception of one's nuclear capabilities and resolve.[27] The chief question raised by the nexus between opaque proliferation and existential deterrence concerns the credibility of nuclear weapon postures that are cloaked in secrecy. How can opaque proliferants achieve their deterrent aims without overt demonstrations of their nuclear prowess and direct threats against adversaries?

The answer to this question can be understood with the help of a model depicting the logic of opaque proliferation and existential deterrence. In this model, there are three main agents: two opaque nuclear powers and a mediator, the international community. The interaction between the agents is captured by two processes: bargaining between the opaque proliferants, largely of an indirect or tacit nature, which signals their resolve *vis-à-vis* one another; and transparency-building, the unconscious function of the mediator, which effectively certifies the capabilities of the opaque proliferants. In South Asia, the opaque nuclear weapon states are India and Pakistan, and the international community is represented by the most powerful state in the nonproliferation regime, the United States.

---

27. Analysts disagree as to the relative weight that should be assigned to the weapons themselves and to the manipulation of the weapons in calculations of deterrence. For Edward Rhodes, "the mere existence of an ability to inflict or withhold tremendous pain is logically not sufficient to result in coercive power: the idea of 'existential deterrence'—the notion that simply because nuclear weapons exist, they deter—is logically false. For nuclear deterrence to operate, the opponent must also believe that the coercer is committed to a strategy that has some unacceptable probability of resulting in nuclear war if deterrence fails." *Power and MADness: The Logic of Nuclear Coercion* (New York: Columbia University Press, 1989), p. 85. To the contrary, on p. 9 of "Existential Deterrence," Bundy writes: "The uncertainties which make existential deterrence so powerful have the further consequence that what either government says it might do, or even believes it might do, in the event of open conflict cannot be relied on either by friends or by opponents as a certain predicter of what it would actually do."

OPACITY AND TACIT BARGAINING

Opaque proliferants signal their resolve to one another through a process of strategic bargainings.[28] As Neil Joeck speculates, adversarial opaque proliferants are forced by their public postures of nuclear denial into a strategic dialogue built primarily on tacit communication,[29] defined by Thomas Schelling as "bargaining in which communication is incomplete or impossible." In tacit bargaining, the positions taken by the two sides are not expressed directly to one another, as in formal negotiations, but rather indirectly, through words or actions intended to signal what one expects of the adversary and what the consequences will be if these expectations are not met. For Schelling, "tacit and explicit bargaining are not thoroughly separate concepts . . . the various gradations from tacit bargaining up through types of incompleteness or faulty or limited communication to full communication all show some dependence on the need to coordinate expectations." The problem, says Schelling, "is to develop a modus vivendi when one or both parties either cannot or will not negotiate explicitly or when neither would trust the other with respect to any agreement explicitly reached."[30]

Following Schelling, Joeck writes: "In the subcontinent, some evidence suggests that India and Pakistan may agree far more than they disagree on nuclear problems. There may be sufficient agreement to allow for cooperative bargaining rather than overt competition that would result in an arms race or war." From this perspective, India and Pakistan "are trying to attain certain goals (security and prestige) that put them on a collision course, while at the same time trying to avoid an outcome (an unrestrained nuclear arms race that could more fundamentally jeopardize their security) that puts them on a cooperative course."[31]

The signalling of intentions between opaque proliferants runs along a communication spectrum from formal negotiations to the

---

28. As Thomas Schelling writes: "To study the strategy of conflict is to take the view that most conflict situations are essentially bargaining situations. They are situations in which the ability of one participant to gain his ends is dependent to an important degree on the choices or decisions that the other participant will make." This interdependence of decision-making is the essence of strategy, in the game-theoretical, not military, sense. See *The Strategy of Conflict* (New York: Oxford University Press, 1963), pp. 3, 5.

29. Joeck, "Tacit Bargaining and Stable Proliferation," p. 77.

30. Schelling, *Strategy of Conflict*, pp. 53, 73.

31. Joeck, "Tacit Bargaining and Stable Proliferation," pp. 80–81, 83.

transmission of intentions via action. In between are at least two other modes of communication: intentions can be transmitted indirectly, by, for example, passing them through an intermediary; or intentions can be signalled through unilateral pronouncements by government officials or by state-controlled or influenced media organs. The latter Schelling terms "passive deterrence," which is achieved by "just letting it be known, perhaps through an innocent leak of information, that a government or other organization simply had nuclear weapons, letting every potential addressee of this 'deterrent threat' reach his own conclusions about what kind of misbehavior, if any, might provoke nuclear activity."[32] Because of the need to preserve secrecy, strategic bargaining between opaque proliferants more often tends toward informal, indirect, or tacit communication. Formal negotiations require, as a baseline for discussion, exchanges of detailed information that opaque proliferants are loath to provide, for fear of compromising their opacity.

THE IMPORTANCE OF THRESHOLDS. In Schelling's conceptualization, tacit bargaining rests in part on unambiguous thresholds that provide the foundation for cooperative behavior. Bargaining thresholds can be topographical, such as the U.S. refusal to bomb north of the Yalu River during the Korean War. Or they can be marked by constraints on behavior, such as the combatants' nonuse of poison gas in World War II. As Schelling says, thresholds owe their "focal character to the fact that small concessions would be impossible, that small encroachments would lead to more and larger ones. One draws a line at some conspicuous boundary or rests his case on some conspicuous principle that is supported mainly by the rhetorical question, 'If not here, where?'" The most durable thresholds are characterized by "their simplicity, uniqueness, discreteness, susceptibility of qualitative definition, and so forth." Once established, they define acceptable limits on conflict. Schelling observes a "kind of virginity . . . about all-or-none distinctions that differences of degree do not have. It takes more initiative, more soul-searching, more argument, more willingness to break tradition and upset expectations, to do an unprecedented thing." Thresholds may be consciously established, or they may "arise by a historical process, even inadvertently or accidentally, and can acquire status just by coming to be recognized over a prolonged period."[33]

---

32. Thomas C. Schelling, "Who Will Have the Bomb?" *International Security*, Vol. 1, No. 1 (Summer 1976), p. 85.

33. Schelling, *Strategy of Conflict*, pp. 75, 111–112, 263; and Schelling, *Arms and Influence* (New Haven, Conn.: Yale University Press, 1966), pp. 132, 156.

India and Pakistan have, through a tacit process of strategic bargaining, established their own nuclear taboo. Both sides are nuclear
weapon–capable, but they apparently have chosen not to deploy
assembled nuclear weapons, a threshold that influences their behavior and lends it predictability. This status quo gives the Indo-
Pakistani nuclear balance a measure of stability that might be eroded
by the open deployment of nuclear weapons, which could lead to an
unbridled and less predictable nuclear arms race. As Schelling writes:
"Once the virgin principle is gone, there is no confidence in any rest-
ing point, and expectations converge on complete collapse. The very
recognition of this keeps attention focused on the point of complete
abstinence."[34]

INADVERTENT TRANSPARENCY-BUILDING. If deterrent intentions can
be signalled by tacit bargaining, capabilities must also be demonstrated in some credible way. The opaque proliferant's adversary must
believe that it is capable of carrying out a nuclear strike. How can the
adversary be convinced of this possibility, given the fact that opaque
proliferants deny possessing nuclear weapons? Paradoxically, the
international nonproliferation community has "solved" this dilemma:
countries like India, Israel, and Pakistan do not have to demonstrate
their nuclear capabilities because the global nonproliferation regime
does it for them. Every time a government with extensive intelligence-
gathering capabilities or a reputable private watchdog organization
calls attention to the opaque proliferant's capabilities, it inadvertently
bolsters the credibility of those capabilities in the eyes of the proliferant's adversaries. When a private organization documents the strides
Pakistan has made in its nuclear program, the credibility of
Islamabad's deterrent is enhanced where it matters most—in New
Delhi. Similarly, when U.S. officials publicly estimate New Delhi's
nuclear capabilities, they enhance the credibility of the Indian deterrent
in Islamabad. Senior U.S. policymakers have repeatedly stated over the
past few years that India and Pakistan can build and deliver nuclear
weapons quickly in the event of a crisis.[35] These pronouncements,

---

34. Schelling, *Strategy of Conflict*, p. 112.

35. See the remarks by Bush administration Director of Central Intelligence
Robert Gates to the Nixon Library Conference, Washington, D.C., March 12,1992;
the testimony of Clinton administration Director of Central Intelligence James
Woolsey in House Committee on Foreign Affairs, Subcommittee on International
Security, International Organizations, and Human Rights, *U.S. Security Policy Vis-
à-Vis Rogue Regimes*, 103d Cong., 1st sess., July 28, 1993; and the comments of
Clinton administration Under Secretary of State for International Security Affairs
Lynn E. Davis in Michael R. Gordon, "South Asian Lands Pressed on Arms," *New
York Times*, March 23, 1994.

intended to pressure the opaque proliferants into reversing their course, instead stamp their nuclear programs with a seal of credibility they would otherwise lack. The piling up of such revelations over the years has the cumulative effect of making an opaque proliferant no less of a perceived nuclear power than a declared nuclear weapon state.

Opacity and Nuclear Weapon Stability

In Chapter 1, I argued that nuclear weapon stability in proliferating regions actually involves two central and distinct issues: the *strategic* interaction between nuclear-capable states and the pressures it creates for preemptive escalation, and *loose nukes*, or the domestic dynamics of nuclear command and control. I concluded that the prospects for crisis stability between nuclear proliferants are good, while the prospects for loose nukes problems are more worrisome. I turn now to a different set of questions. How does opacity influence nuclear weapon stability? More specifically, does opacity increase or decrease pressures for the preemptive use of nuclear weapons? And does opacity enhance the likelihood of accidental or unauthorized nuclear weapon use, or does it dampen this possibility? The answers to these questions are significant in a world where the opaque pattern of second-generation proliferation has fundamentally supplanted the transparent pattern of first-generation proliferation.

OPACITY AND CRISIS STABILITY

To recapitulate, Schelling's "reciprocal fear of surprise attack" describes a situation of escalating tension, which ultimately leads one or both states in a crisis to conclude that the benefits of a preemptive strike outweigh the costs of absorbing a first strike and only then responding.[36] Most analysts believe that opacity increases the prospects for this kind of preemptive escalation. The most ardent proponent of this view is Shai Feldman, who argues that "the proliferation of advanced but covert nuclear weapons programs entails the greatest dangers. Regions where nuclear weapons have been introduced secretly will be the least stable." He continues: "The risks of nuclear proliferation are greatest during the transition stage, right after a primitive nuclear force is obtained. The forces are then small and vulnerable, presenting both appealing targets for preemption and incentives for early use. Clearly a region containing such forces would be extremely unstable." By Feldman's reasoning, opacity prevents

36. See Schelling, *Strategy of Conflict*, pp. 207–229; and Schelling, *Arms and Influence*, pp. 221–259.

states from signalling their intentions, thereby enhancing the possibilities of miscalculation and preemption. Moreover, the limited circle of nuclear decision-makers circumscribes debate, leading to ill-advised and faulty doctrines. Where the military exercises control over nuclear decision-making, preemptive doctrines will predominate. Also, undeclared nuclear forces might push adversary elites into aggressive postures because they underestimate the opaque proliferant's nuclear capabilities and therefore discount the possibility of a nuclear response to aggression. In Feldman's conception, credibility demands an overt nuclear posture. Since "the risks are greatest during the transition" to nuclear weapons, "once a state attains a rudimentary nuclear force, making its eventual transition into a nuclear power inevitable," the more advanced nuclear powers should "manage" this transition into a more stable force posture.[37]

Susan Burns shares Feldman's pessimism about the effects of opacity on crisis stability. She argues that if new proliferants are known to have crossed the line into nuclear weapon deployments, stability is served by bringing their bombs up from the basement. As Burns writes: "Because of the greater certainty regarding the capabilities of an overtly nuclear adversary, a much stronger element of caution would be introduced, substantially decreasing incentives to engage in provocation" that might lead to nuclear war.[38] For Cohen and Frankel the chances of preemptive escalation are increased by the necessarily limited discourse between "primitive" nuclear weapon states. As Frankel writes:

The deep secrecy surrounding the nuclear programs of contemporary proliferators has created a situation where the nuclear "red lines," those thresholds that the enemy is warned not to cross lest a nuclear attack would follow, are not clearly drawn or perceived. Since the nuclear presence is actively denied, the elites of the countries in conflict lack the opportunity to develop a common language of nuclear threats and responses, that delicate, codified grammar of things said and half-said that allow two nuclear armed countries in a crisis fully to understand each other and avoid the irrevocable consequences of misperceptions.[39]

---

37. Shai Feldman, "Managing Nuclear Proliferation," in Jed C. Snyder and Samuel F. Wells, Jr., eds., *Limiting Nuclear Proliferation* (Cambridge, Mass.: Ballinger, 1985), pp. 304–308.

38. Susan M. Burns, "Preventing Nuclear War: Arms Management," in Stephen Philip Cohen, ed., *Nuclear Proliferation in South Asia: The Prospects for Arms Control* (Boulder, Colo.: Westview, 1991), p. 94.

39. Cohen and Frankel, "Opaque Nuclear Proliferation," pp. 32–33; and Frankel, "Nuclear Underworld," p. 125.

AN ALTERNATIVE VIEW. These views of opacity's impact on crisis stability are debatable. As discussed in Chapter 1, nuclear preemption under any circumstances is a dicey prospect, given the insistent logic of first-strike uncertainty. To reiterate, decision-makers contemplating a preemptive strike against an adversary's nuclear forces would require full confidence in their ability to knock out all of the opponent's forces. The survival of one or a few of the adversary's deliverable nuclear warheads would allow a devastating response, an attack that might not be limited to counterforce targets, given the magnitude of the provocation. A less-than-perfect preemptive strike could well be suicidal. History discloses an unblemished record of political leaders resisting the temptation to cripple their enemies' existing nuclear forces. Contrary to the prevailing wisdom, opacity enhances rather than diminishes this caution. After all, opaque nuclear forces are even less attractive targets for a nuclear first strike than transparent ones because they are even more veiled. How many weapons does the opponent have? Are they assembled? If so, where are they located and in what mode? Are they mobile or hidden? Which are real? Which are dummies? If the weapons are unassembled, are the warheads stored near the delivery systems? These are crucial but impossible-to-answer questions, given the limited intelligence capabilities of the second-generation proliferants. In sum, it is difficult to imagine any policymaker in a regional nuclear arms competition giving the green light to a preemptive strike.

Another consideration is that the nuclear discourse between opaque proliferants is not as barren as some analysts make it out to be. As I have argued, although opaque proliferants communicate with one another in different ways than the first-generation nuclear weapon states, the fact remains that they do communicate. Rather than a total absence of discourse between the parties, there is a different type of discourse, one that is less formal, less direct, and often tacit, but still mutually understandable. Over the years this discourse establishes certain fundamental understandings between opaque proliferants. Admittedly, these are not as clear as those between the overt nuclear powers, but they are compelling nonetheless. As these understandings develop, it becomes exceedingly unlikely that decision-makers in opaque nuclear weapon states will fail to comprehend the possibilities that confront them. Opaque proliferants deny possessing nuclear weapons, but they, no less than transparent nuclear powers, manipulate their presumed ability to launch a nuclear strike.

Feldman and Burns apply the logic of stages of nuclear development embodied in first-generation proliferation without realizing the irrelevance of that logic with opaque proliferation. At any given point in time, the opaque proliferant's adversary simply does not know the exact nature of its capabilities. To argue, as Feldman does, that at a certain point of its nuclear weapon development, a country's transition into nuclear weapon status is "inevitable" and can be managed, misses opacity's essential logic; so does Burns's argument about the need to make nuclear postures overt once new proliferants actually deploy nuclear weapons. How do we know when these points of inevitability are reached? Is it when the proliferant can produce a small amount of fissile material? When it can transform that material into bomb cores? When it has nuclear-capable transport aircraft? Advanced fighter bombers? Ballistic missiles? Even in the unlikely event that an adversary could confidently pinpoint these developments, which one would constitute the moment of inevitability?

OPACITY AND LOOSE NUKES. Regarding the domestic control of nuclear forces, opacity is a safety enhancer. One of its chief characteristics is the limited circle of decision-makers and the tight control they exercise over nuclear forces and planning. The obsessive secrecy with which the Indian, Israeli, and Pakistani nuclear establishments oversee their respective nuclear weapon programs should logically reduce the chances of accidental or unauthorized use of nuclear weapons. There is no reason to believe that wider decision-making circles or more open debate would improve an opaque nuclear proliferant's ability to devise the command and control arrangements necessary to prevent accidental nuclear detonations. Opaque nuclear-scientific establishments are composed of the best and the brightest scientists available. They are well aware of the dangers of accidents and have the same, if not better, access to information on accident-proofing as would any larger indigenous group of technical personnel. Indeed, accidents should be less likely in cases where nuclear forces are small, especially where the weapons remain unassembled or stored separately from their delivery systems. As regards unauthorized nuclear use, it is also logical to expect that under nuclear opacity, renegade military officers or terrorists would be hamstrung, not assisted, by their limited access to nuclear plans and programs, and that a wider decision-making circle would increase the risk of weapons falling into the wrong hands. Here, too, the maintenance of small or unassembled nuclear weapon systems would likely thwart, rather than promote, the designs of unauthorized users.

What Does Existential Deterrence Deter?

The most trenchant criticism of opaque nuclear postures is Frankel's contention that opacity erodes the "red lines" that define acceptable and unacceptable behavior in any nuclear deterrent balance. As he says, uncertainty regarding capabilities and doctrines and the limited communication between opaque nuclear adversaries blurs the distinction between tolerable and intolerable provocations. Frankel's point dictates a closer examination of what types of behavior (aside from nuclear strikes) existential deterrence proscribes.

DETERRENCE OF CONVENTIONAL ATTACKS

It is a fundamental tenet of nuclear deterrence theory that nuclear weapons, at a minimum, deter conventional attacks against their possessors. Of course, as with all such theory, this is a question of probability, not certainty. But logic and history both support this principle. On the side of logic, it is difficult to imagine any country running the risk of nuclear devastation for the uncertain gains to be had from an invasion of a nuclear weapon state. As Schelling writes, "some threats are inherently persuasive, some have to be made persuasive, and some are bound to look like bluffs." Threats to defend against conventional invasion by recourse to nuclear retaliation fall into the first category: "the difference between the national homeland and everything 'abroad' is the difference between threats that are inherently credible, even if unspoken, and the threats that have to be made credible."[40] Given opaque proliferants' signalling of intentions and capabilities, described above, there is little reason to suspect that they should be any more prone to conventional assaults on the homeland than overt nuclear weapon states. For such an attack to occur, the invading enemy would have to be woefully ignorant of the proliferant's nuclear status, an unlikely mistake given that it is in the proliferant's interest to get the word out. With nuclear weapons, the natural propensity is to err on the side of caution.

The history of the nuclear era reveals two examples of a nuclear weapon state suffering a conventional invasion: the attack by an Arab coalition on Israel in 1973, and Argentina's attempt to reclaim the Falkland Islands from Britain in 1982. Israel's failure to deter the Arab assault likely stemmed from its then-status as an ambiguous rather than an opaque nuclear power. Although there was strong evidence

---

40. Schelling, *Arms and Influence*, p. 36.

that Israel was pursuing nuclear weapons in the 1960s and early 1970s, the perception of its nuclear weapon capability had not yet taken on the status of conventional wisdom in international politics. Bundy reports that U.S. presidents in the 1960s paid little attention to Israel's nuclear strides, and that it was the 1973 war itself that sharpened Washington's focus on Israel's nuclear potential: "It was only a year later that the CIA reached its firm conclusion that Israeli nuclear weapons existed." The mid-1970s and thereafter saw a flurry of scholarly analyses and media reports, culminating with the famous Vanunu revelations of 1986, all of which contributed to the growing international consensus on Israel's status as a nuclear weapon state.[41] It is difficult to imagine a repeat of 1973, given what Israel's neighbors know today about its nuclear prowess. Furthermore, in neither the Israeli case nor the Falklands attack was the unambiguous homeland of a nuclear weapon state invaded.

DETERRENCE OF LOW-INTENSITY OPERATIONS

While existential deterrence can be expected to deter nuclear and conventional attacks on opaque proliferants, deterrence of the third level of conflict—unconventional war—is more problematic. Cross-border support for secessionist guerrillas operating on an adversary's soil probably cannot be deterred by nuclear threats, existential or otherwise. The credibility of any nuclear posture rests on one's ability to convey to the adversary that his actions affect one's vital interests. In the case of guerrilla operations, tangible national interests may not be directly and openly threatened. National boundaries are not demonstrably crossed by the opponent's regular forces. Territories where guerrillas operate may be disputed, lending at least a veneer of diplomatic cover for the adversary seeking to change the status quo. Moreover, the political disputes that give rise to secessionist struggles typically pre-date, often by decades, the development of nuclear capabilities. Finally, the secrecy and remoteness of low-intensity conflicts give the revisionist state a margin of plausible deniability that may prevent the status-quo power from effectively deterring aggression; deterrent threats ring hollow when the adversary can credibly deny any involvement in the opaque proliferant's internal affairs. In sum, opaque proliferation and existential deterrence logically deter

---

41. Bundy, *Danger and Survival*, pp. 506–507. Mordechai Vanunu was an Israeli technician who exposed the details of his government's nuclear weapon program in extensive interviews with a prominent British newspaper.

against nuclear strikes and conventional attacks across established borders; they should not, however, be expected to deter unconventional operations, especially in disputed territories.

Opaque Proliferation, Existential Deterrence, and Nuclear Weapon Stability

In Chapter 1, I examined the theoretical debate over the consequences of nuclear proliferation. I concluded that fears of crisis instability in proliferating regions are often overblown, but that loose nukes problems are more dangerous. This chapter has analyzed the logic of a specific form of nuclear proliferation, opacity, and its relationship to another important concept, existential deterrence. I first summarized the characteristics of nuclear opacity and then argued that any deterrent effect to be derived from opaque nuclear postures is logically of an existential nature. Next, I argued that nuclear opacity is theoretically more stable than overt proliferation because it enhances crisis stability and makes domestic control of nuclear weapons easier.

After establishing that opacity is theoretically less destabilizing than transparent nuclear proliferation, I turned to an examination of the dynamics of existential deterrence in proliferating regions. I argued that the challenge of demonstrating capabilities and projecting intentions is surmounted by the twin processes of inadvertent transparency-building by the international nonproliferation community and tacit communication between the opaque proliferants themselves. After acknowledging that this is a more tenuous means of establishing deterrent credibility than direct demonstrations of capability and resolve, I examined the problem of nuclear red lines, which some have argued are less distinct under opacity and existential deterrence. I concluded that existential deterrence is likely to deter nuclear strikes and conventional attacks across established borders, but not unconventional operations.

Having explored a number of theoretical disputes bearing on the stability of regional nuclear competitions, I turn now to an empirical examination of South Asia, the region some observers consider to be the likeliest site for a future nuclear war. Chapters 3–6 provide the first-ever detailed examination of the subcontinent's nuclear dynamics, especially during a critical period from December 1986 to May 1990, when two Indo-Pakistani crises erupted as Islamabad and New Delhi were resolutely nuclearizing. The first of these chapters is a historical overview of the India-Pakistan security rivalry.

Chapter 3

The India-Pakistan
Security Rivalry

This chapter provides a concise historical overview of Indo-Pakistani security dynamics. It is neither a comprehensive analysis of Indo-Pakistani relations nor of the South Asian nuclear arms competition; rather, it is a snapshot of these subjects, intended to give the non-specialist reader sufficient contextual knowledge of South Asian security issues to appreciate the case studies that follow.

In the next section, I discuss the causes of the chronic animosity that divides India and Pakistan. I pay special attention to the roots of Hindu-Muslim communalism prior to independence, the genesis of the Kashmir dispute, the extension of the Cold War to South Asia, and the causes of the 1965 and 1971 Indo-Pakistani wars. In the third section, I outline the early history of the South Asian nuclear arms competition. I describe how, in a striking parallel, New Delhi's nuclear program grew out of its defeat in the Sino-Indian war of 1962 and China's 1964 nuclear test, while Islamabad's program was the result of a rout at the hands of India in 1971 and India's own nuclear test in 1974.

The chapter's fourth section is an overview of the political context shaping Indo-Pakistani relations during the 1980s. The first part focuses on how the Soviet occupation of Afghanistan influenced South Asian international politics. The second part looks at an important domestic trend, the decay of Indian democracy, which led to the eruption of secessionist insurgencies in two important Indian states, Punjab and Kashmir. These civil conflicts in states bordering Pakistan had an enormous influence on Indian security calculations during the 1986–87 and 1990 crises, as will be evident in Chapters 4 and 6.

Finally, in the concluding sections of this chapter, I trace the course of South Asian nuclear developments in the early 1980s, paying particular attention to each side's evolving nuclear weapon capabilities, its signalling of those capabilities to the adversary, and its perception of the adversary's own nuclear signals. I also discuss why Pakistan's nascent nuclear facilities were not the target of an Indian preventive strike, which the logic of nonproliferation suggests is a strong possibility during the transition to nuclear weapons. Collectively, these sections help to set the stage for the subsequent case studies.

The Roots of Indo-Pakistani Animosity

Analyzing all of the factors that have contributed to five decades of hostility between the modern states of India and Pakistan would require a book-length treatment in itself.[1] While such an analysis is outside the realm of this study, it will be useful at the outset of this empirical examination of South Asian nuclear dynamics to identify the most significant factors accounting for Indo-Pakistani animosity. Although it might be argued that the differences between Hindus and Muslims are so stark that they alone can explain five decades of poor relations between an Islamic country and its Hindu-majority neighbor, it should be recalled that, for centuries, Hindus and Muslims have coexisted on the subcontinent in relative tranquility. To be sure, there have been episodes of communal violence throughout South Asian history, but Hindu-Muslim carnage on a massive scale is only a twentieth century phenomenon.

THE PRE-INDEPENDENCE PERIOD

What is it about this century that brought out the worst in South Asia's two largest socioreligious communities? Ironically, it was the gradual demise of colonialism and the arrival of self-rule that created a new arena of competition, and thus bloodshed, between Hindu and Muslim Indian nationalists. Under authoritarian British rule, both Hindus and Muslims viewed themselves as victims of imperialism; as a result, their political resentments were generally directed at the British, not at each other. The subcontinent's political history in the first half of the twentieth century is largely the story of a steady devolution of political power from British colonial authorities to Indian nationalists. At first, Hindus and Muslims worked together in the nationalist movement. However, as this movement's successes

---

1. The best work of this kind is Šumit Ganguly's *The Origins of War in South Asia: Indo-Pakistani Conflicts Since 1947* (Boulder, Colo.: Westview, 1986).

brought Indians inexorably closer to self-rule, India's Muslim minority grew increasingly anxious about its political prospects in an independent Indian polity. This concern led eventually to the 1940 demand for "Pakistan," a political homeland for South Asia's Muslims. From that point on, Hindu-Muslim relations plummeted.

As the pace of decolonization increased in the 1940s, so did the intensity of Hindu-Muslim violence.[2] For all intents and purposes, India and Pakistan were born at war. As the British government simultaneously granted India its independence and partitioned the former colony into the new states of India and Pakistan, communal violence marred what was otherwise a celebration of freedom from foreign rule. In the months leading up to independence in August 1947, widespread rioting broke out between Hindus and Muslims (and between Sikhs and Muslims). With the partition of the subcontinent, an estimated fifteen million people migrated across hastily drawn borders.[3] Muslims made their way to the new Pakistan, and Hindus and Sikhs fled to the new India. As these refugees crossed paths, vicious fighting erupted. It is commonly estimated that approximately 500,000 people were killed during the wrenching process of partition.[4]

THE GENESIS OF THE KASHMIR DISPUTE

Two months later, India and Pakistan were at war over the disputed territory of Kashmir.[5] The thorniest issue raised by partition involved the status of the former "princely states," areas that had been ruled by local Indian monarchs under the watchful eye of the British. Over 500 nominally independent princely states occupied more than 40 percent of pre-partition India, which allowed Britain to control large tracts of territory without having to commit precious manpower and resources to their governance. In 1947, a problem arose: what would be the status of these newly "independent" states after the British

---

2. The standard history of this period is W. Norman Brown, *The United States and India and Pakistan* (Cambridge, Mass.: Harvard University Press, 1955).

3. Francis Robinson, ed., *The Cambridge Encyclopedia of India, Pakistan, Bangladesh, Sri Lanka, Nepal, Bhutan and the Maldives* (Cambridge, U.K.: Cambridge University Press, 1989), p. 59.

4. Craig Baxter et al., *Government and Politics in South Asia*, 2nd ed. (Boulder, Colo.: Westview, 1991), p. 37.

5. The following discussion draws on Brown, *United States and India and Pakistan*, pp. 112–173; William J. Barnds, *India, Pakistan, and the Great Powers* (New York: Praeger, 1972), pp. 13–43; and Alastair Lamb, *Kashmir: A Disputed Legacy, 1846–1990* (Karachi: Oxford University Press, 1993), pp. 101–187.

withdrew from the subcontinent? Under the terms of partition, the new Pakistan would be carved from the old India on the basis of a simple formula: Muslim majority areas "located in territories contiguous to Pakistan would accede to Pakistan and the rest would go to India."[6] In the case of the princely states, individual rulers were given sole responsibility for the decision to accede to either India or Pakistan, with the understanding that the option of independence was infeasible.

In the vast majority of cases, accession proceeded smoothly, with princely states joining either India or Pakistan without incident. Kashmir was the most important of three exceptions. In late summer 1947, the communal rioting accompanying partition began to spread from Punjab into Kashmir. While the Kashmiri monarch hesitated on the question of accession, a Muslim revolt erupted in Poonch, in western Kashmir. The Poonch rebels established a provisional government in what they called Azad ("Free") Kashmir. In October, 2,000–3,000 armed guerrillas, mainly Pathans from Pakistan's Northwest Frontier Province, crossed the border between West Pakistan and Kashmir, rallying behind the Azad Kashmiris. The Azad Kashmir Muslims and the Pathan irregulars were supported by the government of Pakistan.[7] These forces made progress toward the state capital of Srinagar, causing the monarch to flee. With his domain on the verge of collapse, he signed Kashmir's accession to India on October 26, 1947. The next day, the Indian government began an airlift of troops and equipment to Srinagar, and in the ensuing fighting, the Indian Army pushed the Muslim insurgents away from the capital. The war soon settled into a stalemate, with the Muslim fighters assisted by infusions of regular Pakistan Army troops.

Meanwhile, on the political front, a Kashmiri Muslim leader, Sheikh Mohammad Abdullah, was installed as prime minister in Srinagar. Sheikh Abdullah led a popular Kashmiri party called the National Conference, but staunchly opposed the idea of accession to Pakistan. Unquestionably the most popular Kashmiri leader of the post-independence era, Sheikh Abdullah was imprisoned by Indian authorities in 1953, and spent most of the next two decades behind bars for activities that New Delhi considered anti-Indian.

---

6. Gowher Rizvi, "India, Pakistan, and the Kashmir Problem, 1947–1972," in Raju G.C. Thomas, ed., *Perspectives on Kashmir: The Roots of Conflict in South Asia* (Boulder, Colo.: Westview, 1992), p. 50.

7. Lamb, *Kashmir*, pp. 124–125; and Brown, *United States and India and Pakistan*, pp. 163–164.

THE ROLE OF THE UNITED NATIONS. In January 1948, India referred the Kashmir conflict to the United Nations, charging that the invasion by Muslim forces from outside the state had been illegal, given Kashmir's accession to India. Pakistani diplomats in New York countered that the Indian government had fraudulently achieved Kashmir's accession. In effect, Pakistan successfully transformed the UN debate from a consideration of specific Indian grievances against Pakistani aggression to a comprehensive consideration of Kashmir's future status.[8] The UN Security Council adopted an April 1948 resolution calling for the removal of all outside military forces from Kashmir and for the holding of a subsequent UN-sponsored plebiscite to decide the state's political future. A UN Commission on India and Pakistan went to Kashmir in July 1948 and, after months of negotiations and continued fighting, arranged a cease-fire between the two sides that went into effect on January 1, 1949. Since that date India has controlled the majority of the former princely state's territory, including Jammu, most of the Vale of Kashmir, and Ladakh. Pakistan controls a smaller area, consisting of the "Northern Areas" of Gilgit and Baltistan, and Azad Kashmir in the western part of the state.

The conditions necessary for a plebiscite never developed, and none has ever been held. Neither country has been willing to compromise on Kashmir, partly for strategic reasons, but also because to do so would be to deny the legitimating ideology on which each state was founded. Pakistan's two-nation theory held that the subcontinent's Muslims could safeguard their political rights only through the formation of a separate country. For Pakistanis, the idea of a Muslim-majority state falling within Indian borders is anathema, as it repudiates the two-nation theory and thus the entire basis for the creation of Pakistan. Indian leaders' secular ideology rests on the successful incorporation of all minorities, including Muslims, into the Indian political order. A Pakistani Kashmir would be an insult to Indian secularism. If Muslims' rights cannot be protected in Kashmir, they are subject to doubt throughout India. Kashmir is a zero-sum test for each state's legitimating ideology: one's validity invalidates the other.

THE COLD WAR'S IMPACT

In the 1950s, the Cold War became another factor in Indo-Pakistani animosity. The security postures of India and Pakistan have always exhibited a profound strategic dissonance. India's regional security

---

8. Brown, *United States and India and Pakistan*, p. 166.

doctrine is exclusionary: it seeks to maintain what New Delhi perceives as South Asia's "natural" balance of power, which by any measure is lopsided in India's favor. The key to this strategy has been to prevent external powers from establishing a foothold in the region, either directly or indirectly at the behest of India's neighbors. Its chief policy expression was the nonaligned stance devised by India's first prime minister, Jawaharlal Nehru. Nonalignment gave India a moral voice in international politics, as well as maximum leverage in its relations with the superpowers; it was also intended to exclude Washington and Moscow from South Asia.

As might be expected, Pakistan's regional security doctrine is the diametrical opposite of India's. Pakistan seeks to deny India's predominance in South Asia by altering the balance of power. It has done so the only way it can: by drawing into the region on its side one or more of the external powers that India seeks to exclude. Pakistan's inclusionary doctrine has at various times sought to involve the United States, China, and influential Islamic nations in its rivalry with India. In the 1950s, the intensifying U.S.-Soviet rivalry provided Pakistan with just the leverage it needed to pursue this strategy. In quick succession, Pakistan linked itself with U.S. strategic planning in a Mutual Defense Assistance Agreement (1954), the Southeast Asia Treaty Organization (1954), the Baghdad Pact (1955—later the Central Treaty Organization), and a bilateral Agreement of Cooperation (1959).[9] According to the 1959 executive agreement, the United States would now regard "as vital to its national interest and to world peace the preservation of the independence and integrity of Pakistan," and, in case of aggression against Pakistan, would "take such appropriate action, including the use of armed forces, as may be mutually agreed upon."[10] With Pakistan's two wings linking regional defense arrangements in East Asia and the Middle East, Washington embarked in the late 1950s on a rapid buildup of the country's armed forces. Indian leaders have charged ever since that U.S. support for Pakistan only emboldens it to challenge India, whereas a Pakistan left to its own devices would have learned to live amicably with its more powerful neighbor.

---

9. See Devin T. Hagerty, "The Development of American Defense Policy Toward Pakistan, 1947–1954," *Fletcher Forum*, Vol. 10, No. 2 (Summer 1986), pp. 217–242.

10. "Agreement of Cooperation Between the Government of the United States of America and the Government of Pakistan," *United States Treaties and Other International Agreements*, Vol. 10, Part 1, 1959 (Washington, D.C.: U.S. Department of State, 1960), pp. 317–319.

THE 1965 INDO-PAKISTANI WAR

India and Pakistan fought a second war over Kashmir in 1965.[11] The 1965 conflict was a preventive war initiated by Pakistan to wrest the disputed territory from India. India had been routed in its 1962 war with China, a defeat that precipitated a substantial Indian military buildup. Indian defense spending "roughly tripled" from 1960 to 1965, while its military manpower increased from 535,000 to 869,000.[12] At the same time, Indian-controlled Kashmir saw a sharp rise in political violence during the early 1960s, owing in part to the blatant manipulation of Kashmiri politics by the Indian government and its acolytes in Srinagar. In 1963, rioting erupted over the theft of a sacred Muslim relic (a hair of the Prophet Mohammad) from a mosque in the Kashmiri capital. Although the relic was quickly recovered, the Indian Army and local police had to quell the rioting by force.

India's 1962 humiliation, its increasing military muscle, and political discontent in Kashmir combined to convince Pakistani leaders that they had a limited window of opportunity to take the disputed territory.[13] Pakistani President Ayub Khan was goaded into war by his ambitious foreign minister, Zulfikar Ali Bhutto. Stanley Wolpert paraphrases Bhutto's rationale for launching a preventive war: "Time was on India's side: with arms pouring in from both superpowers, within two or three years India's military capability would be such that 'Pakistan would be in no position to resist her.' India's 'ultimate objective' was nothing less than the 'destruction' of Pakistan. Thus, the time to 'hit back hard' was 'now,' to make it virtually impossible for India to embark on a total war against Pakistan for the next decade." At the very least, an aggressive Pakistani policy could revive the Kashmir issue by forcing India to the negotiating table.[14]

In the summer of 1965, the Pakistani government infiltrated several thousand armed guerrillas across the cease-fire line to foment rebellion among Kashmiri Muslims. Pakistan's clumsy machinations failed miserably: not only did no popular uprising occur, but India responded in late August by ordering thousands of troops across the

---

11. The following discussion is based on Barnds, *India, Pakistan, and the Great Powers*, pp. 183–208; Ganguly, *Origins of War in South Asia*, pp. 57–93; and Stanley Wolpert, *Zulfi Bhutto of Pakistan: His Life and Times* (New York: Oxford University Press, 1993), pp. 72–99.

12. Barnds, *India, Pakistan, and the Great Powers*, p. 187.

13. Ganguly, *Origins of War in South Asia*, p. 78.

14. Wolpert, *Zulfi Bhutto of Pakistan*, pp. 89, 90.

cease-fire line into Pakistan-controlled Kashmir. These soldiers soon captured several key mountain passes. Faced with the prospect of backing down and losing territory or pressing onward, Ayub Khan chose the latter course. On September 1, a Pakistani armored column crossed the cease-fire line in southern Kashmir, making steady progress and inflicting heavy losses on the surprised Indian forces. Pakistani troops soon threatened India's Achilles' heel, the vital road connecting Srinagar with India proper. In response, Indian leaders dramatically raised the ante with a daring offensive across the Punjab border. By and large, India's armor in Punjab outfought Pakistan's, making progress toward Lahore and Sialkot, while simultaneously blunting a Pakistani counteroffensive aimed at Amritsar. Finally, with each of the battle fronts stalemated, the war was ended through UN intervention on September 22. In terms of political objectives achieved, Pakistan had suffered a grievous loss; its strategy of taking Kashmir by force had been effectively neutralized by a bold Indian counteroffensive.

THE 1971 BANGLADESH WAR

Six years later, India and Pakistan fought another war. The 1971 conflict was the outgrowth of a Pakistani civil war that had erupted in March of that year. The root cause of this civil strife was the severe polarization that had emerged between East and West Pakistan since 1947, which in the late 1960s led to increasingly aggressive Bengali separatism and a correspondingly repressive response by the Punjabi-dominated Pakistani state.[15] As the fighting in East Pakistan escalated in the spring of 1971, the Pakistan Army resorted to extreme brutality, causing Bengali refugees to seek safety in India. These refugees numbered nearly four million by the end of May, when they were arriving in India at a rate of 60,000 per day.[16] Faced with severe political and economic strains imposed by the Bengali refugees, and tempted by the prospect of permanently easing its two-front security threat from Pakistan, New Delhi decided to support the secessionists' aspirations for their own state of Bangladesh—"land of the Bengalis."

15. For an overview of the issues that precipitated the Pakistani civil war of 1971, see Richard Sisson and Leo E. Rose, *War and Secession: Pakistan, India, and the Creation of Bangladesh* (Berkeley and Los Angeles: University of California Press, 1990), pp. 8–34.

16. Ibid., p. 152. The final refugee total may have exceeded eight million. See the discussion on p. 297, n. 36.

In April, the separatists issued a declaration of independence and formed a government-in-exile on Indian soil. New Delhi also set up training camps for the Bengali guerrillas on Indian territory near the East Pakistan border and assisted the insurgents in their operations across the border. In July, the Indian government decided on a war to liberate Bangladesh. By the fall, New Delhi was deploying artillery, tanks, and air power in support of guerrilla operations in East Pakistan. In late November, India "launched simultaneous military actions on all of the key border regions of East Pakistan, and from all directions, with both armored and air support." Having planned a December 6 invasion to capture the East Pakistani capital of Dhaka, Indian leaders were "greatly relieved and pleasantly surprised" when Pakistan launched preemptive air strikes against Indian air installations on December 3. As Richard Sisson and Leo Rose explain: "This date is usually cited for the commencement of the third Indo-Pakistani war, and because of the air strikes, Pakistan is often depicted as having taken the initiative in starting the war. In more realistic, rather than formal, terms, however, the war began on 21 November, when Indian military units occupied Pakistani territory as part of the preliminary phase to the offensive directed at capturing and liberating Dhaka." When the Indian Army finally did invade on December 5, it made rapid progress owing to its vast advantages in logistics, firepower, and popular support. Dhaka fell on December 16, and Bangladesh was born.[17]

The South Asian Nuclear Arms Competition

The 1970s brought a new element to Indo-Pakistani relations: a vigorous nuclear arms competition. South Asia's nuclear programs are links in a proliferation chain extending back to World War II. The first links in the chain were the United States and the Soviet Union. Next, China's 1964 nuclear test and subsequent weaponization were rooted in Beijing's concern over the United States and later the Soviet Union as threatening adversaries. In turn, India's 1974 nuclear test was the product of a long national debate over nuclear weapons in the wake of India's defeat in the China war, and the Chinese test. Pakistan's 1972 decision to pursue nuclear weapons was caused by its defeat in the Bangladesh war, and later reaffirmed by evidence of India's nuclear prowess. Finally, Pakistan's clandestine, but widely reported, efforts to

17. Ibid., pp. 142–144, 210–215.

develop nuclear weapons in the late 1970s and early 1980s provoked a renewed debate in India over the costs and benefits of actually deploying nuclear weapons. Although China remained significant for Indian nuclear planners, the main South Asian nuclear dynamic during the 1980s was an intensified nuclear competition between New Delhi and Islamabad. The rest of this section will briefly trace the early development of each country's nuclear weapon program.

THE EVOLUTION OF INDIA'S NUCLEAR PROGRAM

Indian nuclear research began in 1944, three years before independence. An Indian Atomic Energy Commission was created in 1948, but it was not until 1954 that "steady but modest funding" flowed into research and development under the aegis of a Department of Atomic Energy.[18] The Indian nuclear program's primary objective until the 1962 Sino-Indian war and the 1964 Chinese nuclear explosion was "development for long-term civilian needs."[19] Even so, there were hints of India's subsequent nuclear-option strategy. As early as 1946, in response to a question about the possibility of a future Indian deployment of nuclear weapons, Prime Minister Nehru "stated his hope that India would develop atomic power for peaceful uses but warned that, so long as the world was constituted as it was, every country would have to develop and use the latest scientific devices for its protection."[20]

During the 1950s, a confidential consensus emerged among a small core of Indian leaders that New Delhi should reserve its right to develop nuclear weapons if threatened by a future Chinese nuclear capability. The 1964 Chinese test intensified India's nuclear debate, which was driven by four considerations: the nature of the threat posed by Chinese nuclear weapons, the availability and implications of external nuclear guarantees *vis-à-vis* China, the cost of nuclear weaponization, and the morality of nuclear weapons.[21] Indian analysts' main concern was not an immediate military threat from the Chinese, but the prospect of future political intimidation by Beijing.

18. Onkar Marwah, "India's Nuclear and Space Programs: Intent and Policy," *International Security*, Vol. 2, No. 2 (Fall 1977), p. 98.

19. Raju G.C. Thomas, "India's Nuclear and Space Programs: Defense or Development?" *World Politics*, Vol. 38, No. 2 (January 1986), p. 321.

20. Lorne J. Kavic, *India's Quest for Security: Defense Policies, 1947–1965* (Berkeley and Los Angeles: University of California Press, 1967), pp. 27–28, n. 19.

21. Mitchell Reiss, *Without the Bomb: The Politics of Nuclear Nonp. oliferation* (New York: Columbia University Press, 1988), p. 211.

In 1964, Indian Prime Minister Lal Bahadur Shastri "launched a program to reduce the time needed to build nuclear arms to six months," thereby giving "official sanction to the development of an Indian nuclear weapons option."[22]

Prime Minister Indira Gandhi decided in 1972 to proceed with an Indian nuclear explosion as soon as possible and gave her final approval to the test in 1974. Her decision likely was based primarily on India's changed security environment after 1971 and secondarily on domestic politics. India's security planning *vis-à-vis* China was jarred by U.S. President Richard M. Nixon's 1971 opening to Beijing. Pakistan's role as a conduit in the China initiative and the U.S. tilt toward Pakistan during the 1971 Bangladesh war may have added to New Delhi's perception that India was becoming the target of a U.S.-Pakistan-China security axis. Nixon's dispatch of an aircraft carrier task force toward the Bay of Bengal during the Indian liberation of Bangladesh was especially galling to Indian offficials, who regarded the U.S. move as a loathsome modern variant of gunboat diplomacy. Others have suggested that by 1974 Gandhi's domestic political problems (which led eventually to the "Emergency" of 1975–77) were so acute that the Indian nuclear test was partly designed to bolster her own standing at home.

THE EVOLUTION OF PAKISTAN'S NUCLEAR PROGRAM

Pakistan's nuclear research program was stimulated by U.S. President Dwight Eisenhower's 1953 "Atoms for Peace" proposal and a subsequent exhibition that toured Pakistan touting the advantages of atomic energy in socioeconomic development. Pakistan established its own Atomic Energy Commission in 1956, and its nuclear program during the 1950s and early 1960s was marked by an absence of military considerations. This changed in the mid-1960s, when Bhutto spurred Pakistan's own nuclear-option debate by arguing for a Pakistani response to India's gains in the nuclear field. Bhutto's precise motives, like Indira Gandhi's, remain obscure, but appear to have arisen from a similar combination of international and domestic imperatives. The 1965 Indo-Pakistani war had revived questions about Pakistan's security, especially in view of the country's lack of strategic depth. Also, Bhutto began to mount his own challenge to President Ayub Khan in the wake of the 1965 war, and

---

22. Leonard S. Spector, with Jacqueline R. Smith, *Nuclear Ambitions: The Spread of Nuclear Weapons, 1989–90* (Boulder, Colo.: Westview, 1990), p. 64.

may have perceived that nuclear nationalism would be an effective way to shore up his domestic support at a time when Pakistan's security problems seemed especially acute. Indications are, however, that Bhutto's position on nuclear weapons remained a minority viewpoint until his rise to power after the Bangladesh war.

The Bangladesh debacle reoriented Pakistan's nuclear program, and India's 1974 nuclear test validated this revised posture.[23] In 1972, given the gaping asymmetry that had emerged in Indian and Pakistani military capabilities with the loss of East Pakistan, now-President Bhutto ordered Pakistan's scientific community to begin developing nuclear arms. According to a U.S. Defense Intelligence Agency report, Pakistani military leaders believed that "a small nuclear program would enable the Pakistanis to do in nuclear terms what their ground and air forces could not do in conventional terms: threaten to punish any Indian attack so severely that consideration of such an attack would be deterred from the onset."[24] Bhutto also may have believed that a Pakistani nuclear capability would increase his own domestic standing, as well as Pakistan's stature among the newly wealthy nations of the Islamic, oil-producing Middle East. According to a declassified State Department document, "nuclear explosive design and development work began in Pakistan soon after the 1974 Indian nuclear test."[25] India's 1974 test did not cause, but rather increased, Pakistan's nuclear resolve.

NONPROLIFERATION HURDLES. In the late 1970s, both India and Pakistan ran into trouble with U.S. nuclear nonproliferation laws, as the Carter administration gave higher priority to stemming the spread of nuclear weapons than did its predecessors. The Nuclear Nonproliferation Act of 1978 prohibited U.S. transfers of fissionable material and technology unless the recipient country agreed to full-scope International Atomic Energy Agency (IAEA) safeguards. Complying with the new law required the administration to renegotiate existing U.S. nuclear cooperation commitments, including one to supply low-enriched nuclear fuel to two Indian power reactors.

23. Neil Joeck, "Pakistani Security and Nuclear Proliferation in South Asia," in Joeck, ed., *Strategic Consequences of Nuclear Proliferation in South Asia* (London: Frank Cass, 1986), p. 87.

24. U.S. Defense Intelligence Agency, "Operational and Logistical Considerations in the Event of an India-Pakistan Conflict," Report DDB-2660-104-84, December 1984, p. 52 (National Security Archive).

25. U.S. Department of State, "The Pakistani Nuclear Program," secret briefing paper, June 23, 1984 (National Security Archive).

The outcome was a bitter Indo-American diplomatic impasse that was resolved only in 1983. Also in 1978, intense pressure from the Carter administration caused the collapse of a plutonium reprocessing agreement between France and Pakistan. Then, in 1979, Washington suspended all U.S. economic and military assistance to Islamabad under a law known as the Symington Amendment. The law prohibited U.S. aid to countries that acquire uranium enrichment technology without putting it under IAEA safeguards, unless the president could certify that termination of U.S. assistance would seriously harm vital U.S. interests, and that he had received "reliable assurances" from the recipient country that it will not acquire or develop nuclear weapons.[26]

South Asian Security Issues in the 1980s

The December 1979 Soviet invasion of Afghanistan brought the Cold War to South Asia's doorstep. Literally overnight, the Soviet occupation of Pakistan's northwestern neighbor revived the moribund Pakistani-U.S. security partnership. As one former Carter administration official recalled: "President Carter and others saw this as a qualitative change in Soviet behavior, calling for a global response. Pakistan, now a front-line state, became an essential line of defense and an indispensable element of any strategy that sought to punish the Soviets for their action."[27] Washington and Islamabad quickly began discussions over the terms of renewed U.S. aid for Pakistan. Although Pakistani President Mohammad Zia ul-Haq ultimately rejected Carter's proposal as too limited to meet Islamabad's new security needs, the Reagan administration and Pakistan in 1981 concluded a six-year, $3.2 billion agreement, split evenly between economic and security assistance.

The centerpiece of the 1981 deal was the sale to Pakistan of forty F-16 fighters; these were supplemented by tanks, helicopters, howitzers, and anti-tank missiles. According to Washington's chief negotiator, sophisticated U.S. weaponry would give Pakistan the "ability to handle with its own resources incursions and limited cross-border

26. Richard P. Cronin, *Pakistan: U.S. Foreign Assistance Facts* (Washington, D.C.: Congressional Research Service, 1988), pp. 4–5.

27. Thomas Perry Thornton, "Between the Stools? U.S. Policy Towards Pakistan During the Carter Administration," *Asian Survey*, Vol. 22, No. 10 (October 1982), p. 969.

threats from Soviet-backed Afghan forces," and "keep the Soviets from thinking they can coerce or subvert Pakistan with impunity." The administration recognized that "even with our proposed assistance Pakistan cannot acquire an independent capability to confront the full wave of a direct and massive Soviet attack," but said that its intention was "to raise the cost of potential aggression and to demonstrate that a strong security relationship exists between the United States and Pakistan which the Soviet Union must take into account in its calculations."[28] Thus began a new phase of collaboration between Washington and Islamabad that lasted until 1990. The Reagan Doctrine of rolling back Soviet-supported communist regimes in the developing world garnered Pakistan billions of dollars in U.S. aid; in addition, Washington funneled through Islamabad billions more dollars worth of weapons and supplies for the Afghan resistance. This covert operation was reportedly the U.S. government's largest since the Vietnam War.[29]

Despite its partnership with Islamabad, Washington also drew closer to New Delhi in the 1980s. India's special relationship with the Soviet Union had begun with Josef Stalin's death in 1953 and culminated in the 1971 Indo-Soviet peace and friendship treaty. Moscow played a substantial role in the Indian economy throughout the Cold War, both by extending to New Delhi ample economic assistance, but also by importing Indian manufactured goods, which were uncompetitive on world markets. Furthermore, as India undertook a large military buildup in the late 1970s and 1980s, New Delhi bought most of its sophisticated weaponry from Moscow on concessionary terms. Still, although India refused publicly to condemn the Soviet invasion of Afghanistan in any but the most benign terms, Indian policymakers were privately distressed by Moscow's aggression.

The Indian government had also begun to perceive that its economic relations with the Soviet Union were of limited utility: New Delhi wanted to "grow" its economy in electronics, computers, and telecommunications, areas where Washington could be more useful than Moscow. India began to explore new cooperation with the United States early in the decade. Momentum accelerated when Rajiv Gandhi succeeded his mother as prime minister in 1984.[30] The

---

28. Senate Committee on Foreign Relations, *Aid and the Proposed Arms Sales of F-16s to Pakistan*, 97th Cong., 1st sess., November 12, 1981, p. 7.

29. Bob Woodward and Charles R. Babcock, "U.S. Covert Aid to Afghans on the Rise," *Washington Post*, January 13, 1985.

30. Indira Gandhi was assassinated in October of that year.

younger Gandhi was a former airline pilot, enamored of high technology and responsive to the developmental possibilities of economic liberalization. A May 1985 Memorandum of Understanding in science and technology took India off the U.S. list of "diversion-risk" countries, paving the way for increased investment and technology transfer. One result of this new cooperation was that Washington had more influence in New Delhi than in previous years, when U.S. relations with the two South Asian adversaries were generally perceived in zero-sum terms.[31]

THE REGIONAL CONTEXT

The 1970s had been a decade of relatively peaceful relations between New Delhi and Islamabad. In 1972, India and Pakistan had signed the Simla Agreement, which stipulated that they would settle their political differences peacefully, through bilateral negotiations or any other mutually acceptable means. The Simla Agreement essentially froze the Kashmir dispute. In addition, the asymmetry in power between India and Pakistan after 1971 was such that Islamabad was in no position to challenge the status quo. Finally, the Bangladesh humiliation had prompted a national identity crisis in Pakistan: if Islam was insufficient to maintain unity between the erstwhile East and West Pakistan, would it suffice to keep the rump Pakistan together? In order to shore up Pakistan's Islamic identity and attract some much-needed international support, President Bhutto turned to the Islamic oil-producing states of the Middle East.[32] With Pakistan projecting itself as Southwest Asian rather than a South Asian country, Indo-Pakistani relations eased.

This changed in the 1980s. The most crucial bone of contention was each side's insistent claim that the other was meddling in its internal ethnic disputes. Particularly important for understanding the 1986–87 and 1990 crises was Pakistan's alleged support for the insurgencies that developed in the Indian border states of Punjab and Kashmir. Those civil conflicts are best viewed in the context of a structural transformation of the Indian political system during Indira Gandhi's

---

31. On this thaw between New Delhi and Washington, see Stephen Philip Cohen, "The Reagan Administration and India," in Harold A. Gould and Šumit Ganguly, eds., *The Hope and the Reality: U.S.-Indian Relations from Roosevelt to Reagan* (Boulder, Colo.: Westview, 1992), pp. 139–153; and Dennis Kux, *India and the United States: Estranged Democracies, 1941–1991* (Washington, D.C.: National Defense University Press, 1993), pp. 379–423.

32. See Devin T. Hagerty, "Pakistan's Foreign Policy Under Z.A. Bhutto," *Journal of South Asian and Middle Eastern Studies*, Vol. 14, No. 4 (Summer 1991), pp. 55–70.

rule. Its general characteristics included the increasing centralization of power in New Delhi at the expense of the Indian states; the decline of Indian political, judicial, and administrative institutions, in particular the Congress party; and the consequent evolution of an institutional vacuum increasingly filled by populist and religious demagoguery of a decidedly unsecular tone.[33] The ultimate result of these trends was a series of insurgencies, two of which were at the root of the Indo-Pakistani crises to be examined in Chapters 4 and 6.

South Asian Nuclear Developments, 1980–86

The early 1980s saw the steady maturation of Indian and Pakistani nuclear weapon capabilities, a process made mutually visible by conflicting U.S. policy objectives in South Asia. On one hand, Washington wanted to head off a regional nuclear arms race; on the other, it was intent on aiding the Afghan resistance in its war against the Soviet Red Army. In order to beef up Pakistan's conventional military preparedness and funnel covert assistance to the Afghan guerrillas via Islamabad, the White House had to scale the wall of U.S. nonproliferation laws that had been built in the 1970s. Support for the Afghan cause was also strong on Capitol Hill, but some legislators worried that turning a blind eye to Pakistan's nuclear program could undermine the nonproliferation regime. U.S. policy toward South Asia for most of the 1980s was driven by this tension between a staunchly anticommunist administration whose first priority was punishing the Soviets in Afghanistan, and a small group of powerful congressmen who worried more about the long-term consequences of "allowing" Pakistan to achieve a nuclear weapon capability. The outcome of this domestic political competition was a series of implicit deals in which Pakistan agreed to keep its nuclear progress within the bounds of various markers laid down by Washington. In the process, a great deal of light was shed on Pakistan's nuclear strides, giving them a measure of credibility that Islamabad could not have attained without actually testing a nuclear device.

DEVELOPMENTS FROM 1980–83
Two months after the Soviet Union invaded Afghanistan in December 1979, the Carter administration offered Pakistan $400 million in

---

33. For more detailed analyses of these developments, see Atul Kohli, ed., *India's Democracy: An Analysis of Changing State-Society Relations* (Princeton, N.J.: Princeton University Press, 1988).

security and economic assistance, despite a private State Department assessment that Islamabad was developing nuclear weapon capabilities and "might be able to explode a device as early as 12–18 months hence."[34] In doing so, the administration said it would ask Congress to waive or suspend the Symington Amendment. For their part, Pakistani leaders projected ambiguity about their nuclear goals, but were surprisingly forthright about the means to achieve them. As President Zia said in February 1980: "We are not making any bomb. . . . It is a modest experiment that we are carrying on. . . . We are only trying to acquire technology. It takes particularly long when you have to acquire this technology through backdoor, clandestine methods."[35]

THE LOGIC OF U.S. AID TO PAKISTAN. In September 1981, Washington and Islamabad concluded their six-year, $3.2 billion aid agreement. In shepherding the aid package through Congress, the Reagan administration refined the rationale that had been implicit in Carter's willingness to push nonproliferation to the back burner. A senior State Department official told Congress: "As praiseworthy as the intentions of the Symington Amendment may have been, it is clear that it has failed to stop the Pakistanis from pursuing their nuclear programs. On the other hand, to the extent that it has kept us from helping that nation upgrade its conventional defenses, it may have added to the sense of insecurity that can only heighten pressures to achieve a capacity to develop nuclear weapons." The administration's view was that a "program of support which provides Pakistan with a continuing relationship with a significant security partner and enhances its sense of security may remove the principal underlying incentive for acquisition of the nuclear option." With such a relationship in place, the United States could perhaps convince Pakistan to refrain from taking the nuclear path to security; without it, Washington would "forfeit the opportunity to influence future decisions." This official also made an explicit link between the flow of U.S. aid and continued Pakistani restraint in nuclear testing: "The Government of Pakistan is fully aware that its explosion of a nuclear device would alter the fundamental premises on which an improved security relationship between the two countries is based. It is difficult to see how the United States could go forward with an assistance program for

---

34. U.S. Department of State, Bureau of Near Eastern and South Asian Affairs, "Near East and South Asia Overview—Nuclear Non-Proliferation Policy in NEA," secret report, 1980 (National Security Archive).

35. "Learn a Lesson from History," *India Today*, February 16, 1980, p. 86.

Pakistan under such circumstances."[36] Congress was eventually persuaded of the administration's logic. In December 1981, it passed a provision allowing the president to waive the Symington Amendment for six years if he determined that aid to Pakistan was in the national interest. At the same time, Congress modified another section of nonproliferation law to cut off U.S. aid to Pakistan or any other nonnuclear weapon state that exploded a nuclear device. As long as Islamabad refrained from testing, it would be eligible for U.S. economic and security assistance.[37]

NEW DELHI'S RESPONSE. Meanwhile, New Delhi showed signs of revising its policy of not actually building nuclear weapons, established after its 1974 nuclear test. Morarji Desai, India's prime minister from 1977 to 1979, was Gandhian in temperament and passionately opposed to nuclear weapons; however, when Indira Gandhi returned to power in 1980, she firmly signalled India's resolve to keep its nuclear options open. In September 1981, Gandhi "claimed that India and 'the rest of the world' knew that Pakistan was developing the capacity to build nuclear weapons and would soon explode a nuclear device. She said this might prompt India . . . to explode another nuclear device of its own."[38] In 1982, Gandhi said that India remained "committed to its policy of utilizing atomic energy for peaceful purposes," but if New Delhi deemed a nuclear explosion necessary "for our development and other peaceful purposes, this will be done in the national interest."

Persistent press reports throughout the early 1980s speculated that both countries were making preparations for a nuclear test. A prominent Indian analyst said it was "doubtful if the Indian Government has learnt, or can learn, much about Pakistan's nuclear doings from its own intelligence sources. However, several powers are closely monitoring the Pakistani nuclear programme and some of them, including the US and the Soviet Union, appear to be keeping New Delhi informed. *The government has sometimes echoed CIA predictions.*"[39] One

---

36. House Committee on Foreign Affairs, *Security and Economic Assistance to Pakistan*, 97th Cong., 1st sess., September 16, 1981, pp. 23–24, and November 17, 1981, p. 297.

37. Richard P. Cronin, *The United States, Pakistan and the Soviet Threat to Southern Asia: Options for Congress* (Washington, D.C.: Congressional Research Service, 1985), pp. 29–30.

38. Michael Richardson, "Arms and the Woman," *Far Eastern Economic Review*, September 25, 1981, p. 20.

39. Bhabani Sen Gupta, "Jitters of Ziatomics," *India Today*, February 28, 1983, p. 66 (emphasis added).

prescient analyst raised the possibility that Pakistan had "given up the idea of aping India by actually detonating an underground nuclear device and has instead opted for the Israeli strategy of reaching, or letting the world believe it has reached, a high level of nuclear technology without actually staging a nuclear test."[40]

U.S. PRESSURE AND PAKISTANI OPACITY. This analysis proved to be correct. As a secret State Department document said in March 1983: "We do not expect Pakistan to attempt a test of a nuclear device in the near future." According to this report, Reagan had reiterated to Zia in December 1982 that developing nuclear weapons would be "inconsistent with the continuation of the U.S. security and economic assistance program." As U.S. aid began flowing to Islamabad, Washington was assured by Zia "that Pakistan has no intention of testing a nuclear device of any kind." The State Department averred that "while this movement by the government of Pakistan is insufficient to meet our long-term non-proliferation objectives, it demonstrates that Pakistan may be influenced to move in the proper direction through appropriate U.S. attention to Pakistan's legitimate security need." The State Department further claimed that the U.S. assistance program "is our most effective weapon in dissuading that nation from continuing its nuclear explosives program."[41]

DEVELOPMENTS FROM 1983–85

By 1983, it was clear that even if Pakistan did not test a nuclear explosive device, it would still hedge its bets by quietly developing all of the capabilities needed to keep its options open. A secret State Department assessment found "unambiguous evidence that Pakistan is actively pursuing a nuclear weapons development program. Pakistan's near-term goal is to have a nuclear test capability, enabling it to explode a nuclear device if Zia decides its [sic] appropriate for diplomatic and domestic political gains. Pakistan's long-term goal is to establish a nuclear deterrent to aggression by India, which remains Pakistan's greatest security concern." In the judgment of U.S. intelligence, Pakistan had "already undertaken a substantial amount of the necessary design and high explosives testing of the explosive triggering package for a nuclear explosive device," and was

---

40. Dilip Bobb, "Sinister Nuclear Strategy," *India Today*, November 15, 1981, p. 119.

41. U.S. Department of State, Bureau of Oceans and International Environmental and Scientific Affairs, "Pakistan's Nuclear Program," secret report, March 14, 1983 (National Security Archive).

"now capable of producing a workable package of this kind." Islamabad had not, however, "produced the fissile material necessary for a nuclear explosive device or a nuclear weapon."[42]

PAKISTANI NUCLEAR SIGNALLING. Subsequent events indicated that Pakistani scientists were inching ever closer to this objective. In February 1984, Dr. A.Q. Khan, the head of Islamabad's uranium enrichment program (and known as the father of the Pakistani bomb), announced that "by the grace of God, Pakistan is now among the few countries in the world that can efficiently enrich uranium."

Soon thereafter, President Zia played down Khan's remarks by saying that "Pakistan has acquired a very modest research and development capacity of uranium enrichment . . . for peaceful purposes."[43] This would be the first in a series of Pakistani revelations about Islamabad's nuclear strides, all of which followed the same pattern. First, the eccentric A.Q. Khan would make a splashy public statement announcing some new Pakistani achievement. Next, very senior officials would follow this up by confirming the substance of Khan's remarks, but adding that Pakistan's nuclear program was, of course, entirely for peaceful purposes. Each of these episodes added a layer of credibility to Islamabad's emerging status as a nuclear weapon state, especially in the eyes of many Indians, who were predisposed to believe the worst about their adversary's intentions.

THE U.S. ROLE. As always, Islamabad walked a fine line between demonstrating its nuclear muscle to New Delhi and raising the ire of the U.S. Congress. Evidence that Pakistan was now enriching uranium (though not to weapons-grade) sparked further congressional action to stem a nuclear arms race in South Asia. In March 1984, a Pakistan-specific nonproliferation amendment passed unanimously in the Senate Foreign Relations Committee. The measure required that U.S. aid to Pakistan be cut off unless the president could certify annually that Islamabad did not possess a nuclear explosive device, and was not acquiring technology, equipment, or material for manufacturing or detonating one. The administration quickly notified the committee that it could not meet the latter requirement, and that aid to Pakistan would therefore have to be terminated if the amendment were made law.[44]

Anxious not to hinder the Afghanistan war effort, the committee then adopted a watered-down, administration-backed compromise,

---

42. U.S. Department of State, "Pakistani Nuclear Program."

43. Leonard S. Spector, *Nuclear Proliferation Today* (Cambridge, Mass.: Ballinger, 1984), pp. 98–100.

44. Ibid., pp. 102–103.

which became known as the Pressler Amendment. Henceforth, before aid to Pakistan could be released for the next fiscal year, the president would have to certify annually that Islamabad does not possess a nuclear explosive device, and that "the proposed United States assistance program will reduce significantly the risk that Pakistan will possess a nuclear explosive device." The alternative amendment thus shifted the "standard for terminating assistance from detonation to possession of a nuclear device," but threatened no punishment for Pakistani nuclear research and development that stopped short of that marker. The committee nevertheless claimed that this would send a "clear and unmistakable signal" to Islamabad that "although the United States considers its security relationship with Pakistan of the utmost importance to the national interest of both our nations, the acquisition by Pakistan of a nuclear device would terminate that relationship." In explaining the majority's position, the committee concurred with the administration's view that the aid cut-off required by the original amendment could have convinced the Pakistanis that "the rapid acquisition of a nuclear device is the only way to provide for their national security." In the long term, the committee said, "preservation of our existing program of security assistance to Pakistan is essential for our efforts to discourage that country from obtaining a nuclear capability. Our security assistance is providing an alternative way for Pakistanis to deflect their nuclear ambitions." U.S. efforts to dissuade Pakistan from acquiring nuclear weapons were "making progress."[45]

EVIDENCE OF PAKISTAN'S NUCLEAR STRIDES. Subsequent events proved this to be wishful thinking. In June 1984, three Pakistani nationals—one of them linked to Pakistan's Atomic Energy Commission—were arrested in Houston for smuggling fifty high-speed electronic switches ("krytrons") that could be used to trigger a nuclear warhead. As one U.S. analyst suggested, the krytron affair, "coupled with the statements of Pakistani authorities, could plausibly be related to an elaborate effort to persuade India that Pakistan already had a nuclear weapons capability—if not a weapon in being—and gain the presumed deterrence advantages of a bomb in advance of actually having one." In particular, the smugglers "were exceedingly unmindful of or unconcerned about the consequences of

---

45. Senate Committee on Foreign Relations, International Security and Development Cooperation Act of 1984, 98th Cong., 2nd sess., 1984, S. Rept. 98-400, pp. 7, 19, 58–59, 114. The compromise legislation was signed into law in 1985.

discovery, or incompetent, or both."[46] The krytron arrests inspired Washington to post yet another marker in its efforts to slow the Pakistani nuclear program. In a September 1984 letter to Zia, President Reagan warned of "grave consequences" if Islamabad were to enrich uranium beyond a 5 percent level (93 percent is required for nuclear weapons). Pakistani leaders assured U.S. officials that they would respect this parameter.[47]

INDIA'S RESPONSE. Predictably, the Indian government responded to Pakistan's increased nuclear visibility by stepping up its own nuclear preparations. Just before her death in October 1984, Indira Gandhi called Islamabad's nuclear strides a "qualitatively new phenomenon in our security environment," which added a "new dimension" to Indian defense planning.[48] By the middle of 1985, Gandhi's son and successor, Rajiv, admitted that in light of Pakistan's nuclear progress, India was reconsidering its own commitment not to build nuclear weapons.[49] In June 1985, Rajiv Gandhi was quoted as saying that Pakistan was "very close" to building a bomb; as for India, he said: "In principle we are opposed to the idea of becoming a nuclear power. We could have done so for the past 10 or 11 years, but we have not. If we decided to become a nuclear power, it would take a few weeks or a few months."[50] Four months later, Gandhi said that "Pakistan has either already got the bomb or will get one in a matter of months and may not even need to test it."[51] In October 1985, a high-level U.S. delegation failed to convince the Indian government that Islamabad's nuclear program was not as far along as New Delhi feared. As Gandhi said: "The U.S. seems to believe that Pakistan has not got the enriched uranium yet. We believe they have."[52] The next

---

46. Cronin, *Options for Congress*, pp. 30–31.

47. Leonard S. Spector, *The Undeclared Bomb* (Cambridge, Mass.: Ballinger, 1988), p. 127.

48. Leonard S. Spector, *Going Nuclear* (Cambridge, Mass.: Ballinger, 1987), p. 78.

49. Cronin, *Options for Congress*, p. 28.

50. Maynard Parker, "Rajiv Gandhi's Bipolar World," *Newsweek*, June 3, 1985; and Spector, *Going Nuclear*, p. 78.

51. Spector, *Going Nuclear*, p. 270, n. 21. Gandhi's remark about testing was a reference to reports that China had given Pakistan vital nuclear weapon design information.

52. Patricia J. Sethi and John Walcott, "The South Asia Two-Step," *Newsweek*, November 4, 1985, p. 42; and William Stewart and Ross H. Munro, "An Interview With Rajiv Gandhi," *Time*, October 21, 1985, p. 50.

month, the Indian foreign minister charged that Islamabad had enough weapons-grade uranium for three to five atomic bombs.[53]

PREVENTIVE WAR PRESSURES

Speculation grew in the late 1970s that Pakistan's growing nuclear infrastructure would be disabled by preventive attacks, either from the air or by saboteurs. In August 1979, Carter administration officials said that an interagency task force was debating various options for curtailing Islamabad's nuclear progress, including a covert operation to sabotage the Kahuta uranium enrichment facility.[54] A U.S. analyst reports that "there was a great deal of anxiety in Islamabad in August 1979 that, having failed to influence Pakistani nuclear policy, Washington would shortly undertake covert military action" against Kahuta and other nuclear installations. "This move was expected either through direct U.S. action or as a commando raid by either the Israelis or the Indians. These rumors were taken seriously enough for PAF [Pakistan Air Force] Mirages to overfly the facility and air defenses to be set up on an alert basis."[55] Washington eventually abandoned the idea of disabling Kahuta as "too dangerous and politically provocative."[56]

Three years later, U.S. intelligence officials were quoted as saying that Indian military leaders had in 1981 presented Prime Minister Indira Gandhi with a contingency plan to destroy Islamabad's nuclear facilities. She "decided against carrying out an attack," but "did not foreclose the option of striking if Pakistan appeared on the verge of acquiring a nuclear weapons capability." Gandhi's main concern was reportedly that Islamabad would order reprisal raids against India's own nuclear facilities. Indian spokesmen denied the charges. Meanwhile, President Zia said that Islamabad was concerned about the prospect of an Indian preventive strike but had made "adequate preparations." U.S. offficials confirmed that Islamabad had ringed Kahuta with surface-to-air missiles to ward off Indian bombers.[57] The

---

53. "Foreign Minister Speaks in Parliament on Pak Nuclear Bomb," confidential cable from the American Embassy in New Delhi to the Secretary of State, No. 28599, November 1985 (National Security Archive).

54. Richard Burt, "U.S. Will Press Pakistan to Halt A-Arms Project," *New York Times*, August 12, 1979.

55. Shirin Tahir-Kheli, *The United States and Pakistan: Evolution of an Influence Relationship* (New York: Praeger, 1982), p. 136.

56. Richard Burt, "U.S. Aides Say Pakistan Is Reported to Be Building an A-Bomb Site," *New York Times*, August 17, 1979.

57. Milton R. Benjamin, "India Said to Eye Raid on Pakistan's A-Plants," *Washington Post*, December 20, 1982.

June 1981 Israeli attack on Iraq's Osirak nuclear facility fueled renewed speculation about preventive attacks against Kahuta. As one U.S. official said: "They don't do things as neatly as the Israelis in that part of the world, but we can't rule it out."[58]

Similar rumors surfaced in September 1984, when leaks from a CIA briefing to the Senate Select Committee on Intelligence suggested that Indira Gandhi was again being urged by military advisers to destroy Kahuta preventively. One cause for U.S. concern was the apparent failure of U.S. intelligence to locate two squadrons of Indian Air Force Jaguar fighter bombers, which might have been moved in preparation for a raid across the border.[59] Senior Pakistani officials said that they regarded the possibility of attacks on their nuclear installations as a "serious threat," and had taken "appropriate defensive measures." They added that Islamabad would view such strikes as "naked aggression," which would leave "no alternative but to retaliate."[60] According to one account, Pakistani leaders also "sent an explicit message to New Delhi through diplomatic channels": if India attacked Kahuta, the PAF would "strike every nuclear installation in India, civilian as well as military," raising the possibility of massive radiation poisoning. This unconfirmed report claims that the Pakistani threat forced New Delhi to back down.[61] Indian officials at the time pointed out that a preventive strike would "legitimise an action to which India would itself be vulnerable," but conceded that, "in a purely theoretical sense, some people may be looking at such scenarios."[62] The following year, in response to a reporter's question about whether India might emulate the Israeli strike against Osirak, Prime Minister Rajiv Gandhi claimed that India had not considered such an attack. He added: "And we do try not to behave like the Israelis."[63]

---

58. Robert Manning, "Hanging by the Bomb," *Far Eastern Economic Review*, December 4, 1981, p. 22.

59. Don Oberdorfer, "U.S. Sees India-Pakistan Rifts Not as Signals of Imminent War," *Washington Post*, September 15, 1984. Other sources suggested that the Jaguars were simply obscured by cloud cover.

60. Don Oberdorfer, "Pakistan Concerned About Attack on Atomic Plants," *Washington Post*, October 12, 1984.

61. William E. Burrows and Robert Windrem, *Critical Mass: The Dangerous Race for Superweapons in a Fragmenting World* (New York: Simon and Schuster, 1994), pp. 349–350.

62. Robert Manning, "Talking Up the Tension," *Far Eastern Economic Review*, October 4, 1984, p. 27.

63. Parker, "Rajiv Gandhi's Bipolar World," p. 42.

THE INDIA-PAKISTAN NUCLEAR NON-ATTACK AGREEMENT. In December 1985, India and Pakistan announced an agreement not to attack each other's nuclear facilities. Gandhi "apparently initiated the no-attack proposal in an effort to lay the issue to rest."[64] New Delhi had evidently determined that the potential costs of striking Kahuta outweighed the benefits. An analysis prepared for the State Department's Bureau of Intelligence and Research in 1984 had alluded to several unpalatable possibilities that would likely dissuade India from attacking Kahuta: the "exposure of Indian territory to the resulting radiation," the "danger of Pakistani retaliation," escalation to a general war, international sanctions, and an embargo on oil imports from Pakistan's Islamic allies in the Middle East.[65]

Indo-Pakistani Nuclear Dynamics in the Early 1980s

This overview of South Asian nuclear developments in the early 1980s lends empirical support to several of the theoretical arguments I made in Chapters 1 and 2. First, it demonstrates the main incentive for nuclear opacity: the fear of punishment by the nonproliferation community, or in this case, the United States. Renewed U.S. aid to Pakistan was contingent on explicit assurances that Islamabad would not "embarrass" Washington by conducting a nuclear explosive test. Although Pakistan exceeded other markers, such as enriching uranium to a level above 5 percent, testing a nuclear device would have been too dramatic a gesture for the U.S. Congress to ignore. Islamabad understood this: while it repeatedly broke the game's minor rules, it never violated the major one. Subsequent charges that U.S. complacency "let" Pakistan develop nuclear weapons in the 1980s must be seen in this light. It was never a question of Islamabad either achieving or not achieving a nuclear capability; if it wanted one badly enough, it would get it. The real issues were whether Washington could slow Islamabad's nuclear progress until such time as Pakistani leaders viewed nuclear weapons as unnecessary for Pakistani security, and keep Pakistan's nuclear weapon capabilities within certain parameters until that time. These goals have been partially realized: on one hand, Islamabad to this day views its nuclear

---

64. Spector, *Going Nuclear*, p. 81.

65. U.S. Department of State, Bureau of Intelligence and Research, "India-Pakistan: Pressures for Nuclear Proliferation," Report 778-AR, February 10, 1984 (National Security Archive).

option as integral to Pakistani security; but on the other, Pakistan has slowed its nuclear program after attaining a rudimentary weapon capability, with the result that a full-blown South Asian nuclear arms race has been averted.

Second, this overview of the 1980–86 period illustrates the U.S. role in transparency-building, especially in the case of Pakistan. The Reagan administration's struggle to keep aid flowing to Pakistan in the face of spirited congressional opposition inevitably generated detailed information about Islamabad's nuclear strides. In turn, much of what Indian leaders knew about the Pakistani nuclear program they gleaned from the statements and estimates of U.S. officials, made public in media reports and open congressional proceedings. Indian analysts repeatedly cited leaked U.S. intelligence judgments as authoritative evidence of Pakistani nuclear developments. Islamabad no doubt appreciated the credibility this increased visibility lent to its nascent nuclear weaponization.

Finally, the early history of the Indo-Pakistani nuclear arms competition lends further support to the argument I made in Chapter 1 that preventive attacks against possibly nuclear states are extremely unlikely. As is apparent from Indian calculations in the early 1980s, too many potential costs outweigh the uncertain benefits of preventive strikes against nuclearizing states: general war, reprisals against one's own nuclear facilities, international sanctions, and, in the case of neighbors, radioactive fallout drifting across borders. It would have been irresponsible for Indian military planners not to have contemplated preventive attacks against Pakistan's uranium enrichment facility at Kahuta; however, the fact that the political leadership ultimately thought better of the idea adds weight to an already impressive historical pattern of restraint in this area.

INDIA'S AND PAKISTAN'S NUCLEAR STATUS IN 1986
By the end of 1986, India had for the first time acquired weapons-usable plutonium free of nonproliferation controls, and was also known to be working on improved weapon design.[66] The Indian Army chief, General K. Sundarji, said in February 1986: "There are enough indicators to suggest that Pakistan has achieved or is close to achieving a nuclear weapons capability." Sundarji vowed that the

---

66. Spector, *Going Nuclear*, p. 73.

Indian Army would "not be made to fight in a disadvantageous situation, and was gearing its organization, training, and equipment for the possibility of military operations in a nuclear environment.[67]

In July, a secret State Department memo said that "Pakistan continues to pursue a nuclear explosives capability. . . . If operated at its nominal capacity, the Kahuta uranium enrichment plant could produce enough weapons-grade material to build several nuclear devices per year. . . . Our assessment remains, however, that Pakistan does not possess a nuclear explosive device."[68] A November *Washington Post* story quoted U.S. intelligence sources as stating that Pakistan had enriched uranium to 93.5 percent. In a remark that reverberated around South Asian defense circles, another source said that Pakistan was "two screwdriver turns" away from having an assembled atomic bomb.[69] This was the strategic context for the first India-Pakistan crisis of South Asia's nuclear era, which erupted in late 1986. That crisis is the subject of Chapter 4.

67. Inderjit Badhwar, "The Thinking Man's General," *India Today*, February 15, 1986, p. 78.

68. "Official Visit of Pakistani Prime Minister Mohammed Khan Junejo: Background and Talking Points," secret memorandum from the U.S. Department of State to Henry A. Kissinger, July 1986 (National Security Archive).

69. Bob Woodward, "Pakistan Reported Near Atom Arms Production," *Washington Post*, November 4, 1986.

Chapter 4

Nuclear Weapons and the 1986–87 Brasstacks Crisis

The first crisis of South Asia's nuclear era erupted in December 1986 and January 1987. From a high point marked by the Zia-Gandhi nuclear non-attack agreement of December 1985, Indo-Pakistani relations had degenerated to their lowest ebb since the Bangladesh war. In the autumn of 1986, a series of Indian military exercises called Brasstacks started a spiral of competitive mobilization. By January 1987, both countries' military forces were on alert, with Indian and Pakistani armored formations poised near sensitive areas along the international frontier. As President Zia later told an interviewer, "neither India nor Pakistan wanted war but we could have easily gone into war."[1] Just as quickly as it began, though, the crisis abated. By the end of January, Islamabad and New Delhi were negotiating over the withdrawal of troops from border areas. In early February, the two sides agreed to a phased demobilization of forces that was implemented over the next few months. Thereafter, Indo-Pakistani relations returned to their normally tense, but not critical, state.

In this chapter, I chronicle and then analyze the 1986–87 Brasstacks crisis. My main conclusion is that evolving Indian and Pakistani nuclear weapon capabilities had little discernible influence on the outcome of the crisis. The dire predictions of the logic of nonproliferation were, of course, not realized, nor is it readily evident that nuclear deterrence prevented war. As was explored extensively in Chapters 1 and 2, the vast majority of the literature on the consequences of proliferation—and its subset on nuclear opacity—suggests

---

1. Interview with Mohammad Zia ul-Haq, "Neither India Nor Pakistan Wanted War, But We Could Have Easily Gone Into War," *The Telegraph* (Calcutta), February 22, 1987.

that crises erupting during the transition to nuclear weapons should be extremely dangerous, perhaps even the most perilous scenario one can imagine.[2] Given this conventional wisdom, the fact that the Brasstacks crisis did not evolve into a nuclear crisis is significant.

The chapter is organized as follows. In the next section, I discuss the political context shaping South Asian international politics in 1986–87. Then I present a chronological overview of the Brasstacks crisis. In the fourth section, I analyze the crisis, paying particular attention to four questions: 1) What were New Delhi's intentions in conducting Brasstacks? 2) What was it about the Indian exercises that so alarmed Pakistani leaders? 3) What was the significance of nuclear weapon capabilities for the outcome of the crisis? and 4) Why was the crisis ultimately resolved peacefully, if not because of nuclear deterrence? In the chapter's conclusion, I more closely examine the implications of my judgment that nuclear weapon capabilities had little impact on the outcome of the crisis.

Background: The India-Pakistan Security Rivalry in 1986–87

At the global level, the U.S.-Soviet Cold War continued unabated in 1987, although the first tentative signs of a thaw were evident. The most important South Asian manifestation of the superpower competition was the ongoing war in Afghanistan. By 1987, some 120,000 Soviet soldiers were pitted against an increasingly well-armed collection of Afghan resistance groups. Early in the war, Moscow had taken advantage of the insurgents' lack of air defenses by pursuing a scorched-earth policy. Through a combination of high-altitude bombing and helicopter search-and-destroy operations, the Soviets were able to depopulate much of rural Afghanistan. By 1987, an estimated one million Afghans had been killed, five million were refugees in Iran and Pakistan, and two million more were internal exiles swept into Kabul and other cities where they were more easily controlled and less of an asset to the resistance. In 1986, the United States began supplying the Afghan insurgents with Stinger surface-to-air missiles, which dramatically changed the complexion of the fighting by neutralizing

---

2. See the comments of David Gompert and John Weltman in Chapter 1. It is unsurprising that Gompert, a proliferation pessimist, is nervous about the prospect of bitter adversaries putting the finishing touches on their nuclear weapons "in the heat of conflict." But even Weltman, a deterrence optimist, concedes that the evolution of a "mutually stable weapons posture" may only be gradual, and that "hostilities involving nuclear weapons" might erupt in the meantime.

the effectiveness of the feared Soviet Mi-24 Hind helicopter gunship. This was the beginning of the end for the Soviets' ill-fated occupation of Afghanistan; Afghan resistance and his own domestic imperatives soon caused Soviet leader Mikhail Gorbachev to search for a way to stanch the Red Army's "bleeding wound."[3]

The United States and Pakistan were determined to encourage this kind of thinking in Moscow by maintaining a united front against Soviet aggression. In the mid-1980s, Washington annually supplied hundreds of millions of dollars-worth of covert military assistance to the Afghan insurgents via their Pakistani supporters. Moreover, Washington and Islamabad agreed in 1986 to renew their own economic and military aid relationship. Pakistan would receive another $4.02 billion in U.S. assistance from 1988 to 1993, provided that the Reagan administration could continue to overcome the objections of legislators who warned that Pakistani nuclear weapons were too high a price to pay for victory in Afghanistan. As the follow-on aid package made its way through the U.S. legislative process in 1987, it shed more light than ever before on the rapid progress Pakistani scientists had made in developing nuclear weapons. This increased transparency was not altogether objectionable to Islamabad, because it lent Pakistan's nuclear weapon capabilities a measure of credibility they otherwise would have lacked. I will document this phenomenon in Chapter 5.

THE REGIONAL CONTEXT

Regionally, the relative amity of Indo-Pakistani relations in 1985 gave way to increasing tension in 1986. The major source of political conflict on the eve of Brasstacks was each side's alleged support for ethnic insurgencies on the other's territory. Islamabad accused New Delhi of fomenting political violence in the southern Pakistani province of Sindh, which had seen an influx of migrants since Pakistan gained independence in 1947. The first wave of settlers were *muhajirs* (refugees) from India, who fueled the commercial and industrial growth of Karachi, Pakistan's largest city. Later settlers included Punjabis and, especially during the Afghanistan war, Pathans and Afghans. Sindhi nationalism grew in the 1970s, as a response to what ethnic Sindhis perceived as their increasing subordination to outsiders. In 1983, an opposition coalition called the Movement for the Restoration of Democracy launched violent

3. Devin T. Hagerty, "Afghanistan's Islamic Insurgency," Fletcher School of Law and Diplomacy, Tufts University, October 2, 1987 (author's files).

disturbances against the Zia regime. This agitation soon took on a regionalist tone, with Sindhis demanding greater provincial autonomy, reduced disparities in economic development, more equitable distribution of federal government funds, and increased representation in the military and civil services. In 1986, mass rioting pitted ethnic Sindhis and *muhajirs* against Punjabis, Pathans, and Afghans. Throughout, Pakistani leaders accused the Indian government of inciting violence between the various groups.[4] As will be discussed below, Pakistan's main security concern during the Brasstacks crisis was closely linked to the instability in Sindh.

Similarly, India's main fear during Brasstacks concerned the Sikh insurgency that had raged in the Indian state of Punjab since the early 1980s.[5] In 1981, the Akali Dal—the main Sikh political party—had launched a sustained agitation against the Congress party and the Indian government. Sikh leaders hoped to resolve certain long-standing disputes, the most important of which concerned the status of Chandigarh, which had been the capital of both Punjab and the neighboring state of Haryana since the old state of Punjab was linguistically reorganized in 1966. As negotiations between Sikh leaders and Indira Gandhi's government failed to bear fruit, the Sikh political movement descended into militancy. With the violence escalating, extremist Sikh leaders turned the Golden Temple in Amritsar—Sikhism's holiest shrine—into a sanctuary and base of operations. Some called for the creation of Khalistan—an independent Sikh state. In June 1984, the Indian Army launched Operation Bluestar, an assault on the Golden Temple and other Sikh temples where militant leaders had taken refuge. An estimated 600–1,000 people were killed in the three-day siege. The Indian Home Ministry claimed that the Sikh insurgency was a prelude to the creation of Khalistan, supported by "neighboring and foreign powers," which would have "crippled the armed forces in any future confrontation across the borders."[6]

---

4. For details of the ethnic conflict in Sindh, see Craig Baxter et al., *Government and Politics in South Asia*, 2nd ed. (Boulder, Colo.: Westview, 1991), pp. 182–184; and Shahid Javed Burki, *Pakistan: The Continuing Search for Nationhood*, 2nd ed. (Boulder, Colo.: Westview, 1991), pp. 73–74.

5. The following discussion draws on Robert L. Hardgrave, Jr. and Stanley Kochanek, *India: Government and Politics in a Developing Nation*, 5th ed. (Fort Worth, Texas: Harcourt Brace Jovanovich, 1993), pp. 152–160. I have also profited from reading Paul R. Brass, "The Punjab Crisis and the Unity of India," in Atul Kohli, ed., *India's Democracy: An Analysis of Changing State-Society Relations* (Princeton, N.J.: Princeton University Press, 1988), pp. 169–213.

6. Salamat Ali, "The 'Hidden Hand'," *Far Eastern Economic Review*, June 28, 1984, p. 14.

In October 1984, Indira Gandhi was murdered by two Sikh members of her security detail. In the assassination's aftermath, some 2,700 Sikhs were slaughtered in Delhi's worst violence since partition. Gandhi was succeeded by her son, Rajiv, who in December won the prime ministership in his own right. In August 1985, the government reached an agreement with moderate Sikh leaders that conceded their main demands, including the transfer of Chandigarh to Punjab, which was slated for early 1986. In September 1985, the Akali Dal won a majority in state assembly elections, whose 67 percent turnout indicated strong support for the accord. However, the Congress soon reneged on the deal, for fear of damaging its electoral prospects elsewhere in northern India. The agreement's collapse unleashed renewed terrorism in Punjab: there had been 64 terrorist killings in the state during 1985; that number rose to 620 in 1986, and to 883 in 1987.[7]

The Sikh insurgency cast a chill over Indo-Pakistani relations, and the violence in Punjab provided the immediate political backdrop for the Brasstacks exercises. In February 1986, the Indian foreign minister told his colleagues in the Indian Parliament that the government had hard evidence of Pakistani support for Sikh extremists in Punjab. Soon thereafter, New Delhi abruptly canceled a planned visit to Pakistan by Rajiv Gandhi, warning Islamabad that its meddling in Punjab was a serious obstacle to the normalization of relations.[8] In late summer 1986, New Delhi announced plans to seal the Indo-Pakistani border in order to prevent the entry of Sikh terrorists from Pakistan. India would create a five-mile-wide security belt along the border, and routine policing of the area would henceforth be the responsibility of the Indian army, instead of local and paramilitary security forces.[9] Indian military movements during the Brasstacks crisis were largely an outgrowth of New Delhi's sensitivity to the instability in Punjab and its wider implications for the integrity of the Indian union.

THE DOMESTIC CONTEXT

Domestically, both India and Pakistan were governed by relatively strong leaders in 1987. The Congress had won a landslide victory in

---

7. Atul Kohli, *Democracy and Discontent: India's Growing Crisis of Governability* (Cambridge, U.K.: Cambridge University Press, 1990), p. 369.

8. Mohan Ram, "The Warmth Wears Off," *Far Eastern Economic Review*, March 27, 1986, p. 34.

9. Salamat Ali, "Cause for Confrontation," *Far Eastern Economic Review*, August 21, 1986, p. 30.

the 1984 national election, garnering an all-time high of 77 percent of the seats in the Lok Sabha, India's lower house of parliament. In office, Rajiv Gandhi's government was plagued by the same over-centralization and personalization of power that had characterized his mother's rule. The fact that he reshuffled his cabinet twenty-seven times in five years[10] also created an impression of indecisiveness at the top. All in all, though, Gandhi's huge parliamentary majority and unchallenged personal stature left little doubt as to who was in charge in New Delhi.[11] In Pakistan, President Zia led the country with a firm hand while taking the first tentative steps toward democracy. In 1985, Zia had allowed "party-less" elections, hand-picked a civilian prime minister, Mohammad Khan Junejo, and ended martial law. While he allowed Junejo a fair amount of independence in the day-today running of the government, Zia kept a tight grip on Islamabad's national security decision-making.[12]

Chronological Overview of the Crisis

The 1986–87 crisis was precipitated by a series of Indian military exercises known collectively as Brasstacks. These exercises culminated in March 1987 with Brasstacks IV, Indian Army maneuvers involving two armored divisions, one mechanized division, and six infantry divisions. Brasstacks IV was South Asia's largest ever military exercise, comparable in scale to similar North Atlantic Treaty Organization (NATO) maneuvers in Europe. Although the Indian government consistently maintained that Brasstacks IV was a routine army exercise, it used more divisions and more armor than any previous Indian maneuvers. Brasstacks IV took place in the Rajasthan desert near the Pakistani border, which Indian officials claim is the only part of the country with enough fallow land to accommodate large-scale ground exercises without disrupting agriculture and incurring huge expenses to compensate farmers. The stated objective of Brasstacks IV was to test new concepts of mechanization, mobility, and air support devised by the Indian chief of the army staff (COAS),

---

10. Baxter et al., *Government and Politics in South Asia*, p. 70.

11. The corruption scandals that emerged later in 1987 tainted the prime minister's image and severely eroded his authority. See Hardgrave and Kochanek, *India*, pp. 265–269.

12. Burki, *Pakistan*, pp. 72–85.

General K. Sundarji. A graduate of the U.S. Command and General Staff College at Fort Leavenworth, Kansas, Sundarji was enamored of U.S. air-land battle doctrines emphasizing deep offensive thrusts supported by aggressive air cover.[13]

Brasstacks IV was intended to simulate an Indian response to a Pakistani ground offensive, testing the Indian Army's strategy of "offensive-defense." According to one study of the crisis, the political scenario underlying the exercise was that "insurgency in Kashmir had reached unmanageable proportions." At the same time, "an announcement declaring the existence of the independent Sikh nation of Khalistan is made by Sikh militants encouraging Pakistan to make a 'final push' to detach" both Kashmir and Punjab from India.[14] The military scenario was that Red Land (Pakistan) has crossed the international border and advanced twenty kilometers into Blue Land (India). Blue Land then launches a counteroffensive, testing both its ability to defend territory and to strike back in response. For this purpose, General Sundarji had created an organizational hybrid, the Reorganized Army Plains Infantry Division (RAPID), which would in theory be able to hold land defensively while retaining sufficient mobility to carry out a counteroffensive.[15]

PAKISTANI CONCERNS

As Pakistani officials received intelligence information in 1986 regarding the planned exercises, they grew increasingly nervous. As early as August, well before Indian troops had begun moving into the exercise area in Rajasthan, the Pakistani director general of military operations (DGMO) contacted his Indian counterpart via their hotline to ascertain New Delhi's intentions. The Indian side claimed there had been no need to inform the Pakistanis about the forthcoming exercises, since no Indian troops had yet moved to the exercise

---

13. Information on Brasstacks IV comes from my interviews with General K. Sundarji and a former senior Indian decision-maker who was closely involved in the Brasstacks crisis. See also Manoj Joshi, "From Maps to the Field," *The Hindu* (Madras), March 29, 1987; and Keith Flory, "Getting Closer to Brasstacks," *The Statesman* (Calcutta), March 7, 1987.

14. Kanti P. Bajpai et al., *Brasstacks and Beyond: Perception and Management of Crisis in South Asia* (Urbana-Champaign: Program in Arms Control, Disarmament, and International Security, University of Illinois, 1995), pp. 36–37. This study was the product of an oral history project incorporating interviews with Indian, Pakistani, and U.S. decision-makers.

15. Interview with Sundarji.

area.[16] In November 1986, Indian Army soldiers began assembling in Rajasthan; also that month, at a meeting of the South Asian Association for Regional Cooperation (SAARC) in Bangalore, India, Pakistani Prime Minister Junejo suggested that SAARC members agree to certain confidence-building measures, such as prior notification of significant troop movements. Junejo's speech reflected Pakistani concerns about the magnitude of Brasstacks. In a meeting with Junejo during the conference, Rajiv Gandhi objected to Pakistani references to Indian troop movements, which he explained were a prelude to routine exercises, not to an invasion of Pakistan.[17] President Zia recalled later that when Junejo had asked Gandhi about the scale of Brasstacks, the Indian prime minister had replied that New Delhi would decrease the size of the exercise.[18]

In any event, Islamabad took little comfort from Gandhi's pledges of peaceful intent. The day after the SAARC summit ended, the Pakistani DGMO again sought promises from his Indian counterpart that New Delhi's intentions were benign. He also requested that the scope of Brasstacks be curtailed and that the operational area of Brasstacks IV be clearly defined, so as to alleviate Pakistani concerns about a surprise offensive launched under the guise of training maneuvers. The Indian DGMO repeated New Delhi's now standard position that Brasstacks was a routine exercise and therefore no cause for alarm. Pakistan's DGMO received the "definite impression" from this call that the size of Brasstacks would be reduced, and that the operational area would be modified in light of Pakistan's anxiety.[19] Zia recalled later that the Indian DGMO had told the Pakistani DGMO in November that Brasstacks had been modified to run from north to south instead of east to west (parallel rather than perpendicular to the Pakistani border).[20] The Indian COAS, General Sundarji, calls this "nonsense," stating that all Indian military exercises, including this one, were structured to run north-south. Sundarji also claims that the Indian DGMO had provided to his Pakistani counterpart sufficient

16. Prem Shankar Jha, "Indo-Pak Relations: Clue to a Riddle," *Hindustan Times*, February 3, 1987.

17. Salamat Ali, "Sophistry at Summitry," *Far Eastern Economic Review*, November 27, 1986, p. 30.

18. Interview with Zia, "Neither India Nor Pakistan Wanted War."

19. Dilip Bobb and Inderjit Badhwar, "Back from the Edge," *India Today*, February 28, 1987, pp. 42–43.

20. Interview with Zia, "Neither India Nor Pakistan Wanted War."

reassurance that New Delhi had no offensive designs against Pakistan.[21] On December 2, the Pakistanis again expressed their apprehension about Brasstacks, but to no avail. Finally, on December 8, Islamabad informed New Delhi that because of its concerns about Brasstacks, Pakistan would extend its own winter exercises.[22]

PAKISTANI MILITARY MOVEMENTS. Pakistan's exercises involved two distinct groupings of army units. The exercise *Saf-e-Shikan* was carried out in the Bahawalpur area by the First Armored Division and the 37th Infantry Division of Pakistan's Army Reserve South. The Flying Horse maneuvers, involving the Sixth Armored Division and 17th Infantry Division of the Army Reserve North, took place in the Jhelum-Chenab corridor. In December, the Army Reserve South completed its training but remained in the Bahawalpur area "in combat ready formation." Meanwhile, *Saf-e-Shikan* was renamed Sledge Hammer, and the Army Reserve North moved to the Gujranwala area in the Ravi-Chenab corridor, west of the Shakargarh salient. Both Pakistani reserves were also supplemented with additional infantry and armor.[23] In addition, claiming that the Indian military had ignored its repeated requests for information about Brasstacks, Pakistan stepped up its surveillance of border areas and placed several of its military cantonments on alert.[24] Islamabad also kept its forward air bases activated (ready to refuel and rearm aircraft) and dumped ammunition and mines into forward areas. According to Zia, Pakistan took these precautions so as not to be "caught with our pants down," if India was indeed thinking in terms of a surprise attack.[25]

INDO-PAKISTANI MILITARY DYNAMICS

By mid-December, then, India and Pakistan were locked into a tense military standoff, a dangerous situation made even more perilous by the fact that, between December 8, 1986 and January 23, 1987, the DGMO hotline was not used. Developments during this crucial period brought India and Pakistan to the brink of war. At the end of December, the Indian government received a piece of intelligence

---

21. Interview with Sundarji.

22. Bobb and Badhwar, "Back from the Edge," pp. 42–43.

23. Bajpai et al., *Brasstacks and Beyond*, p. 41.

24. Suzanne Goldenberg, "Indian Maneuvers Provoke New Fears," *United Press International*, December 15, 1986.

25. Interview with Zia, "Neither India Nor Pakistan Wanted War."

information that it considered less than 100 percent reliable, but still cause for concern. The information suggested that Pakistan was considering a plan whereby Sikh secessionists inside the Golden Temple in Amritsar would announce the formation of an independent Khalistan. Pakistan would quickly recognize the new state and the secessionists would ask for its assistance. Islamabad would oblige by launching a pincer movement into India and slicing off the Amritsar area north of the Beas River. Indian intelligence suggested that Pakistan's Army Reserve North would cross the border near Pathankot, and the Army Reserve South would invade near Ferozepur. The area carved from India in this pincer movement could be defended easily, as it is surrounded on nearly all sides by either Pakistani territory or the Beas. Sundarji recalls calculating that if this were indeed Pakistan's plan, the Indian military should see the movement of the Army Reserve South from the Bahawalpur exercise area north toward Okara. While the Army Reserve South posed no threat near Bahawalpur, moving north would put it in a position to join the Army Reserve North in the pincer movement that Indian intelligence suggested Pakistan was contemplating.[26]

PAKISTAN'S NORTHWARD FEINT.   In late December and early January, Pakistan did in fact move the Army Reserve South from its Bahawalpur exercise area, north across the Sutlej River to Multan, and thence to the Okara area across from Fazilka in India.[27] The Army Reserve South crossed the Lodhran Bridge over the Sutlej in the second week of January, before moving northeast toward the Punjab border. The Pakistan Army was now at least theoretically positioned to carry out the pincer movement that was the Indian military's source of concern. In mid-January, Sundarji recalls, the Indian Army received "very firm" indications from an "exceedingly reliable source" that Pakistan's Army Reserve South had moved north of the Sutlej, and then northeast toward Okara. This was, for Sundarji "the most important piece of this jigsaw. . . . The principal requirements for a Pakistani offensive were in place."[28] Because of competing intelligence estimates within the Indian government, Prime Minister Gandhi apparently was not convinced that the Pakistani Army Reserve South had moved northeast toward the Indian border until January 22, more than two weeks after the fact.[29] At this time,

26. Interview with Sundarji.

27. Interview with former Pakistani foreign secretary Abdul Sattar. Sattar was Islamabad's chief negotiator during the 1987 troop disengagement talks.

28. Interview with Sundarji.

29. Interview with former senior Indian decision-maker.

General Sundarji recommended to Gandhi that the Indian Army take defensive positions along the border from Jammu down through Punjab. India's military forces were then placed on alert, and Indian soldiers were rushed to Punjab to seal the frontier.[30] An Indian official said publicly that the objective of the Punjab deployments was to "prevent any possibility of a surprise attack on the Indian positions," in view of the fact that Pakistan had moved its Army Reserve South so close to the border.[31]

DIPLOMATIC MOVES

At the same time, the Indian government informed representatives of the United States, the Soviet Union, and Pakistan that its Punjab deployment was a purely defensive move. Pakistan's ambassador to India, M. Humayun Khan, was summoned to the foreign office and told that New Delhi considered the movement of Pakistani forces, especially armor, "offensive and provocative." Indian officials demanded that Pakistan return its army units to normal locations.[32] Ambassador Khan denied that Pakistani forces had taken up offensive positions near the Indian border or that Islamabad had moved any armored divisions at all.[33] In response to India's Punjab deployments, Pakistan put its own forces on alert[34] and proposed, both through the Indian ambassador in Islamabad and via the DGMO hotline, that representatives of the two sides meet to discuss de-escalating the crisis.[35] On January 24, India agreed to open negotiations with Pakistan, stating categorically that it had no intention of invading its neighbor.[36] The next day, as President Zia headed off for a previously scheduled trip to Kuwait, Prime Minister Junejo spoke with Rajiv Gandhi on the telephone, further easing tensions.[37]

---

30. Interview with Sundarji.

31. Denholm Barnetson, "India Forces on Red Alert at Pakistan Border," *United Press International*, January 23, 1987. Also see Sanjoy Hazarika, "India Puts Military on Full Alert, Citing a Pakistani Troop Buildup," *New York Times*, January 24, 1987.

32. Bajpai et al., *Brasstacks and Beyond*, p. 35.

33. "India Not To Attack Pak," *Indian Express*, January 25, 1987.

34. Richard M. Weintraub, "India and Pakistan Move Military Units to Sensitive Frontier," *Washington Post*, January 25, 1987.

35. Oliver Wates, "Pakistan Blames Unprecedented Indian Exercises for Tensions," *Reuters*, January 24, 1987.

36. Robert Mahoney, "Indian Troops Take Up Positions on Pakistan Border," *Reuters*, January 24, 1987.

37. Bajpai et al., *Brasstacks and Beyond*, p. 44.

The two sides held talks at the foreign secretary level from January 31 to February 4. In the final agreement, New Delhi and Islamabad promised not to attack each other, to avoid provocative actions along the border, and to pull out their units from the Ravi-Chenab corridor within fifteen days.[38] This first phase of troop withdrawals, involving only Pakistan's Army Reserve North in northern Punjab and the Indian troops facing it across the border, began on February 11 and was completed by February 19. Two days later, Zia traveled to India in what was widely hailed as a gesture of "cricket diplomacy." He used the occasion of an India-Pakistan cricket match in Jaipur, the capital of Rajasthan, to meet with Rajiv Gandhi and signal his country's peaceful intentions. During his visit, Zia denied that Pakistan had supported the Sikh secessionists in India, and offered New Delhi an Indo-Pakistani pact whereby each side would renounce support for separatist movements on the other's territory.[39] Although nothing came of his offer, Zia's visit and its favorable coverage by the Indian media brought the Brasstacks crisis to a symbolic conclusion. In March, agreement was reached on a second round of troop withdrawals, this one from the Rajasthan border area.[40] Meanwhile, India went ahead with Brasstacks IV under the watchful eyes of the international press and diplomatic corps.[41] Ironically, by the time of the actual maneuvers, the Brasstacks crisis had been laid to rest. Subsequently, all Indian and Pakistani forces were returned to their normal peacetime positions.

THE A.Q. KHAN AFFAIR

The Brasstacks crisis brought in its wake a series of revelations about Islamabad's nuclear program that essentially confirmed Pakistan's status as a nuclear weapon state. On January 28, the eve of the first meeting between Indian and Pakistani negotiators, Pakistani scientist A.Q. Khan reportedly asserted that Pakistan had achieved the capability to build nuclear weapons. Khan allegedly told Indian journalist Kuldip Nayar: "What the CIA has been saying about our possessing the bomb is correct and so is the speculation of some foreign

---

38. For the text of the agreement, see "Indo-Pak Accord to De-Escalate Border Tension," *The Statesman* (Calcutta), February 5, 1987.

39. *United Press International,* February 23, 1987.

40. Raja Asghar, "India, Pakistan Agree to Withdraw 250,000 More Troops," *Reuters,* March 2, 1987.

41. Steven R Weisman, "On India's Border, A Huge Mock War, *New York Times,* March 6, 1987.

newspapers. . . . They told us that Pakistan could never produce the bomb and they doubted my capabilities, but they now know we have done it." Nayar also reported that Khan said: "The word 'peaceful' associated with a nuclear program is humbug. There is no peaceful bomb. After all, there is only a weak, transparent screen between the two. Once you know how to make reactors, how to produce plutonium—all that Pakistan has mastered as well—it becomes rather easy to produce nuclear weapons." Most ominously, Khan was alleged to have warned that "nobody can undo Pakistan or take us for granted. We are here to stay and let it be clear that we shall use the bomb if our existence is threatened."[42]

DELAYED SIGNALS. In a strange twist of fate, Kuldip Nayar's report of his discussion with A.Q. Khan was not published until March 1. By that time, of course, the Brasstacks crisis had simmered down, but Nayar's story unleashed a new torrent of charges and countercharges regarding the status of the Pakistani nuclear program, the circumstances of the January 28 conversation, and the implications of Khan's alleged remarks. Khan immediately denied Nayar's main point—that Islamabad had achieved the capability to build nuclear weapons. In various statements distributed to news agencies by the Pakistani government, the scientist called the Nayar article "mischievous, false and concocted" and "an attempt to malign Pakistan." He also maintained that his remarks had been "taken out of context to mislead the world into believing that Pakistan possesses a nuclear weapon." Khan continued: "Pakistan's enrichment research is solely aimed at the development of fuel-grade uranium for our future power reactors. The government of Pakistan has made it abundantly clear that it has no desire to produce nuclear weapons." A Pakistani foreign ministry spokesman added that, in light of the story's delayed publication, Nayar "obviously needed time to craft his fabrication"; the objective of this hoax, Islamabad charged, was to sabotage the follow-on U.S. aid program for Pakistan, which was due for consideration on Capitol Hill that very week. As the Pakistani ambassador to Washington put it: "We are fully aware of the repercussions on Pakistani-U.S. relations if we go nuclear. There is no doubt in our minds and never has been."[43]

---

42. "Nuke Scientist Says Pakistan Has the A-Bomb, Later Denies Report," *United Press International*, February 28, 1987; and Steven R. Weisman, "Report of Pakistani A-Bomb Causes a Stir in the Region," *New York Times*, March 2, 1987.

43. "Pakistan Denies It Has Nuclear Bomb," *United Press International*, March 2, 1987; Weisman, "Report of Pakistani A-Bomb Causes a Stir"; and Valerie Strauss, "Ambassador Denies Pakistan is Making Nuclear Bomb," *Reuters*, March 2, 1987.

Although Nayar and Khan agreed that they had indeed met on January 28, they disagreed about the nature of their conversation. Khan said that Nayar had come to his house along with a Pakistani newspaper editor who wished to drop off a wedding invitation. The two journalists stayed for tea, and the three men had "an informal conversation about nuclear nonproliferation," but discussed none of the subjects Nayar reported. Khan claimed he had never given an actual interview to Nayar, and "never used the words attributed to me." According to the scientist, Nayar "misused my hospitality and has, unfortunately, indulged in unfair and bad journalism." Nayar countered that his "appointment" with Khan was "fixed beforehand" and "for 70 minutes we spoke of the bomb and nothing else." Nayar also claimed that Khan refused to let him tape-record the interview.[44]

The situation soon grew muddier. On March 3, *The Muslim*, one of Pakistan's leading English-language dailies, published an editorial that appeared to confirm Nayar's version of the meeting, and suggested the rationale for Khan's bold statements. The editorial was written by the newspaper's editor, Mushahid Hussain, who had accompanied Kuldip Nayar to A.Q. Khan's home. In the piece, Hussain said: "The message given by Dr. A.Q. Khan . . . is directed against all those detractors of the Islamic bomb. To the Indians, it is a 'hands-off' message at a time when New Delhi has been carrying out massive warlike exercises all along our eastern border." It was also, he said, a "signal to the Americans not to link the nuclear issue with the aid package since the former is now a fait accompli." Hussain wrote that "for too long the government here had been denying what is obvious to most." The newspaper felt that "the national interest has been served" by A.Q. Khan's message.[45]

The regime in Islamabad reacted immediately. It banned government advertisements in *The Muslim*, cut off the editor's telephone, put his house under surveillance, and forbade him to leave the country. It also forced the newspaper to print a statement saying Khan's purported remarks were a fake. Within a day of publishing the editorial, Hussain resigned his position and diluted his confirmation of the controversial story, saying that the meeting between Nayar and

44. "Pakistan Denies It Has Nuclear Bomb"; "Pakistan's Nuclear Bombshell,"*India Today*, March 31, 1987; and Weisman, "Report of Pakistani A-Bomb Causes a Stir."

45. "Bomb Controversy," *The Muslim* (Islamabad), March 3, 1987, quoted in Leonard S. Spector, *The Undeclared Bomb* (Cambridge, Mass.: Ballinger, 1988), p. 371.

Khan was a "general chat" and that "there was no interview of any sort."[46] The real nature of the January 28 meeting was further obscured when it was discovered that much of what was represented by Nayar as part of their "interview" was actually an "unattributed, nearly verbatim repetition of an article Khan had written six months earlier" in a Pakistani newspaper. Though Nayar claimed Khan had urged him to consult the previously written material, the reporter's unorthodox use of it raised questions about his own credibility.[47] The larger implications of this bizarre episode will be discussed in Chapter 5.

Analyzing the Brasstacks Crisis

INDIAN INTENTIONS

New Delhi's Brasstacks exercises grew out of routine meetings between Rajiv Gandhi and his senior defense advisers in late 1985. After being briefed on the military's readiness to meet potential threats, Gandhi asked when the services had last tested India's overall capacity to mobilize for war. Told that this had never actually been done, Gandhi ordered his advisers to investigate the feasibility of doing so. It soon became apparent, though, that the costs of mobilizing the country's transportation infrastructure—railways, trucks, shipping, and airliners—for such purposes would be prohibitive. As a result, Gandhi's initial idea was scaled down to simulate the larger movement of men and matériel, with the final implementation of the plan to rely mainly on the piecemeal use of India's extensive rail system in short bursts over an extended period of time.[48]

General Sundarji's position is that the downsized Brasstacks was simply one in a series of regular triennial maneuvers, which posed no

---

46. Rod Nordland, "A Pakistan Bombshell," *Newsweek*, March 16, 1987, p. 45; Shahid-ur-Rehman Khan, "Pakistani Journalist Says Khan Did Indicate His Country Has Bomb," *Nucleonics Week*, March 12, 1987, p. 13; Steven R. Weisman, "Pakistan Stiffens on Atom Program," *New York Times*, March 22, 1987; and Asrar Ahmed, "Pakistan Editor Quits in A-bomb Controversy," *United Press International*, March 4, 1987.

47. Spector, *Undeclared Bomb*, p. 134.

48. Interview with former senior Indian decision-maker. This is the likely source of the miscommunication between Gandhi and Junejo at Bangalore in November 1986: apparently Gandhi referred to New Delhi having already downsized the exercises from his original idea. Junejo, having no way of knowing what Gandhi's early thinking was, assumed that his Indian counterpart was referring to future plans for scaling back Brasstacks.

threat whatsoever to Pakistan. Brasstacks IV was intended to test the Indian military's ability to defend territory in the face of a Pakistani ground invasion, and then to turn the tide with an offensive into Pakistan. According to the Indian Army's version of events, the main goal of Brasstacks IV was to subject Sundarji's concepts of mobility, mechanization, and offensive-defense to scrutiny under war-like conditions. Sundarji himself claims that the crisis erupted because Islamabad misread Indian intentions, feared that an Indian invasion was pending, and made preparations for war. From then on, he says, an "action-reaction" process took over, with both countries "feeding each other's fears."[49] This is the most benign explanation of the Brasstacks crisis: India's conduct of "normal" exercises raised alarm bells in Pakistan; subsequently, the logic of the security dilemma structured both sides' behavior, with each interpreting the other's defensive moves as preparations for offensive action. From this standpoint, the real danger was that India and Pakistan might stumble inadvertently into a war neither really wanted.

ULTERIOR MOTIVES? The authors of *Brasstacks and Beyond* suggest that India's military exercises "may have had much larger goals than merely to test out the preparedness of the Indian Army; these appear to have been open-ended, in that there was a degree of 'let's see what happens' tone about Brasstacks." This study maintains that "the 'bigness' of this exercise appears to have fascinated" Rajiv Gandhi, "because he wanted it to be larger than any other held earlier in the South Asian subcontinent. It would seem that it had no larger political or strategic objective in mind although it was believed by some that he wished to strike a heroic posture and impress the neighbors." According to this account, as Brasstacks evolved, a debate emerged within the Indian military. On one side was a group that believed that "Pakistan would never cease its hostility towards India as this emanated from the inner logic of its very existence; thus, Pakistan's anti-India policies were not temporary or tactical. For this reason, the logic ran, Pakistan's decades-long animus against India should be decisively crushed." Another group opposed this course, believing it lacked a compelling political objective. The authors of *Brasstacks and Beyond* conclude: "The suspicion that India had larger objectives in conducting Exercise Brasstacks needs to be seen against this backdrop of conflicting beliefs."[50]

---

49. Interview with Sundarji.

50. Bajpai et al., *Brasstacks and Beyond*, pp. vi, 19–20.

Was there more to Brasstacks than meets the eye? A senior Indian decision-maker who was involved in the crisis pointedly disputes this notion: "Brasstacks came out of a mobilization concept; it was not a whimsical . . . 'let me check out my big toys this morning' concept at all. . . . it was a very logical idea." This source continues: "To the best of my knowledge, at no point in time was Brasstacks IV intended as an excuse to go to war with Pakistan or to create reasons for Pakistan to go to war with us." Asked about the "let's see what happens" thesis, he responds, "No, no, no. . . . These are not credible scenarios for countries."[51] That having been said, Brasstacks was like any other military exercise in that it sent a distinct message to the potential adversary, in this case Pakistan. As early as November 1986, a senior Indian offficial admitted privately that Brasstacks was useful in pressuring Pakistan to be more flexible on certain diplomatic issues.[52] According to at least one "key planner" of the exercises, they were "plainly designed to counter Pakistan's pressure, via subversion and the training of dissident Sikhs, on the Punjab. A military exercise aimed at Pakistan's own weak point—the province of Sindh—would be a fitting riposte to Pakistan, and a threat (with echoes of 1971) that there might be more to come."[53]

Brasstacks and Beyond points to the fact that the DGMO hotline was not used for forty-five days as evidence of a "hidden agenda" underlying the exercises, the implication being that if everything were aboveboard, if Brasstacks were simply a set of training exercises, the Indian side should not have been inhibited from using the hotline to reassure the Pakistanis that their borders were secure.[54] There is also evidence that during the hotline talks which did take place in November and December 1986, the Indians were "less than candid"and provided "information that was clearly open to interpretation."[55] This is certainly consistent with an intention to send warning signals; after all, if the Indians meant to convey a message of strength and resolve, they would hardly be eager to reassure the Pakistani side of their benign intent. However, manipulating the hotline in this fashion is not necessarily evidence that Brasstacks was aimed at sparking a war. Convincing support for that thesis is still lacking.

---

51. Interview with former senior Indian decision-maker.
52. Hazarika, "India Puts Military on Full Alert."
53. Bajpai et al., *Brasstacks and Beyond*, p. 17.
54. Ibid., p. 28.
55. Bobb and Badhwar, "Back from the Edge," p. 42.

PAKISTANI PERCEPTIONS AND RESPONSE

It is easy to identify the source of Pakistan's alarm about Brasstacks. In a nutshell, some senior Pakistani leaders feared that Indian forces were assembling in Rajasthan under the guise of exercises, but that their real purpose was to launch a surprise offensive across the border into Sindh. The Indian goal, according to this scenario, would be to cut off Punjab and the capital from Sindh and the commercial port of Karachi, by snapping the vital north-south road and rail links. Sindh had been racked by separatist violence since 1983; Islamabad believed that the Indian intelligence agency—the Research and Analysis Wing (RAW)—was behind the fighting in Sindh, no less than New Delhi thought Pakistan's Inter-Services Intelligence (ISI) was fomenting insurgency in Indian Punjab. At least some Pakistani officials feared that India might be able to harness this anti-Pakistan sentiment and oversee the establishment of an independent nation carved from southern Pakistan.[56]

Several senior Pakistani offficials have spoken out about Islamabad's perception of Brasstacks and what the maneuvers might mean for Pakistani security. According to President Zia himself, Islamabad was first and foremost concerned with the sheer size and location of Brasstacks, whose two corps, including both of India's armored divisions, gave Pakistani leaders the "jitters." In late 1986, Pakistani officials at various levels tried to ascertain from their Indian counterparts exactly what the scope and nature of Brasstacks would be; they also urged Indian officials to scale down the exercises, or at least to define their parameters so as to reassure the Pakistan Army that a surprise attack was not looming. During these conversations, Indian officials repeatedly dissembled or, in the case of Rajiv Gandhi, made what Pakistani leaders viewed as promises to circumscribe Brasstacks that were not kept. In turn, the failure of Indian officials to be more forthcoming about the details of Brasstacks only increased Islamabad's suspicion that there might be more to the maneuvers than New Delhi claimed.[57]

According to Abdul Sattar, the former foreign secretary who led the Pakistani delegation to the Brasstacks de-escalation talks, Pakistani intelligence suggested that the Indians thought Zia was "on his last legs" politically, and that Sindh was ripe for a repeat of the 1971 war. Once again, Pakistani officials feared, an opportunity had

---

56. See Bajpai et al., *Brasstacks and Beyond*, pp. 19, 35, 37, 38–39.

57. Interview with Zia, "Neither India Nor Pakistan Wanted War"; Bobb and Badhwar, "Back from the Edge," p. 42; and interview with Abdul Sattar.

presented itself for India to humiliate Pakistan. Sattar remembers that this scenario was neither accepted nor rejected outright by the political leadership, which did wonder whether General Sundarji was being "adventurous," but chose to wait and see what Indian capabilities might develop.[58] Pakistani leaders' thinking was profoundly shaped by past relations with India, especially their experiences with war in 1965 and 1971. As President Zia said: "We feel that India has not . . . yet been reconciled to the existence of Pakistan. . . . There is some lurking suspicion in the minds of some Indian leaders about the existence of Pakistan. Is it going to last? . . . Is it going to collapse?"[59] For Pakistani policymakers, the Bangladesh war was sufficient evidence that India could indeed take advantage of ethnic discord in Pakistan, go on the offensive, and "liberate" a vast chunk of territory. Sattar also recounts that after the ambitious Indian riposte across the Punjab border in 1965, the Pakistani foreign office was roundly criticized for underestimating that very possibility; the career diplomatic service did not want to be embarrassed again. At the time, Sattar himself believed that the chance of war was not high but that Islamabad could not rule it out.[60]

PAKISTAN'S NORTHWARD FEINT EXPLAINED. In early January, Islamabad surprised New Delhi by moving its southern armored reserve from the Bahawalpur area northeast to the Punjab border, across from the Indian city of Fazilka. According to Sattar, Pakistan moved these divisions because it could not hope to match the Indian buildup in Rajasthan, and so feinted in another direction to ease the pressure created by the assembled Brasstacks units.[61] The logic behind this move was that if India wanted to invade Pakistan from its Brasstacks exercise area, no amount of Pakistani reinforcements would be able to repulse the offensive. Given this assesment, it would be better from Islamabad's standpoint to threaten India at its own weak point in Punjab, where an insurgency was already raging. If an Indian attack did develop in the south, Pakistan Army forces would at least be in place to strike across the Punjab border, thus ensuring themselves a draw in the fighting and enhanced leverage in the postwar bargaining. Pakistan could then swap its gains in Punjab for Indian gains in Sindh.

---

58. Interview with Sattar.

59. Interview with Zia, "Neither India Nor Pakistan Wanted War."

60. Interview with Sattar.

61. Ibid.

THE INDIAN RESPONSE. After the Army Reserve South's feint, New Delhi worried, in turn, that the Pakistan Army was now in a position to carry out a daring pincer movement that could decapitate part of Indian Punjab, and perhaps even turn it over to a newly declared independent state of Khalistan. Despite the fact that the Indian Army had taken measures to ensure that the Punjab frontier would be adequately defended during the Brasstacks exercises in Rajasthan, the Indian government ordered a massive airlift of soldiers to Punjab, where they took up defensive positions along the border. According to Sundarji, New Delhi had to respond defensively or risk humiliation; if nothing were done and Pakistan did invade Indian Punjab, the outcry in India would be fierce. He recalls telling Prime Minister Gandhi: if the Pakistan Army occupies Amritsar, "we'll never live it down." Sundarji says that the Indian Army had no intention of attacking Pakistan in January 1987, but "there was every intention of going for a counteroffensive should the Pakistanis attack us."[62]

POLITICAL-MILITARY DYNAMICS. This is the composite dynamic that drove the Brasstacks crisis: India and Pakistan had already fought three wars. Each government was extremely sensitive to the other's meddling in its internal ethnic conflicts, which posed fundamental challenges to its delicate national fabric. Zia's offer of a mutual non-intervention pact with India in the immediate aftermath of the crisis illustrates his recognition that cross-border meddling in domestic conflicts was the primary cause of Indo-Pakistani hostility. As the chess game unfolded, the two sides became enmeshed in a competitive dynamic dominated by the logic of the security dilemma: what each side viewed as its own precautionary, defensive moves were interpreted by the other side as threatening, offensive preparations. Because each country had compelling historical evidence for the other's malign intentions, it had no choice but to make decisions that erred on the side of caution. As Sattar acknowledges, these scenarios caused "totally distorted" perceptions, but the two leaderships were intensely worried about being surprised and humiliated by their counterparts across the border.[63]

THE *FAUX* NUCLEAR DIMENSION OF THE BRASSTACKS CRISIS

The main nuclear dimension of Brasstacks—such as it was—revolves around the controversial conversation between Pakistani scientist

---

62. Interview with Sundarji.
63. Interview with Sattar.

A.Q. Khan and Indian journalist Kuldip Nayar on January 28, 1987. Absent this discussion and the resulting imbroglio over Khan's alleged remarks, there would be little discernible relationship between the crisis and the South Asian nuclear arms competition. The conventional interpretation of Khan's reported remarks is that they were intended to "convey a not very subtle message to the Indians: any attempt to dismember Pakistan would be countered with the bomb."[64] While this likely was Khan's intention, a much more significant question arises: were his comments part of a wider, purposeful attempt by Islamabad to send a nuclear deterrent threat to New Delhi?

The A.Q. Khan "interview" does not seem to have been part of an officially sanctioned effort by the government of Pakistan to deter India from aggression with the threat of nuclear retaliation; rather, it fits the nuclear signalling pattern described in Chapter 3. Khan's bluster may have been tacitly accepted by the government, which may have found the ambiguity created by his remarks useful in keeping New Delhi off balance. But if Islamabad had intended to send a serious nuclear deterrent threat to New Delhi at the height of the Brasstacks crisis, it would hardly have assigned the task to the "boy who cried wolf"; Zia likely would have chosen someone from his own inner circle for the job, in order to signal a clear distinction between Khan's characteristic braggadocio and the government's utter sincerity in this particular case. Moreover, with the U.S. aid package up for congressional consideration in the months ahead, Islamabad had every reason to keep a lid on damaging disclosures about its nuclear ambitions. Washington had committed $4.02 billion worth of assistance to Islamabad, resources that Pakistan desperately needed. Pakistan's security challenges were daunting to say the least: it was surrounded by its much larger adversary, India; an Afghanistan occupied by the Soviet Red Army; and an unpredictable, post-revolutionary Iran. U.S. aid was facing stiff opposition on Capitol Hill, where Pakistani officials were actively lobbying for an extension of the Symington Amendment waiver. Islamabad's retaliation against the journalist Mushahid Hussain is suggestive of its sensitivity on this score.

As would be expected, Indian and Pakistani officials differ in their retrospective assessments of whether the threat was of official origin. A retired senior Pakistani diplomat denies that Khan's claims were

---

64. Seymour M. Hersh, "On the Nuclear Edge," *New Yorker*, March 29, 1993, p. 59.

part of a purposeful government effort at deterrence, adding that the scientist is a loose cannon, and "no one can control him." This source also points out that Kuldip Nayar sought out A.Q. Khan, and not vice versa, which would have been an odd way for the government to send signals to an adversary under crisis conditions.[65] In General Sundarji's view, the Kuldip Nayar interview was a "clumsy effort at signalling": the Pakistanis expected that the reporter would rush back to New Delhi and pass the word, but instead he waited for an attractive publishing opportunity.[66] These conflicting perspectives are unsurprising: the Pakistani viewpoint maintains plausible deniability, and thus Pakistani nuclear opacity, while the Indian interpretation is consistent with New Delhi's standard assumption that all pronouncements from across the border are part of a government conspiracy. In any event, the A.Q. Khan message had no impact on the resolution of the Brasstacks crisis, because it was transmitted after the crisis was over.

EXISTENTIAL DETERRENCE? More broadly, little evidence has yet come to light suggesting that nuclear weapon capabilities played any existential deterrent role in Indian and Pakistani crisis behavior in 1987. General Sundarji remembers that during Brasstacks, Islamabad was "exceedingly careful not to do anything which would make us attack." Even in Kashmir, where border skirmishes were common, the guns fell silent. Indian intelligence picked up Pakistani orders to their commanders on the ground not to take any action that could be construed by Indian military planners as an attack. Sundarji interprets this caution as an indication that the Pakistani leadership did not want to get into a war with India before they had weaponized their nuclear program.[67] Another view is that planners in Islamabad were particularly sensitive to the prospect of any conflict escalating to the nuclear level, and so took measures to make sure that no fighting broke out. The evidence unearthed to date does not warrant such a conclusion.

Senior officials on both sides concur that Brasstacks was essentially a prenuclear weaponization crisis, i.e., that Indian perceptions had not matured to the point where India viewed Pakistan as a "real" nuclear weapon state. Sattar claims that Islamabad's nuclear weapon capabilities had not yet "flowered" in early 1987; they were "nascent," he says, "not yet actual."[68] Sundarji agrees with this assessment: "We knew they were near to it, but our best information at that point of time was

---

65. Interview with former senior Pakistani diplomat.

66. Interview with Sundarji.

67. Ibid.

68. Interview with Sattar.

that they had not weaponized." He believes that Indian aggression would not have caused a Pakistani nuclear response, but that Islamabad might have tried to bluff such a response by making "veiled" threats. Sundarji further maintains that "we perhaps would have called their bluff at that point in time."[69] A senior Indian decision-maker confirms that the threat of Pakistan using nuclear weapons in a conflict was never a subject of discussion in Indian leadership circles.[70]

WHY WAS THE CRISIS RESOLVED PEACEFULLY?

If existential nuclear deterrence was not the key to conflict resolution, what explains South Asia's "non-war" of 1987? The main reason why the Brasstacks crisis did not escalate to actual military hostilities was the fact that no underlying political dynamic pushed the two sides toward war. To be sure, the crisis developed in a context of each side's intense sensitivity to the other's cross-border meddling in strife-torn areas. As discussed above, instability in Sindh and Punjab was close-ly linked to the two governments' main security concerns. However, these were essentially *defensive* calculations. Neither country's ethnic turmoil could be resolved by *offensive* action against the other; indeed, a Pakistani invasion of Indian Punjab or an Indian thrust into Sindh would have multiplied, rather than diminished, the attacking side's security challenges.

CONVENTIONAL DETERRENCE? Alternative explanations, grounded in international relations theory, fail to explain why India and Pakistan did not fight a war in 1987. One possibility is that Islamabad and New Delhi were deterred from aggression by each other's conventional military capabilities. In the most sophisticated theory of conventional deterrence, John Mearsheimer distinguishes between the attrition strategy, in which "the attacker is primarily concerned with overwhelming a stubborn defense in a series of bloody set-piece battles," and the blitzkrieg strategy, which utilizes armor to drive deep into enemy territory without bogging down in major engagements. According to Mearsheimer's theory, "if a potential attacker believes that he can launch a successful blitzkrieg, deterrence is very likely to fail." On the other hand, "if a potential attacker believes that he can secure a decisive victory only by means of an attrition strategy, deterrence is very likely to obtain."[71]

---

69. Interview with Sundarji.

70. Interview with former senior Indian decision-maker.

71. John J. Mearsheimer, *Conventional Deterrence* (Ithaca, N.Y.: Cornell University Press, 1983), pp. 34–36, 53, 63–64.

In 1987, Pakistan clearly had no capability of launching a successful blitzkrieg against India. Pakistan's ambassador to India acknowledged as much at the height of the crisis, when he said: "There can be no question of Pakistan wanting a military conflict. We are fully aware of the military equation between the two sides."[72] Conditions were much more favorable for an Indian invasion of Pakistan. A comprehensive analysis of the subcontinental military balance written in the months leading up to the crisis suggests that India could have launched a successful blitzkrieg against Pakistan if the political leadership had deemed such a course desirable. According to this analysis, dated May 1986, "Islamabad's receipt of U.S. military equipment has done little to alter marked asymmetries in Indo-Pakistani strength levels. India continues to enjoy an overwhelming numerical and qualitative advantage in most weapon categories." India's offensive strike capability, "in concert with close air support and interdiction operations by the Indian Air Force, would permit rapid advances into Pakistan." Pakistan's security problems were "compounded by a lack of strategic depth and poor defensive terrain adjacent to Pakistan's economic and cultural heartland."[73] Employing Mearsheimer's theory, since India's chances of carrying out a successful blitzkrieg were so favorable, conventional deterrence cannot explain New Delhi's decision not to pursue a war against Pakistan in 1987.

LEARNING FROM THE PAST? Another possible explanation for South Asia's non-war of 1987 is that the two sides had learned from their past experience that war between them does not pay.[74] There is clear evidence that South Asia's revisionist power, Pakistan, had grown more realistic in the 1980s about the costs and benefits of war with India. President Zia was a tank commander during the 1965 war, and thus a firsthand witness to the futility of forcibly trying to wrest Kashmir from India.[75] The Pakistan Army's resolve not to take any

---

72. Mahoney, "Indian Troops Take Up Position on Pakistan Border."

73. Jerrold F. Elkin and W. Andrew Ritezel, "The Indo-Pakistani Military Balance," *Asian Survey*, Vol. 26, No. 5 (May 1986), pp. 518–519, 522, 529.

74. The classic treatment of learning and statesmanship is the chapter entitled "How Decision-Makers Learn from History," in Robert Jervis, *Perception and Misperception in International Politics* (Princeton, N.J.: Princeton University Press, 1976), pp. 217–287. See also Philip E. Tetlock, "Learning in U.S. and Soviet Foreign Policy: In Search of An Elusive Concept," in George W. Breslauer and Philip E. Tetlock, eds., *Learning in U.S. and Soviet Foreign Policy* (Boulder, Colo.: Westview, 1991), pp. 20–61.

75. For a discussion of the numerous peace and arms control initiatives forwarded by Islamabad to New Delhi during the Zia period, see Robert G. Wirsing, *Pakistan's Security Under Zia, 1977–1988* (New York: St. Martin's, 1991), pp. 98–101.

action that would provoke Indian aggression in 1987 illustrated its belief that a fourth Indo-Pakistani war would have been disastrous for Pakistan. But this explanation does not fit the Indian experience. If anything, Indian leaders may have learned from history that in some circumstances, war with Pakistan *does* pay. In 1965, India successfully neutralized Pakistan's invasion with a bold offensive of its own. In 1971, New Delhi launched a blitzkrieg that turned East Pakistan into Bangladesh, forever erasing India's vulnerability to a two-front invasion, and rendering Pakistan an international cripple for the next decade. Why should Indian leaders have learned from these experiences that war does *not* pay? Instead, their composite lesson should logically have been that there are certain intolerable circumstances under which the forceful application of offensive military doctrines can ease the occasional security challenge by a smaller but determined neighbor. In sum, then, we are left with the simplest, most mundane explanation for South Asia's non-war of 1986–87: no political dispute was deemed so intractable that either side viewed war as the best possible solution.

Implications for Theory

I have argued in this chapter that the impact of nuclear weapons on the 1986–87 Brasstacks crisis was neutral: Indian and Pakistani nuclear capabilities neither exacerbated nor dampened tendencies toward war in January 1987. On the face of it, this interpretation provides little support for the logic of nonproliferation or for the logic of nuclear deterrence; that having been said, though, its implications are still important. In an intellectual context where all but a few analysts share the view that crises that erupt during the transition to nuclear weapons should be extremely destabilizing, a case refuting that consensus should, at a minimum, cause those in the majority to reconsider their views. This is especially so in light of the fact that the 1986–87 Indo-Pakistani crisis was practically a textbook example of the type of situation that most alarms proliferation analysts. It might be objected that, since Brasstacks unfolded prior to the weaponization of Indian and Pakistani nuclear capabilities, its outcome is irrelevant to the debate about the consequences of proliferation. However, we only know that Brasstacks was a pre-weaponization crisis in retrospect; because of their respective governments' nuclear opacity, Indian and Pakistani policymakers in 1986–87 had no way of knowing for sure what their adversaries' true nuclear capabilities were. Not only do proliferation pessimists and some deterrence optimists consider the process of military nuclearization to be a dangerous transition, but the extant literature on opaque proliferation strongly suggests that opacity should also undermine crisis stability.[76] Taken as a whole, then, the conventional wisdom on the consequences of nuclear proliferation would have us believe that crises that erupt between covertly nuclearizing Third World states, especially those with a long history of warfare, should lead to intense pressures for each side to preemptively destroy the other's nuclear weapon capabilities, by either nuclear or conventional attacks. Despite the predominance of this thinking in proliferation scholarship, no Indian or Pakistani decision-maker during the Brasstacks crisis has intimated that his government even considered such a course of action. In sum, although it does not lend empirical support to the logic of nuclear deterrence,"[77] the Brasstacks case casts doubt on the logic of nonproliferation, as well as the standard analytical perspective on opacity and nuclear weapon stability.

The Brasstacks crisis had one other nuclear dimension that remains to be explored. In this context, it was a cause rather than a consequence of Indian and Pakistani decision-making. South Asia's near war of 1986–87 apparently accelerated both governments'—but especially Islamabad's—nuclear weaponization efforts. At the same time, India's and Pakistan's evolving nuclear capabilities were made increasingly evident to one another through the process of inadvertent transparency-building described in Chapter 2. In the three-year period after Brasstacks, the United States and the rest of the nonproliferation community grew increasingly concerned about New Delhi's and Islamabad's nuclear progress. In an effort to inhibit their nuclear programs, Washington, in particular, shed a great deal of light on the strides being made by Indian and Pakistani nuclear scientists. In doing so, the U.S. government inadvertently lent credibility to New Delhi's and Islamabad's nuclear deterrent postures—an effect quite the opposite of that intended. The result was that during the next Indo-Pakistani crisis, which is the subject of Chapter 6, neither side had any doubt that the other was an actual, not aspiring, nuclear weapon state. First, however, Chapter 5 will examine this process of inadvertent transparency-building between 1987 and 1990.

---

76. See the discussion of opacity and nuclear weapon stability in Chapter 2.

77. I had earlier speculated that New Delhi's and Islamabad's nuclear capabilities may have contributed to conflict resolution during the Brasstacks crisis. See Devin T. Hagerty, "The Power of Suggestion: Opaque Proliferation, Existential Deterrence, and the South Asian Nuclear Arms Competition," *Security Studies*, Vol. 2, Nos. 3/4 (Spring/Summer 1993), p. 275.

Chapter 5

The Legacy of Brasstacks: South Asian Proliferation Dynamics, 1987–90

The most important consequence of the 1986–87 Brasstacks crisis was that it quickened the pace of nuclear proliferation in South Asia. Brasstacks particularly increased Islamabad's determination to achieve a nuclear deterrent *vis-à-vis* its larger neighbor; and New Delhi, in response, moved closer to weaponizing its own nuclear capability. Since India had conducted a nuclear explosive test in 1974, Pakistani decision-makers never doubted that New Delhi could deploy nuclear weapons if it made the essentially political decision to do so. But Pakistan had never tested a nuclear explosive device; therefore, Islamabad had to work much harder to make its maturing capabilities credible in the eyes of Indian officials. Their efforts were especially pronounced during the period between the resolution of the Brasstacks crisis in January 1987 and the next Indo-Pakistani crisis, which erupted in January 1990.

During this interregnum, India increasingly perceived Pakistan to be a full-fledged nuclear weapon state, largely for two reasons. First, Islamabad engaged in an intensified nuclear signalling campaign in the aftermath of the Brasstacks crisis. Second, Washington's heightened scrutiny of Pakistan's nuclear program shed light on, and thus lent credibility to, the developing Pakistani weaponization capability. These two processes are the subject of this chapter. In the next two sections, I document the evolution of Islamabad's nuclear signalling and Washington's inadvertent transparency-building[1] from 1987 to 1990. Then I describe the beginnings of a South Asian nuclear deterrence discourse during the same period. In the chapter's final section, I briefly set the stage for an analysis of the 1990 Kashmir crisis

---

1. See the theoretical discussion of this phenomenon in Chapter 2.

by outlining India's and Pakistan's perceived nuclear weapon capabilities at the close of the 1980s.

The Impact of Brasstacks on South Asian Nuclear Developments

Although Indian and Pakistani nuclear weapon capabilities apparently had little effect on the outcome of the crisis, Brasstacks strongly influenced the course of subsequent South Asian nuclear developments. In the months after January 1987, Islamabad sped up its efforts to acquire a rudimentary nuclear deterrent. At the same time, it increased the transparency of those efforts by continuing the pattern of nuclear signalling established by Pakistani scientist A.Q. Khan. First, senior Pakistani officials would make bold public statements touting their country's nuclear strides. Next, the United States would condemn Pakistan's flouting of the nonproliferation regime. Finally, Islamabad would halfheartedly retract the remarks or claim they had been misinterpreted. In each case, Pakistani leaders' manipulation of their nuclear opacity gave Islamabad's nuclear capabilities another layer of credibility in Indian eyes. In turn, New Delhi indicated more insistently that it would match any nuclear weaponization by Islamabad.

As Pakistan raised its nuclear profile in 1987, the United States was an unwitting accomplice. Throughout the year, various congressional committees considered the follow-on, $4.02 billion U.S. aid package for Islamabad. Continued U.S. assistance depended on clearing the various statutory hurdles devised by the Congress to prevent Islamabad from developing nuclear weapons. As the Pakistan aid proposal worked its way through the legislative process in 1987, Islamabad's nuclear activities became the focus of intense U.S. scrutiny and media attention. Ironically, this increased visibility served to enhance the credibility of Islamabad's nuclear deterrent, rather than to dampen its nuclear ambitions. The result of Pakistani nuclear signalling and the transparency lent by public discussion of Islamabad's nuclear capabilities was that, by the time of the next Indo-Pakistani crisis in 1990, Pakistan had emerged in the eyes of Indian leaders as a real nuclear power, no less than if it had detonated a nuclear explosive device.

U.S. TRANSPARENCY-BUILDING IN THE WAKE OF BRASSTACKS

On February 16, 1987 (after the Brasstacks crisis had been defused, but before the publication of the A.Q. Khan story), the U.S. ambassador to Pakistan, Deane Hinton, made an important speech at Islamabad's Institute of Strategic Studies. Hinton noted "developments in Pakistan's nuclear program which we see as inconsistent with a purely peaceful program. Indications that Pakistan may be seeking a weapons capability generate tension and uncertainty." Hinton questioned whether India and Pakistan could ever derive deterrent security from their nuclear capabilities, since neither "can, in the foreseeable future, hope to afford the secure delivery systems (for example, missiles in hardened silos or ballistic missile submarines) needed to be confident of what is known in the jargon of nuclear deterrence as a 'secure second-strike capability'." Regarding the Pressler Amendment,[2] Hinton said it was "open to question" whether President Reagan could continue to certify Pakistan as nuclear weapon-free "were we to conclude that Pakistan had in hand, but not assembled, all the needed components for a nuclear explosive device." Hinton ended his speech by saying: "The recent 'war scare' was bad enough. How would the leaders and the general public have felt had there been a 'red alert' proclaimed while Pakistan or India or both were believed to have or known to have nuclear weapons in their arsenals?"[3]

Hinton's circumspect language implied two U.S. judgments about Pakistan's nuclear prowess: first, that it had not possessed deliverable nuclear weapons during the Brasstacks crisis (thus confirming the Indian assessment); and second, that Islamabad had acquired, or nearly acquired, all of the necessary components to build nuclear weapons, but had not yet made the political decision to assemble them into a bomb. Hinton's warning that Pakistan might not meet the Pressler standard even in the absence of final bomb assembly was a message to both Islamabad and the U.S. Congress. To Islamabad, it said: Stop where you are or face a possible aid cut-off. To Capitol Hill, it said: Look how hard we in the administration are trying to get the Pakistanis to refrain from developing nuclear weapons. Indian officials responded to Hinton's speech by stating that they believed "reports that Pakistan had put together the components of a nuclear bomb but stopped short of assembling one."[4]

---

2. As discussed in Chapter 3, the Pressler Amendment requires the president to certify annually that Pakistan does not "possess a nuclear explosive device," as a condition for the release of U.S. assistance to Pakistan.

3. "Text of Ambassador Hinton's Speech on Nuclear Non-Proliferation at the Institute of Strategic Studies in Islamabad," February 15, 1987, Unclassified Cable No. 03500 from the U.S. Embassy in Islamabad to the United States Information Agency in Washington, D.C.

4. Steven R. Weisman, "Pakistan's Nuclear Aims Worrying U.S.," New York Times, February 20, 1987.

On February 24, the Carnegie Endowment for International Peace in Washington, D.C. released a comprehensive study of the South Asian nuclear arms competition, which suggested that Pakistan had reached the "nuclear-weapons threshold." The report said that Pakistan either possessed all of the components necessary for "one or several atom bombs," or was "just short" of this goal because it had not yet produced enough weapons-grade uranium.[5] The Carnegie report generated wide international press coverage and the Indian response was not long in coming. On February 27, when India's Parliament discussed the Pakistani nuclear threat, several legislators "urged the government to review its nuclear policy in light of what they called Pakistan's capacity to make and deliver a nuclear device." Indian Foreign Minister N.D. Tiwari assured them that India was keeping a close eye on Pakistan's nuclear program, and would take appropriate action if Islamabad actually built a nuclear weapon.[6]

RESPONSES TO THE A.Q. KHAN AFFAIR

When the A.Q. Khan story broke on March 1, it set off a furor in India. A Ministry of External Affairs spokesman called Khan's remarks "another confirmation of what has already been known *because of news reports in the United States.*"[7] Back in Washington, a senior State Department official told Congress that the administration viewed A.Q. Khan's statements as "inaccurate."[8] Other U.S. policymakers said privately, though, that they did not doubt the accuracy of the Kuldip Nayar piece, but had "decided to ignore it publicly on the basis of Khan's denial."[9] A State Department official summed up the prevailing U.S. view of Pakistan's nuclear program: "We think they have the capability of producing one [nuclear bomb]

5. David B. Ottoway, "U.S. Warns Pakistan on Testing Nuclear Device," *Washington Post*, February 25, 1987.

6. Andrew Tamowski, "India 'Seriously Concerned' By Pakistan Atom Bomb Report," *Reuters*, March 1, 1987.

7. Steven R. Weisman, "Report of Pakistani A-Bomb Causes a Stir in the Region," *New York Times*, March 2, 1987 (emphasis added). See also "It's Confirmation of Pak's Nuclear Capability," *The Hindu* (Madras), March 3, 1987.

8. House Committee on Foreign Affairs, Subcommittee on Asian and Pacific Affairs, *Foreign Assistance Legislation for Fiscal Years 1988–89* (Part 5), 100th Cong., 1st sess., March 5, 1987, p. 475.

9. Nayan Chanda, "Yes, We Have No Bomb," *Far Eastern Economic Review*, March 12, 1987, p. 34.

now, but we're convinced they don't have one yet."[10] According to *India Today*, policymakers in New Delhi viewed the A.Q. Khan interview as "a carefully calculated and specifically directed message with the covert blessings of Pakistan's military establishment." Said one official: "It is impossible that a man as heavily guarded and as important to Islamabad as Dr. Khan could meet an Indian journalist for over an hour to discuss their nuclear programme without some sort of green signal from the military leadership."[11] An influential nuclear trade publication described the atmosphere in New Delhi: "The report triggered renewed pressures on the government here to reassess the country's defense options including nuclear weapons. The pressures are coming primarily from members of Parliament, newspaper editors and columnists, and some civilian planners in the defense and foreign ministries." In response, Prime Minister Gandhi asked these ministries to "make a fresh assessment of Pakistan's nuclear status in the light of Khan's quoted statements."[12] As if to signal India's own nuclear weapon capabilities to Pakistan, an official at the Bhabha Atomic Research Center said that India had enough plutonium to build "as many bombs as the country needs. What is required is the political will to do so."[13] Gandi confirmed that India had not yet built nuclear weapons, but said that "if we decided to become a nuclear power, it would take a few weeks or a few months."[14] A U.S. official provided independent corroboration of India's nuclear posture, telling a congressional panel that "while India is deeply concerned about Pakistan's nuclear program, it has so far not felt compelled to respond by acquiring nuclear weapons itself."[15] India's patience was limited, though. Defense Minister K.C. Pant said in April that "the emerging nuclear threat to us from Pakistan is forcing us to review our options."[16]

---

10. David B. Ottoway, "Pakistani A-Bomb Seen Likely," *Washington Post*, March 8, 1987.

11. "Pakistan's Nuclear Bombshell," *India Today*, March 31, 1987.

12. Vyvyan Tenorio and Shahid-ur Rehman, "Pakistan Denies It Has Bomb, But Tensions Rise in India," *Nucleonics Week*, March 5, 1987, p. 8.

13. Leonard S. Spector, *The Undeclared Bomb* (Cambridge, Mass.: Ballinger, 1988), p. 90.

14. Vyvyan Tenorio, "India Faces Rising Pressure for Arms Race with Pakistan," *Christian Science Monitor*, March 9, 1987.

15. House Committee, *Foreign Assistance Legislation, 1988–89*, p. 423.

16. Spector, *Undeclared Bomb*, p. 95.

TRANSPARENCY-BUILDING DURING THE PAKISTAN AID DELIBERATIONS
Congressional hearings on the Pakistan aid package began the week after the A.Q. Khan story emerged. On March 5, Robert Peck, a deputy assistant secretary of state for Near Eastern and South Asian affairs, told a House subcommittee that the president could not obtain "reliable assurances" from Islamabad that Pakistan was not seeking to manufacture nuclear weapons, as required by the Symington Amendment.[17] The same day, Senator John Glenn demanded in a letter to the president that U.S. aid to Pakistan be terminated "until you have received reliable assurances from the Pakistanis that they have ceased producing nuclear explosive materials." According to Glenn, the available evidence "points to the conclusion that all the components and the means for assembling a working nuclear explosive device are in Pakistan's possession."[18] Despite this, the administration remained staunchly opposed to a cessation of aid. As Peck told Congress: "We have been down the cutoff road before and know that any action which would cut off, curtail, or cast doubt on the continuation of our assistance would be counter-productive, because it would grievously undercut our influence over Pakistan's nuclear decision-making."[19]

An opinion issued by the State Department's legal adviser implied that Glenn's assertion was correct, but it sent contradictory signals about the definition of "possession" under the Pressler Amendment. The opinion first noted that "the statutory standard is whether Pakistan possesses a nuclear explosive device, not whether Pakistan is attempting to develop or has developed various relevant capacities. . . . A distinction must therefore be drawn between the ability to achieve possession of a nuclear explosive device, and actual possession of such a device." This implied that as long as Pakistan stopped short of assembling a device, it would not risk losing U.S. aid.

---

17. House Committee, *Foreign Assistance Legislation, 1988–89*, pp. 471–473. In another exchange, Rep. Stephen Solarz asked Robert Peck: "If we were to put such a provision into law in which as a condition for our aid the President would have to report that he was satisfied that they were not producing nuclear weapons material or otherwise attempting to acquire nuclear weapons, do you think that the President would be able to provide such assurances to the Congress so that the aid could go forward?" Peck responded: "I doubt that the President could. Certainly not under present circumstances."

18. John H. Cushman, Jr., "Glenn Cites Fear of a Pakistani A-Bomb," *New York Times*, March 6, 1987.

19. House Committee, *Foreign Assistance Legislation, 1988–89*, p. 423.

However, the opinion further maintained that "a state may possess a nuclear explosive device, and yet maintain it in an unassembled form for safety reasons or to maintain effective command and control over its use or for other purposes. The fact that a state does not have an assembled device would not, therefore, necessarily mean that it does not possess a device under the statutory standard.[20] In other words, Pakistan *did* run the risk of losing U.S. aid, even if it did not assemble an actual nuclear device.

THE INDO-PAKISTANI NUCLEAR DISCOURSE

Despite this ambiguity, one thing was perfectly clear in New Delhi: Pakistan had all the components it needed to build a nuclear weapon. Indian policymakers carefully monitored the Pakistan aid package's progress through the U.S. legislative process and drew their own conclusions. As one official said in mid-March: "Every indication we have is that Pakistan is only two screwdriver turns away from possessing the bomb."[21] For their part, Pakistani leaders encouraged this perception. In a *Time* magazine interview released on March 24, President Zia admitted that "Pakistan has the capability of building the Bomb. You can write today that Pakistan can build a bomb whenever it wishes. Once you have acquired the technology, which Pakistan has, you can do whatever you like." Zia added, however, that Islamabad had no intention of building nuclear weapons: "What's the difficulty about building a bomb? We have never said we are incapable of doing this. We have said we have neither the intention nor the desire."[22]

Rajiv Gandhi's inevitable response ignored Zia's disclaimer. He said: "We have known for years now that they were close to making a weapon and had the intention to make a weapon."[23] On India's nuclear ambitions, Gandhi said: "We intend meeting President Zia's threat. We will give an adequate response." The Indian prime minister further pledged to keep New Delhi's options "open at the moment. We would still like an option where we would not go nuclear. We do not want to go nuclear."[24] In a May interview, Gandhi

---

20. Ibid., pp. 487–488.

21. "Zia Calls for Nuclear Dialogue with India," *Reuters*, March 21, 1987.

22. Ross H. Munro, "Knocking at the Nuclear Door," *Time*, March 30, 1987, p. 42.

23. Jack Payton, "Gandhi: U.S. Let Pakistan Build Nuclear Bomb," *St. Petersburg Times*, March 27, 1987.

24. Spector, *Undeclared Bomb*, p. 95.

cited "clear evidence that Pakistan is going ahead full steam with its nuclear weapons program. *Statements have been made by their nuclear scientists, and the statements of their leaders have done nothing to dispel fears.*"[25] Pakistan's nuclear signals were being received.

MORE U.S. TRANSPARENCY-BUILDING

In July 1987, a Canadian citizen of Pakistani descent, Arshad Pervez, was arrested in Philadelphia for attempting to export to Pakistan twenty-five tons of special steel alloy used to enrich uranium.[26] This new evidence of Islamabad's determination to develop nuclear weapons nearly derailed the Pakistan aid package, and in the process further increased the transparency of Islamabad's nuclear activities. As U.S. proliferation expert Leonard Spector told *India Today:* "The whole equation in the subcontinent has changed and an element of militarisation has begun to accompany the technical capabilities."[27] Approval of future U.S. aid to Pakistan required an extension of the Symington Amendment[28] waiver, which was due to expire on September 30. Before the Pervez arrest, the relevant congressional committees had recommended only a two-year waiver, instead of the six-year extension requested by the Reagan administration. Islamabad's attempted nuclear smuggling put this plan on hold, and Congress allowed the Symington waiver to expire at the end of September.[29] U.S. aid to Islamabad was suspended as of October 1, sending a strong signal to the world—especially New Delhi—that Pakistan was a de facto nuclear weapon state.

Despite unambiguous evidence of Islamabad's resolve to develop nuclear weapon capabilities, the Reagan administration argued strenuously that aid to Pakistan should be restored. Administration

---

25. Pranay Gupte, "'We Don't Have the Bomb': An Interview with Rajiv Gandhi," *Forbes*, May 18, 1987, p. 156 (emphasis added).

26. Pat Towell, "Nuclear-Materials Incident Jeopardizes Aid to Pakistan," *Congressional Quarterly Weekly Report*, July 25, 1987, p. 1668.

27. Shekhar Gupta, "The Nuclear Heist," *India Today*, July 31, 1987, p. 101.

28. As discussed in Chapter 3, the Symington Amendment prohibits U.S. assistance to countries that acquire unsafeguarded uranium enrichment technology. Congress can vote to allow the president to waive the law if he determines that termination of U.S. aid would seriously harm vital U.S. interests and if he has received "reliable assurances" from the recipient country that it will not acquire or develop nuclear weapons.

29. Nayan Chanda, "Congress Puts Aid on Ice," *Far Eastern Economic Review*, October 29, 1987, p. 24.

officials claimed that cutting aid would send the wrong signal to the Soviets, who appeared increasingly anxious to find a way out of their Afghanistan quagmire. As one policymaker told a congressional committee: "Provision of U.S. assistance bolsters Pakistan's resistance to Soviet intimidation" and "reaffirms the credibility of our security commitment to Pakistan."[30] U.S. officials also recognized that strict conformity with their own laws might have unintended effects on South Asian nuclear developments. As one said, in a comment that captures the essence of U.S. transparency-building:

We should also keep in mind the likely Indian reaction. If the U.S. cuts off assistance to Pakistan because of an inability to meet a particular nuclear certification, many Indians will see this both as confirmation that Pakistan has crossed the nuclear threshold, and as removing any external restraint on Pakistan's nuclear program. Indeed, without the restraining force of U.S. assistance, Pakistan is more likely to move ahead in additional areas of proliferation concern. The pressure on India's leaders to move forward quickly with a dedicated nuclear weapons program is likely to be nearly irresistible. Legislation intended to bolster our non-proliferation efforts in South Asia could thus have the paradoxical effect of accelerating a nuclear arms race instead.[31]

Eventually, arguments like these prevailed. In December 1987, Congress extended the president's authority to waive the Symington Amendment for thirty months and authorized the first installment of new assistance. Aid to Pakistan began flowing again. The president had earlier conveyed to Congress his annual determination that "Pakistan does not possess a nuclear explosive device," as required by the Pressler Amendment. In doing so, Reagan said his judgment had "taken into account the fact that the statutory standard as legislated by Congress is whether Pakistan possesses a nuclear explosive device, not whether Pakistan is attempting to develop or has developed various relevant capacities."[32] According to a U.S. diplomat,

30. House Committee on Foreign Affairs, Subcommittees on Asian and Pacific Affairs and on International Economic Policy and Trade, *The Implications of the Arshad Pervez Case for U.S. Policy Toward Pakistan*, 100th Cong., 2nd sess., February 17, 1988, p. 21.

31. House Committee on Foreign Affairs, Subcommittees on Arms Control, International Security, and Science; Asian and Pacific Affairs; and International Economic Policy and Trade, *Pakistan and United States Nonproliferation Policy*, 100th Cong., 1st sess., October 22, 1987, pp. 15–16.

32. Richard P. Cronin, *Pakistan: U.S. Foreign Assistance Facts* (Washington, D.C.: Congressional Research Service, 1988), p. 8.

Islamabad had "acquired the technical capabilities needed to possess a nuclear explosive device," but had not "made the political decision to do so, and some essential steps remain to be taken, if the political decision were made."[33] The White House had chosen to embrace the more lenient interpretation of the Pressler Amendment earlier offered by the State Department lawyers.

A CRITICAL YEAR. All in all, 1987 was a critical year for the South Asian nuclear arms competition. In the wake of Brasstacks, senior Pakistani officials boldly asserted that Islamabad was capable of building nuclear weapons. Their statements continued a pattern that was too consistent to be inadvertent. Pakistan's nuclear signalling might have been interpreted in New Delhi as sheer bluster, had it not been accompanied by a steady stream of U.S. revelations about Islamabad's nuclear transgressions. The combination of Pakistani signalling and U.S.-generated transparency enhanced the credibility of Islamabad's nuclear weapon posture. Former senior CIA official Richard J. Kerr recalls that the U.S. government had an "intelligence basis" not to certify the Pakistanis as nuclear weapon–free "from 1987 on."[34] That the Indian government's estimates closely reflected those of the United States is not in doubt: Indian Foreign Secretary J.N. Dixit revealed in 1992 that New Delhi has also known since 1987 that Pakistan could assemble a nuclear weapon.[35]

The Maturation of South Asian Nuclear Capabilities, 1988–90

The years 1988 and 1989 brought several important developments in the South Asian nuclear arms competition. First, continuing revelations about the Indian and Pakistani nuclear weapon programs erased any lingering uncertainty about whether New Delhi and Islamabad could build nuclear weapons on short notice. Both sides continued to produce fissionable material, and both pushed ahead with qualitative improvements in their ability to assemble nuclear weapons. Second, New Delhi and Islamabad conducted preliminary testing of ballistic missiles that were at least theoretically capable of carrying nuclear warheads, although the actual deployment of these missiles remained a future, not an immediate, prospect. Each side's awareness of the other's missile development strides also contributed

---

33. House Committee, *Arshad Pervez Case*, pp. 21–22.

34. Seymour M. Hersh, "On the Nuclear Edge," *New Yorker*, March 29, 1993, p. 60.

35. George K. Tanham, *Indian Strategic Thought: An Interpretive Essay* (Santa Monica, Calif.: RAND Corporation, 1992), p. 81, n. 5.

to the perception that it was now dealing with a nuclear-armed neighbor. Finally, Pakistani leaders and some Western proliferation experts began to suggest that a rudimentary nuclear deterrent balance was evolving in South Asia. Islamabad encouraged this perception because it implied that Pakistan had achieved a security "equalizer" with India.

CONTINUED U.S. TRANSPARENCY-BUILDING

In the area of capabilities, 1988 and 1989 brought more of the same transparency-building process that was evident in the immediate aftermath of Brasstacks. In March 1988, journalist Hedrick Smith wrote a long article detailing the status of South Asia's nuclear programs. According to Smith, the prevailing U.S. government estimate was "that it would take Pakistan at most a few weeks or months to assemble a bomb," although some officials believed it to be more "a matter of hours or days." Smith wrote that the "different estimates largely depend on officials' uncertainty over whether the Pakistanis have yet taken one of the final steps—precision machining the uranium metal core." The article quoted U.S. Representative Stephen Solarz as saying that Islamabad has "the nuclear equivalent of a Saturday night special. It may not be technically elegant, but it's capable of doing the job." By the end of 1987, wrote Smith, "Pakistan had produced enough fissionable weapons-grade uranium for four to six atomic bombs, and India enough plutonium for about 40."[36]

In a summary assessment of the situation as of mid-1988, Leonard Spector wrote:

Between late 1986 and mid-1988 Pakistan almost certainly crossed the nuclear weapons threshold in the limited sense that it acquired the essentials for a small number of nuclear weapons, while India, which conducted its first and only nuclear test in 1974, declared that it was reconsidering the stance it has taken since that date against building nuclear arms.

For the moment, both remain in the early stages of nuclearization, with India's program by far the more extensive. Neither nation has deployed a nuclear force, and, indeed, neither may possess a completely fabricated nuclear device. It appears, however, that both have all of the essentials needed to manufacture atomic bombs and to deliver them by aircraft during any crisis lasting more than several weeks.[37]

36. Hedrick Smith, "A Bomb Ticks in Pakistan," *New York Times Magazine*, March 6, 1988, p. 77.

37. Spector, *Undeclared Bomb*, pp. 69–70.

In late 1988, U.S. officials reportedly confirmed that Pakistan had obtained a nuclear weapon design from China. They also said that New Delhi was stockpiling nuclear material and conducting weapon design research, "but as far as we know, the two parallel tracks have not been merged."[38]

In November 1988, President Reagan again certified that Pakistan did not "possess a nuclear explosive device." This time, though, the White House warned: "The Congress should be aware that as Pakistan's nuclear capabilities grow, and if evidence about its activities continues to accumulate, this process of annual certification will require the president to reach judgements about the status of Pakistani nuclear activities that may be difficult or impossible to make with any degree of certainty."[39] U.S. officials characterized the certification decision as a "very close call," which reflected political concerns rather than scientific judgments. At one level, Washington did not want to precipitate a cessation of U.S. aid to Pakistan with Soviet troops still occupying Afghanistan. At another, the State Department hoped to allow some breathing room for the newly elected Benazir Bhutto government and the incoming Bush administration to narrow U.S.-Pakistani differences.[40]

BENAZIR BHUTTO IN OFFICE

Anxious to improve relations with India and to please its supporters in Washington, the new Bhutto government agreed to impose some restraints on Islamabad's nuclear program. In December 1988, Bhutto and Indian prime minister Rajiv Gandhi finally signed the nuclear non-attack agreement that Gandhi and Zia had verbally concluded three years earlier. The pact committed India and Pakistan to "refrain from undertaking, encouraging or participating indirectly or directly in any action" to destroy or damage each other's nuclear power and research facilities, uranium enrichment plants, and other nuclear installations. Each country was required to notify the other annually of the exact location of its nuclear facilities.[41] Bhutto also made two

---

38. Nayan Chanda, "See No Evil," *Far Eastern Economic Review*, January 5, 1989, p. 12.

39. Leonard S. Spector with Jacqueline R. Smith, *Nuclear Ambitions: The Spread of Nuclear Weapons, 1989–1990* (Boulder, Colo.: Westview, 1990), p. 101.

40. President Zia was killed in a plane crash in August 1988. Benazir Bhutto was elected prime minister and took office in December 1988.

41. Warren H. Donnelly, *Pakistan and Nuclear Weapons* (Washington, D.C.: Congressional Research Service, 1990), p. 7.

secret promises to Washington: first, that Pakistan would stop enriching uranium to weapons grade; and, second, that it would not convert its existing stock of weapons-grade uranium from gas to metal, which could then be machined into bomb cores.[42] Thus, by 1989 Pakistan's nuclear weapon potential was essentially frozen, with all of the components in place, but as yet unassembled. Meanwhile, a *Time* magazine cover story on India's emergence as a great power said: "A top Indian official conceded that New Delhi deliberately fosters ambiguity about its nuclear capabilities, but offhand remarks suggest that India has atomic-weapons components on the shelf and a special team ready to assemble them. An official close to the Prime Minister claims that India can produce a nuclear bomb 'overnight'."[43]

BHUTTO'S WASHINGTON VISIT. With the withdrawal of Soviet forces from Afghanistan in February 1989, the U.S. government could afford to take a tougher line on Pakistan's nuclear program. During a June state visit to Washington, Benazir Bhutto was given a detailed briefing on Pakistan's nuclear progress by CIA Director William H. Webster. The briefing demonstrated both the extent of the program, which U.S. officials feared was being concealed from Bhutto, and Washington's knowledge of its intricate details.[44] Webster also "drew the line that defined the possession of a 'nuclear explosive device.' If Pakistan turned highly enriched uranium gas to metal, he warned, it would cross the line."[45] This would precipitate a cessation of U.S. aid under the Pressler Amendment. If an aid cutoff was the stick, Washington also offered Bhutto a carrot to strengthen her domestic position: sixty new F-16s for the Pakistan Air Force.[46] The administration argued that its "willingness to cooperate with the new government's efforts to

---

42. Hamish McDonald, "Destroyer of Worlds," *Far Eastern Economic Review*, April 30, 1992, p. 23. See also "Pakistan Missile Flap Ongoing," *Associated Press*, May 13, 1994.

43. Ross H. Munro, "Superpower Rising," *Time*, April 3, 1989, p. 16.

44. It is uncertain what Bhutto knew about the nuclear program during her first term in office. On taking power in December 1988, she was quoted as saying: "I do not think that Pakistan has a nuclear bomb. I hope it does not. Our party manifesto very clearly advocates a peaceful nuclear program." Donnelly, *Pakistan and Nuclear Weapons*, p. 5. Pakistan's former army chief, Mirza Aslam Beg, claims that Bhutto's ignorance did not last long: I had at least five meetings with her. Two months after Benazir Bhutto had taken over, we had a detailed examination of the program." See "Pakistan Missile Flap Ongoing."

45. William E. Burrows and Robert Windrem, *Critical Mass: The Dangerous Race for Superweapons in a Fragmenting World* (New York: Simon and Schuster, 1994), p. 81.

46. Pat Towell, "Bhutto, on Visit, Moves to Ease U.S. Worries Over Policies," *Congressional Quarterly Weekly Report*, June 10, 1989, p. 1415.

modernize its fighter force will contribute to Pakistan's sense of security and assure the Pakistani public that the country's defense needs can be met effectively by a civilian democratic government."[47] In her speech before a joint session of Congress, Bhutto said: "Speaking for Pakistan, I can declare that we do not possess nor do we intend to make a nuclear device. That is our policy."[48] Bhutto's trip bought Pakistan some time. In October 1989, President Bush certified, with the now standard caveats, that Pakistan did not possess a nuclear explosive device.[49] The next month, Congress extended the Symington Amendment waiver from April 1990 to April 1991.

SOUTH ASIA'S MISSILE ERA BEGINS. The 1988–89 period also saw India and Pakistan test-fire nuclear-capable ballistic missiles. In February 1988, New Delhi tested the *Prithvi*, which was reported to have a range of 150 miles when carrying a 2,200-pound warhead. In February 1989, Islamabad announced that it had tested the *Hatf I* and *Hatf II*, which could carry an 1,100-pound payload 50 and 186 miles, respectively. Then, in May 1989, India test-fired the *Agni*, an intermediate-range missile, which could loft a 2,200-pound warhead about 1,500 miles. None of these missiles was actually deployed during the period covered by this study, but each successive milestone contributed to the mutual perception of progressive nuclear weaponization.[50]

Nuclear Deterrence in South Asia?

During the late 1980s, influential Pakistanis and some Western proliferation experts began to discuss the operation of a nuclear deterrent balance between Islamabad and New Delhi. In July 1987, Mushahid Hussain, the journalist who had accompanied Kuldip Nayar to his meeting with A.Q. Khan, suggested that "with Pakistan's nuclear capability serving as a deterrent against India, emergence of a nuclearised South Asia is on the horizon where a new 'balance of terror' between Pakistan and India will maintain parity

47. House Committee on Foreign Affairs, Subcommittees on Arms Control, International Security and Science, and on Asian and Pacific Affairs, *The Proposed Sale of F-16s to Pakistan*, August 2, 1989, p. 20.

48. Benazir Bhutto, "The Policies of Pakistan: Nuclear Problems and Afghanistan," *Vital Speeches of the Day*, June 7, 1989, p. 553.

49. Don Oberdorfer, "Pakistan Has No A-Bomb, Bush Informs Hill," *Washington Post*, October 12, 1989.

50. Robert D. Shuey et al., *Missile Proliferation: Survey of Emerging Missile Forces* (Washington, D.C.: Congressional Research Service, 1989), pp. 71–72; and Spector, *Nuclear Ambitions*, pp. 74, 102–103.

and peace. If the bomb can stabilise Soviet-American ties or help maintain peace in Europe, why not in South Asia too?"[51] In 1988, Spector wrote: "Pakistan's recent *de facto* nuclearization, together with India's pre-existing nuclear weapons capability, has created a form of crude, undeclared nuclear deterrence between two regional powers in which, so far, neither is thought to have integrated nuclear arms into its military posture or doctrine."[52]

This view of South Asia's nuclear balance was lent credibility at the highest levels. Pakistan's President Zia said of India's nuclear capabilities: "If they create ambiguity, that ambiguity is the essence of deterrence. The present programs of India and Pakistan have a lot of ambiguities, and therefore in the eyes of each other, they have reached a particular level, and that level is good enough to create an impression of deterrence."[53] Former Pakistan Army chief Mirza Aslam Beg recalls that Pakistan froze its nuclear program in 1989 only after deciding that "we had acquired a meaningful low-level deterrence capability and that this capability was good enough to deter India, which had a larger capability."[54] During this period, India's strategic community tended to resist the notion that India and Pakistan were deterred from war by each other's nuclear capabilities. For Indian leaders to have acknowledged the operation of a nuclear deterrent balance in South Asia would have been tantamount to ceding Pakistan's claim of strategic equality with India. This is anathema in New Delhi, which has always maintained that it keeps its nuclear options open to meet potential threats from China, not from Pakistan.

As General K. Sundarji said in May 1988: "Against Pakistan, our dissuasive and riposte capabilities are good. Our major problem is going to be China. Pakistan we can take care of *en passant.*"[55]

Summary: The Impact of the Brasstacks Crisis

During the Brasstacks crisis of 1986–87, Pakistan's nuclear status was uncertain. Apart from a small circle of Pakistani decision-makers, very few people knew conclusively whether Islamabad had achieved

---

51. Mushahid Hussain, "Nuclear Non-Proliferation Issues," *Strategic Studies* (Islamabad), Vol. 10, No. 4; and Vol. 11, No. 1 (Summer–Autumn 1987), p. 65.

52. Spector, *Undeclared Bomb*, pp. 13–14.

53. Ibid., p. 145.

54. "Pakistan Missile Flap Ongoing."

55. "General K. Sundarji: Disputed Legacy," *India Today*, May 15, 1988, p. 39.

the capability to explode nuclear weapons. The main legacy of the Brasstacks crisis was that, three years later, Pakistan's nuclear status had changed: by 1990, Pakistan had evolved into a de facto nuclear weapon state. While the exact nature of Islamabad's nuclear capabilities continued to be shrouded in secrecy, the nonproliferation community—and India—no longer doubted that Pakistan could build and deploy nuclear weapons if and when its leaders made the political decision to do so. Leonard Spector's summary assessment was that "India and Pakistan are currently capable of deploying small nuclear forces comprised of atomic bombs that could be delivered by advanced fighter-bombers, with India's capabilities being considerably greater than Pakistan's. Neither country is believed to have integrated nuclear weapons into its military forces, however, and it is possible that neither has manufactured complete nuclear devices."[56] A late 1989 *Washington Post* editorial expressed the nonproliferation community's conventional wisdom: South Asia, it said, was now the "likeliest place in the world for a nuclear war."[57] This, then, was the strategic backdrop for the second Indo-Pakistani crisis in three years, which is the subject of Chapter 6.

---

56. Spector, *Nuclear Ambitions*, p. 59.
57. "The Next Nuclear War," *Washington Post*, October 13, 1989.

Chapter 6

Nuclear Weapons and the 1990 Kashmir Crisis

The late 1980s marked the dawn of a new era in South Asia's international relations. Developments at the global, regional, and domestic levels sharply intensified the India-Pakistan rivalry. These three political streams reached their confluence in the spring of 1990, with the eruption of the second Indo-Pakistani crisis of South Asia's nuclear era. Analysts disagree over the nature and seriousness of the Kashmir crisis, in particular, whether New Delhi and Islamabad were on the brink of war and what, if any, nuclear dimension shaped their behavior. I will analyze these questions below, but it will suffice at the outset to say that there was a possibility of war between India and Pakistan in 1990, and that no decision-maker in Islamabad or New Delhi could rule out the slimmer, but not negligible, chance that such a war might involve the use of nuclear weapons.

This chapter is organized as follows. First, I discuss the background of the crisis, especially the insurgency in Kashmir that was its root cause.[1] Then I provide a chronological overview of the crisis as it evolved in the spring of 1990. The remainder of the chapter is devoted to an analysis of the nuclear dimensions of the crisis. First, I present the conventional interpretation, which suggests that India and Pakistan nearly fought a nuclear war in 1990. I then criticize that analysis, arguing instead that Islamabad and New Delhi were deterred from war—nuclear and conventional—by their recognition of each other's nuclear weapon capabilities and the possibility that any direct military hostilities between them might have escalated to a nuclear exchange, i.e., existential deterrence.

---

1. For a more detailed treatment, see Šumit Ganguly, "Explaining the Kashmir Insurgency: Political Mobilization and Institutional Decay," *International Security*, Vol. 21, No. 2 (Fall 1996), pp. 76–107.

This was not a nuclear crisis per se; it was a political crisis between two hostile Third World neighbors who had already fought three wars and who were secretly developing nuclear weapons. The command and control arrangements governing their rudimentary nuclear capabilities were either extremely crude or nonexistent[2] —circumstances that the logic of nonproliferation suggests should be fraught with peril. In other words, the 1990 Kashmir crisis was a hard test for the logic of nuclear deterrence, a test which, happily, it passed convincingly.

Background: The Kashmir Dispute in 1990

At the global level, the rapidly ending Cold War had serious repercussions for India and Pakistan as the 1990s began. The Soviet defeat in Afghanistan had cut the legs out from under the U.S.-Pakistani strategic partnership, allowing submerged policy differences to resurface. The most important of these disagreements concerned Pakistan's continued development of nuclear weapons, which replaced the Afghan war effort as the foremost issue for U.S. decision-makers concerned with Pakistan. India's strategic relationship with the Soviets also suffered. As Moscow's attention turned inward and its rivalry with Washington evolved into a tentative partnership, India lost its value as a bulwark of pro-Moscow sentiment in the Third World. When Gorbachev's initial reforms plunged the Soviet economy into depression, Moscow was forced to rethink the generous terms under which it had structured its economic and military ties with Third World allies. Indian trade with the Soviet Union— previously conducted in rupees, which diminished New Delhi's requirements for hard currency—was put on a more conventional commercial footing. The terms of Soviet military sales to India also grew less attractive. In sum, as the new decade began, both New Delhi and Islamabad were losing their moorings in the international system.

Regionally, the turn of the decade heralded the reemergence of the Kashmir dispute, which quickly plunged Indo-Pakistani relations into another tailspin. In the mid- to late 1980s, political agitation against the central government in New Delhi had grown among the

---

2. For a speculative discussion of possible Indian arrangements for the use of nuclear weapons, see Stephen Peter Rosen, *Societies and Military Power: India and Its Armies* (Ithaca, N.Y.: Cornell University Press, 1996), pp. 251–253.

Muslims of Kashmir. By 1989, Muslim militants in the Vale of Kashmir were in open rebellion, and, in the years since, a full-blown secessionist insurgency has raged against the Indian state. The insurgency poses dangers for India as the defender of the status quo and opportunities for Pakistan as the revisionist challenger. The escalating war between Indian security forces and Kashmiri militants radically transformed Indo-Pakistani relations by giving the two governments their first compelling reason to shed blood since the Bangladesh war two decades earlier. Moreover, it sharply raised the level of antagonism between India and Pakistan just as their foreign policy establishments were struggling to adapt to the new structure of global politics. Kashmir is viewed by many non–South Asians as the potential flashpoint for a fourth Indo-Pakistani war, which could be the first major war between two nuclear weapon states.

Domestically, political developments in South Asia were no less dramatic. On the surface, the election of prime ministers Benazir Bhutto in 1988 and V.P. Singh in 1989 were positive strides for democracy on the subcontinent. Bhutto's ascent to power was a big step in the restoration of democracy in Pakistan, begun cautiously by President Zia in 1985, and continuing, unsteadily, in the 1990s. Singh's triumph over Rajiv Gandhi in 1989 marked only the second time in history that India's dominant Congress party had been removed from office, and the uneventful transfer of power in New Delhi was widely interpreted as signalling the robustness of Indian democracy. Both elections were applauded by Western analysts, steeped in their appreciation of the vitality of liberal democracies and their putative international concomitant, the absence of war between such political systems.[3]

Below the surface, however, the domestic political pictures were more volatile. After 1988, Pakistan was effectively ruled by a troika of leaders, of whom the inexperienced Bhutto was the weakest. The other two centers of power revolved around the president, Ghulam Ishaq Khan (a long-time civil servant and Zia's finance minister), and the chief of the army staff (COAS), General Mirza Aslam Beg. While they were content to let the charismatic Bhutto represent Pakistan on the world stage, she chafed under their continued dominance of vital national security issues like the nuclear program and relations with

---

3. On the "democratic peace" debate, see Michael E. Brown, Sean M. Lynn-Jones, and Steven E. Miller, eds., *Debating the Democratic Peace* (Cambridge, Mass.: MIT Press, 1996).

India. In New Delhi, V.P. Singh's leadership credentials were stronger than Bhutto's, but his position was equally tenuous. Before taking power, Singh had occupied senior government posts—first as Rajiv Gandhi's finance minister, then as defense minister. Despite his personal stature, though, Singh's government was a fragile coalition, forced to rely on the rightist Bharatiya Janata Party (BJP) for support in parliament. Once in power, it was immediately buffeted by a number of contentious issues, including Kashmir, that severely weakened its authority. Ultimately, both governments collapsed in the face of challenges from conservative pressure: Bhutto was deposed by Ghulam Ishaq in August 1990, and Singh resigned three months later.

The interaction of these global, regional, and domestic developments made South Asia extremely unstable in 1990. The Kashmir conflict reignited just as India and Pakistan were losing the support of former Cold War patrons, and were only beginning to grope their way toward an accommodation with new global realities. Adding to this combustible mix, each country's political leadership was weak and had limited experience managing Indo-Pakistani relations. For all of the animosity evident between President Zia and the two Gandhis during the 1980s, one can also discern a degree of mutual familiarity and grudging respect. In 1990, not only were the new Indian and Pakistani prime ministers inexperienced and unfamiliar with one another, but their internal positions were subject to relentless pressures from the political right. Prior to 1990, Indo-Pakistani relations were hostile but manageable; in the 1990 crisis, they plunged into a seemingly endless cycle of harsh mutual recrimination.

GENESIS OF THE INSURGENCY

After the Simla Agreement of 1972, discussed in Chapter 3, the Indo-Pakistani dispute over Kashmir lay dormant. Pakistan, having lost about half of its territory and population in the Bangladesh war, was in no position to challenge India in Kashmir. To be sure, both sides continued to press their claims to the disputed territory. New Delhi maintained that Kashmir was an integral part of the Indian union, its status as such legitimized by both its incorporation into the Indian constitution and decades of democratic Kashmiri political activity within the Indian federation. Islamabad disagreed: Kashmir remained disputed territory, its status unresolved according to either the operative UN resolutions or the more direct Indo-Pakistani negotiations envisioned by the Simla signatories. Indeed, divergent interpretations of the Simla Agreement itself had become one more area of Indo-Pakistani disagreement. For India, Simla had fundamentally supplanted the UN resolutions as a point of reference for resolving the Kashmir dispute. After all, Indian leaders reasoned, the two parties had pledged to work directly with one another, implicitly abandoning extra-regional diplomacy. For Pakistan, Simla supplemented but did not replace the UN resolutions on Kashmir. While it pledged Pakistan not to alter the territorial status quo uni-laterally, it did not rule out external mediation if both New Delhi and Islamabad agreed to seek it. In any event, the Line of Actual Control (LAC) had become the de facto boundary between the Indian and Pakistani parts of Kashmir.

DEVELOPMENTS IN THE 1970S AND 1980S. In the mid-1970s, Indira Gandhi and Sheikh Abdullah finally made their peace; 1977 saw Kashmir's first-ever free election, which brought the sheikh to power as the state's chief minister. In the 1980s, however, the decline of India's "Congress party system" and the death of Sheikh Abdullah had disastrous consequences for Kashmir. The sheikh was succeeded in 1982 by his son, Farooq Abdullah. State assembly elections were held again in 1983, prior to which Indira Gandhi offered to form an electoral alliance with Farooq and his National Conference party. He refused, and the ensuing campaign was marred by violence. The National Conference won a convincing victory by sweeping the heavily Muslim Vale of Kashmir, while the Congress fared well in predominantly Hindu Jammu. Despite the fact that Farooq had been popularly elected chief minister, the Congress worked furiously to destabilize his government. Farooq further alienated Indira Gandhi by trying to unify India's opposition parties on the sensitive issue of center-state relations. His behavior went directly against the grain of her centralizing drives, as a consequence of which Farooq was brand-ed pro-Pakistan and anti-India. In July, the Congress ousted Farooq Abdullah as Kashmir's chief minister by inducing the defection of a bloc of his loyalists in the state assembly. He was replaced by his brother-in-law, G.M. Shah, while Indian paramilitary forces were rushed to Kashmir to keep the peace. The 1984 coup ignited a cycle of political degeneration that would increasingly alienate young Muslims from Indian democracy.

Following Indira Gandhi's death later that year, Farooq Abdullah did a political flip-flop that severely strained his own credibility with Kashmiris. After Kashmir's governor ousted the G.M. Shah regime in March 1986, Farooq demanded new state assembly elections. As a condition for restoring him to power in Kashmir, new prime minister Rajiv Gandhi insisted that Farooq's National Conference join the Congress in an electoral alliance and governing coalition. Unlike in 1983, Farooq accepted the offer, asserting to his followers that by doing so he could increase the flow of resources for economic development to Kashmir. The 1987 election thus pitted a Congress National Conference alliance against a coalition of smaller parties calling itself the Muslim United Front. As in 1983, Farooq Abdullah was easily elected chief minister, but the elections were clearly rigged by the victors, further alienating young Muslims whose experience with Indian democratic practice had now gone sour twice in less than three years.[4] The new government was inefficient and corrupt. Adding to the disgruntlement caused by the political machinations of 1984 and 1987, many well-educated Muslim youths who had been denied their voice in Kashmiri politics were also unable to find decent jobs. By 1988, political estrangement blended with economic angst to produce a critical mass of alienated Kashmiri Muslims. Anti-government agitation erupted in the form of sporadic violence and organized strikes. Militants set off bombs in Srinagar, and security forces became murder targets. By 1989, young Kashmiri Muslims were assassinating policemen, judges, and other government officials with impunity.

From Domestic Insurgency to International Crisis

Robert Oakley, the U.S. ambassador to Pakistan during the 1990 crisis, remembers that prior to that year, Kashmir was not a major irritant in Indo-Pakistani relations: "Kashmir was so calm it was not discussed. . . . there was a series of meetings during 1989 between the two prime ministers and the defense ministers and the foreign ministers and the foreign secretaries—no one raised Kashmir. Punjab always; but Kashmir, no."[5] This situation changed dramatically in early 1990. As the Vale of Kashmir descended into anarchy, forty years of antagonism exploded in mutual fury. New Delhi accused

---

4. See Inderjit Badhwar, "A Tarnished Triumph," *India Today*, April 15, 1987, pp. 76–78; and Inderjit Badhwar, "Farooq Under Fire," *India Today*, September 15, 1987, pp. 42–47.

5. Michael Krepon and Mishi Faruqee, eds., *Conflict Prevention and Confidence Building Measures in South Asia: The 1990 Crisis*, Occasional Paper No. 17 (Washington, D.C.: The Henry L. Stimson Center, 1994), p. 5. This is a transcript of a meeting convened by the Stimson Center to discuss the 1990 crisis. Participants included the 1990 U.S. ambassadors to New Delhi and Islamabad, and South Asian diplomats and military officers.

Pakistan of waging an unconventional war with India, by arming and training Kashmiri Muslim "terrorists." Islamabad responded that it provided only diplomatic and moral support for the Kashmiri "freedom fighters," but eschewed military or other material assistance. Pakistani leaders further charged that the Kashmir insurgency was the product of decades of Indian abuses in the state, not of Pakistani meddling. Most commentators agreed that the primary cause of the Kashmir insurgency could be found in India's domestic affairs. Pakistani support for the militants was typically viewed as an important, but secondary, factor in the Kashmir equation.[6]

V.P. Singh was installed as prime minister on December 2, 1989, after pledging in his campaign against the Congress to solve the myriad ethnic disputes that had scarred the Indian body politic in the 1980s. His message was one of national healing in the wake of Hindu-Muslim communalism, caste conflicts, and sustained political-military competition between New Delhi and disaffected 'elements in practically every corner of India. Anxious to turn his words into deeds, Singh appointed as his home minister a Kashmiri Muslim, Mufti Mohammed Sayeed. On December 8, Sayeed's daughter was kidnapped by Kashmiri militants and held hostage until the government released five imprisoned guerrillas. Political kidnappings were hardly unusual, but the circumstances of this particular abduction seemed dramatically. to illustrate the advanced state of political decay in Kashmir.

From this point on, Kashmir descended into chaos. The militants undertook larger operations like ambushes of military convoys and open engagements with Indian security forces. In January 1990, the government resolved to fight fire with fire: New Delhi sent to Kashmir a former governor of the state, Jagmohan, known for his law-and-order approach to militancy. Jagmohan's appointment signalled New Delhi's resolve to pacify Kashmir with sticks rather than carrots; as he put it, "the best way of solving the crisis is to assert the authority of the State and create an impression that, no matter what the cost, the subversionists and their collaborators will be firmly

---

6. See, for example, "The Enemy Within," *India Today* (editorial), March 31, 1990, p. 11; Šumit Ganguly, "Avoiding War in Kashmir," *Foreign Affairs*, Vol. 74, No. 1 (Winter 1990/91), pp. 63, 65; M.J. Akbar, *Kashmir: Behind the Vale* (New Delhi: Viking, 1991), p. 215; "Crossfire: Kashmir," *India Today*, August 31, 1991, pp. 77–87; and George Fernandes, "India's Policies in Kashmir: An Assessment and Discourse," and Jagat Mehta, "Resolving Kashmir in the International Context of the 1990s," in Raju G.C. Thomas, ed., *Perspectives on Kashmir: The Roots of Conflict in South Asia* (Boulder, Colo.: Westview, 1992), pp. 286, 394–395.

dealt with and eliminated."[7] Farooq Abdullah resigned, New Delhi imposed presidential rule on the state, and Jagmohan began a sustained crackdown of curfews and house-to-house searches in an attempt to imprison or kill as many militant leaders as possible. By this time, the secessionist movement had begun to affect every aspect of life in the state. Local businesses had already suffered severe losses owing to the dwindling flow of tourists; now, insurgent-imposed shutdowns and government curfews brought economic activity to a virtual standstill, as New Delhi flew in thousands of paramilitary soldiers to implement Jagmohan's crackdown.[8] On January 20, growing tension between the militants and security forces exploded into what would be the first of many spasms of mass violence, with Srinagar police spraying bullets into a crowd of demonstrators. An estimated 32 people were killed, among a total of roughly 100 killed in the two weeks after New Delhi's imposition of direct rule over the state.[9]

INTERNATIONAL IMPLICATIONS

The events of January 1990 transformed the Kashmiri insurgency from a mainly Indian affair into renewed Indo-Pakistani conflict. Ambassador Oakley remembers that the initial popular uprising in Kashmir was "primarily spontaneous." He adds, however, that "Pakistan, willy-nilly, began to play a much more active role. Unofficially, groups such as Jamaat-i-Islami [an Islamic political party] as well as ISI [Pakistan's main espionage organization] and the Pakistan Army, began to take a more active role in support of the Kashmiri protests. Training camps of various kinds multiplied. . . . There was much more activity. There were more people and more material going across the border from Pakistan into Kashmir."[10] Still, Prime Minister Bhutto maintained a temperate stand on the deteriorating situation, hoping that the rapprochement she had begun with Rajiv Gandhi would continue under his successor. In early January, Bhutto sent envoy Abdul Sattar to New Delhi to explore ways to maintain the relative amity that had developed since her election in 1988. According to Sattar, the subject of Kashmir was raised only

---

7. Inderjit Badhwar, "Asserting Authority," *India Today*, February 28, 1990, p. 31.

8. See Pankaj Pachauri and Zafar Meraj, "Drifting Dangerously," *India Today*, January 15, 1990, pp. 8–13; and Shekhar Gupta, "Militant Siege," *India Today*, January 31, 1990, pp. 22–32.

9. "Kashmir: Echoes of War," *The Economist*, January 27, 1990, p. 33; and "Kashmir: Fighting Words," *The Economist*, February 3, 1990, p. 32.

10. Krepon and Faruqee, *1990 Crisis*, p. 6.

briefly during his meetings with V.P. Singh, who told him that New Delhi was concerned about reports of Pakistani support for the militants in Kashmir. Sattar says he was "taken aback" by the rising concern over Kashmir in the Indian media, which at that time were more strident than the government in their accusations of Pakistani complicity in the uprising.[11]

As the conflict intensified, Pakistan's opposition parties beseeched Benazir Bhutto to take a stronger stand in support of the Kashmiri insurgents. On January 20, the day of the Srinagar massacre, Pakistan's ruling troika met to discuss the Kashmir situation. Bhutto later parried Indian charges of Pakistani complicity in the insurgency by declaring that Kashmiri militancy was indigenous; unable any longer to resist pressure from conservative elements urging a more aggressive posture, she loudly proclaimed the Kashmiris' right to self-determination.[12] In early February, during deliberations in Pakistan's National Assembly, opposition politicians called on the government to pursue a *jihad* (holy war) in Kashmir. On February 10, the leader of Jamaat-i-Islami urged the government to build nuclear weapons in order to meet the Indian threat.[13]

Meanwhile, Indian behavior led some observers to speculate that New Delhi was raising its nuclear profile, perhaps to send a deterrent message to Pakistan. For one newsweekly, V.P. Singh's appointment of Raja Ramanna—a former chairman of India's Atomic Energy Commission—as minister of state for defense "can only mean that India has decided to give higher priority to its nuclear weapons and missile-development programs." In February, Singh "said India would have to review its peaceful nuclear policy if Pakistan employed its nuclear power for military purposes." Singh also "told newsmen that Pakistan's going nuclear would bring about a radical change in the security environment in the region. If this were to happen, 'we will have to take stock of the situation and act accordingly'." An influential nuclear trade publication suggested that Singh's actions meant that India was quietly increasing its nuclear preparedness.[14]

---

11. Interview with Abdul Sattar.

12. S. Viswam and Salamat Ali, "Vale of Tears," *Far Eastern Economic Review*, February 8, 1990, pp. 19–21.

13. Malcolm Davidson, "Bhutto Says Pakistan Does Not Want War With India Over Kashmir," *Reuter Library Report*, February 10, 1990.

14. "Echoes of War"; "Indian Prime Minister on His Country's Nuclear Policy," *Xinhua General Overseas News Service*, February 21, 1990; and "Iyengar, Ramanna Appointments Open Bomb Speculation in India," *Nucleonics Week*, February 22, 1990.

MILITARY MOVEMENTS

By this time, conventional military preparations had begun on both sides of the border. For purposes of clarity, these activities can be grouped into three regions: Kashmir, Punjab, and the border between Rajasthan and the Pakistani provinces of Punjab and Sindh. Early in the insurgency, the Indian government began to supplement its security forces in Kashmir and Punjab with reinforcements, primarily infantry, from the Indian Army. Its chief concern in these areas, according to then-COAS V.N. Sharma, was to stem the infiltration of Pakistan-backed Sikh and Kashmiri terrorists into India. As Sharma told an interviewer in 1993: "Terrorist groups backed by agencies in Pakistan were able to attack railway stations and vital installations which could affect any military movement on our side. . . . Therefore, there was need for the Indian army to go in there to take care of the communication lines and other bottlenecks so that if there was a military flare-up, we could conveniently move our fighting forces from locations deep in the country to the border areas."[15]

According to Sharma, tank units of Pakistan's 2nd Corps had moved into the desert region of Bahawalpur and Bhawalnagar, across the border from the Indian states of Punjab and Rajasthan. In addition, he claims, parts of Pakistan's 1st Corps, including a tank division, had moved into the Shakargarh salient, just across the border from the vital road linking Jammu to Punjab. Indian military planners were concerned, too, about residual deployments of Pakistan Army forces after a late 1989 integrated air-land exercise; *Zarb-i-Momin*, the largest military exercise in Pakistan's history, had begun on December 9 in Punjab. According to General Beg, it tested a new Pakistani ground strategy: "In the past we were pursuing a defensive policy; now there is a big change since we are shifting to a policy of offensive defence. Should there be a war, the Pakistan Army plans to take the war into India, launching a sizeable offensive on Indian territory."[16] *Zarb-i-Momin* was Beg's response to General Sundarji's Brasstacks exercises of 1986–87. It included seven infantry divisions, one armored division, and a squadron of Apache attack helicopters, in an attempt to demonstrate Pakistan's conventional military prowess and to send a firm dissuasive message to the Indian military.[17] After the

---

15. "It's All Bluff and Bluster," *Economic Times* (Bombay), May 18, 1993.

16. Mushahid Hussain, "Pakistan 'Responding to Change'," *Jane's Defence Weekly*, October 14, 1989, p. 779; and Malcolm Davidson, "Pakistani Army Chief Vows to Stay Out of Politics," *Reuter Library Report*, December 10, 1989.

17. Salamat Ali, "The Counter-Punch," *Far Eastern Economic Review*, October 26, 1989, p. 25.

exercise was over, says Sharma, "we found that these troops were not going back to their peace stations, but they were staying on in the exercise area which is quite close to the international border and the cease-fire line in Jammu and Kashmir." The Indian assessment of these military movements "was that Pakistan was keeping troops ready as a back up support to the increased terrorist activities, in Indian territory, across the border and could take full advantage of terrorist successes to support military intervention."[18]

Further south, according to Sharma, the Indian army in February sent two new tank units for training at its field firing range at Mahajan, in Rajasthan. With Brasstacks fresh in their minds, Pakistani planners grew alarmed that the Indian armored units at Mahajan were "ginning up another large exercise of that nature, or, indeed, preparing to launch an attack from the training range."[19] U.S. officials relayed these concerns to the Indian defense ministry; its representatives explained their version of events and invited U.S. officials to take a closer look at the situation on the ground. U.S. defense attachés in New Delhi believed that the Mahajan training activity was normal for that time of year, when the cool weather makes it comfortable to conduct maneuvers in the desert. Moreover, Sharma told U.S. Ambassador William Clark that the Indian Army could not launch an effective offensive against Pakistan from Mahajan, and Clark's embassy staff concurred.[20]

The U.S. air attaché in New Delhi, Colonel John Sandrock, remembers that "what was unusual from our perspective was the deployment of additional troops in Kashmir as a result of the reported crossborder infiltration from Pakistan into Kashmir and then along the border, south through the rest of Jammu and Kashmir and into the [Indian state of] Punjab." These forces consisted of both regular Indian Army soldiers and troops from the paramilitary Border Security Force. The BSF had the "primary responsibility for border security," while the army's role was to "act as a back-up" in the event of "real hostilities." According to Sandrock, there was no evidence that the army's activities included the movement of tanks and artillery, which appeared to corroborate the Indian claim that the "buildup of forces on the border was to prevent cross-border infiltration and did not constitute a buildup of forces preparing for any hostile action against Pakistan."

---

18. "Bluff and Bluster."

19. Comments of the U.S. ambassador to New Delhi, William Clark, in Krepon and Faruqee, *1990 Crisis*, p. 3.

20. Interview with William Clark.

U.S. military attachés in New Delhi took the first of several reconnaissance trips in February, confirming their impression that Indian forces were not preparing for an offensive military thrust. U.S. attachés in Pakistan undertook a similar series of fact-finding missions on their side of the border, also finding little unusual military activity. Of special importance, one of the attachés noted, was that the two Pakistani strike corps were not on the move, and that the Pakistan Air Force's forward operating bases had not been opened.[21]

A WAR OF WORDS

Meanwhile, the war of words between New Delhi and Islamabad escalated another notch. On March 13, as massive demonstrations continued in Srinagar, Bhutto traveled to Pakistan-held Kashmir, where she promised a "thousand-year war" in support of the militants. The Pakistani prime minister also announced the creation of a $4 million fund to support the "freedom fighters" across the LAC.[22] Though the material effect of such support would be slight, it raised the symbolic ante. V.P. Singh quickly responded that India would react decisively against Pakistani intervention in Kashmir: "I do not wish to sound hawkish," he told the Indian parliament, "but there should be no confusion. Such a misadventure would not be without cost."[23]

OPPOSITION PRESSURE. In early April, the opposition BJP's national executive committee passed a resolution urging the Indian government to "knock out the training camps and transit routes of the terrorists." The BJP contended that "Pakistan's many provocations amount to so many acts of war today. It is literally carrying on a war against India on Indian territory." The party further argued that the doctrine of "hot pursuit is a recognized defensive measure."[24] Former Prime Minister Rajiv Gandhi added to the clamor by urging the government to take "some very strong steps on Kashmir." He added, obliquely, "I know what steps are possible. I also know what is in the pipeline and what the capabilities are. The question is, does the government have the guts to take strong steps?"[25]

---

21. Krepon and Faruqee, *1990 Crisis*, pp. 13–19.

22. Raja Asghar, "Bhutto Predicts Victory for Kashmir Independence Campaign," *Reuter Library Report*, March 13, 1990.

23. Moses Manoharan, "Indian Leader Tells Pakistan to Stay Out of Kashmir Uprising," *Reuter Library Report*, March 13, 1990.

24. "Crush Pak Camps: BJP," *Times of India*, April 8, 1990.

25. David Housego, "India Urged to Attack Camps in Pakistan Over Strife in Kashmir," *Financial Times*, April 9, 1990.

Over the next week, V.P. Singh made a series of forthright public statements intended both to deter any adventurism Islamabad might be contemplating and to neutralize his opposition within India. On April 10, he warned Indians to be "psychologically prepared" for war. Addressing Islamabad, he said: "Our message to Pakistan is that you cannot get away with taking Kashmir without a war. They will have to pay a very heavy price and we have the capability to inflict heavy losses." Singh claimed that Islamabad had moved its radar systems to the border, made operational its forward air bases, and mined the frontier with India. Pakistan's strategy, he charged, was to avoid direct confrontation, while continuing to destabilize India by fanning the flames of violence in Kashmir. If this were successful, a limited Pakistani intervention might follow, to consolidate whatever gains the insurgents had made. Finally, as if to dispel any notion that Pakistan's nuclear weapon capabilities would give Islamabad a deterrent umbrella under which to carry out offensive operations against India, Singh said that if Pakistan deployed nuclear weapons, "India will have to take a second look at our policy. I think we will have no option but to match. Our scientists have the capability to match it."[26]

THE PAKISTANI RESPONSE. Pakistan's leading English-language daily called the Indian prime minister's warning "one of the most serious ever hurled at this country in recent years."[27] On April 11, General Beg convened a meeting of his corps commanders to carry out a "detailed threat assessment." Beg told his subordinates that India had deployed a strike force of up to 100,000 men within fifty miles of the border in Rajasthan. He was referring to the Indian Army units that had been on winter exercises in the Mahajan area, which Pakistani officials now stated had been extended. Pakistan Army sources estimated that the Indian units were deployed in such a way as to "halve India's normal mobilisation time to one week." In addition, Islamabad noted that India continued to move paramilitary forces into Kashmir. One reporter wrote: "The concern in Islamabad is that India might be preparing an attack on Pakistani Kashmir on

26. David Housego and Zafar Meraj, "Indian Premier Warns of Danger of Kashmir War," *Financial Times*, April 11, 1990; Coomi Kapoor, "Indian Threat of Armed Reprisals," *The Times* (London), April 11, 1990; Tony Allen-Mills, "India Ready for War After Hostages Are Executed," *The Independent* (London), April 12, 1990; Mark Fineman, "India's Leader Warns of an Attack by Pakistan," *Los Angeles Times*, April 15, 1990; and "VP Urges Nation to Be Ready as Pak Troops Move to Border," *Times of India*, April 11, 1990.

27. "Unwarranted Bellicosity," *Dawn* (Karachi), April 12, 1990.

the pretext of destroying Kashmiri 'freedom fighter' training camps. There is also concern that a simultaneous attack might be launched into Sindh province, where the only road and rail link between north and south Pakistan is located about 40 km from the Indian border." On April 14, a senior Pakistani official told a parliamentary committee that the country's military forces were on a "high state of preparedness and vigilance to meet any external threat." He continued: "If, out of sheer frustration, India dragged Pakistan into military confrontation, it would find that Pakistan has the full capability of meeting the Indian invasion by mobilising all its national resources."[28]

Indian intelligence officials confirmed that New Delhi was putting more men, matériel, and arms into Kashmir. New Delhi claimed that these reinforcements were a response to Pakistan's buildup on its side of the LAC. Diplomats in New Delhi "said forces on both sides of the border were on a higher than normal state of alert, but several levels lower than would indicate imminent hostilities."[29] Indian officials denied Beg's claim regarding the formation of an Indian strike force in Rajasthan, saying that their units had retreated to "normal positions" after the winter exercise.[30] Western military analysts reported no major troop mobilization near the international frontier, but speculated that by extending their exercises, Indian planners may have positioned tanks and heavy artillery near the border. In the words of one analyst, "everything the Indians have been doing fits under the category of defensive preparedness, but some of it is ambiguous."[31]

INDIAN THINKING. On April 14, Singh elaborated on the logic of these preparations in a discussion with journalists. "Singh said . . . that Pakistan is preparing to launch an attack across India's western border, where he asserted that Pakistan has deployed new armored

---

28. "Indian Threats Demand Vigilance," *Dawn* (Karachi), April 12, 1990; James Clad and Salamat Ali, "Will Words Lead to War?" *Far Eastern Economic Review*, April 26, 1990, pp. 10–11; Malcolm Davidson, "Pakistan Condemns Indian Premier's Talk of War Over Kashmir," *Reuter Library Report*, April 11, 1990; Malcolm Davidson, "Kashmir Row Sparks Dangerous Period for India and Pakistan," *Reuter Library Report*, April 13, 1990; and "Pakistan Ready to Meet Indian Invasion, Minister Says," *Reuter Library Report*, April 14, 1990.

29. "Indian Troops Reinforced Near Kashmir Border With Pakistan," *Reuter Library Report*, April 12, 1990.

30. Davidson, "Dangerous Period for India and Pakistan."

31. Steve Coll, "Indian Troops, Separatist Violence Aggravate Kashmir Crisis," *Washington Post*, April 13, 1990.

regiments and sophisticated radar. Singh added that Pakistan's army and air force were on 'red alert' along" the LAC, and that Pakistani artillery had been moved to forward positions across from Kashmir and Punjab. Singh "said his intention was to avert war: 'Many wars have been prevented by a timely warning. It is indecision and confused signals that have usually triggered a conflict'." Claiming that political jockeying among Pakistan's ruling troika made it difficult to know exactly who was in charge there, Singh said: "Had anyone been in control, it would not have been necessary for me to issue a public warning." Still, sentiment was growing among influential Indians for strikes against Pakistan. Home Minister Sayeed, for example, argued that war "would be fully justified if the objective of freeing Kashmir from the stranglehold of the secessionists was achieved." BJP leader L.K. Advani took an even stronger line, warning that Pakistan would "cease to exist" if it attacked India.[32]

One Indian strategist took a more sanguine view of the prospects for war. In an *India Today* interview, retired army chief K. Sundarji suggested that the likelihood of war was low due to the influence of nuclear deterrence on Indian and Pakistani leaders. He said: "Any sensible planner sitting on this side of the border is going to assume Pakistan does indeed have nuclear weapons capability. And by the same token, I rather suspect the view from the other side is going to look very similar." Sundarji acknowledged that "on the other side, there may be the odd person who has kidded himself into believing that they have the nuclear weapon capability and we don't," but called this view "stupid. The sooner they wake up to this reality, the better."[33]

THE CONVENTIONAL MILITARY EQUATION. By mid-April 1990, the disposition of military forces near the Indo-Pakistani border and the LAC in Kashmir was as follows: in Kashmir, India had deployed up to 200,000 troops, drawn from both the army and paramilitary forces. These soldiers supplemented some 17,000 local Jammu and Kashmir police. The outside security forces often clashed with the local police, whose loyalties they suspected. Pakistan had deployed a smaller force of at least 100,000 soldiers in Azad Kashmir. The Indian and Pakistani forces were reported to be "eyeball to eyeball" across the

---

32. Fineman, "India's Leader Warns of an Attack by Pakistan"; "The Makings of a Bloody, Old-Fashioned War," *The Economist*, April 21, 1990, p. 35; Steve Coll, "Assault on Pakistan Gains Favor in India," *Washington Post*, April 15, 1990; and "Indian Forces Battle Moslems in Kashmir," *Chicago Tribune*, April 16, 1990.

33. "If Pushed Beyond a Point By Pakistan, We Will Retaliate," *India Today*, April 30, 1990, p. 76.

LAC, in some cases as close as 200 meters apart. Demonstrating the heightened tension, the United Nations Military Observer Group in India and Pakistan reported a quadrupling of border violations in the January–March period of 1990, over the same period in 1989.[34]

In Punjab, Indian and Pakistani infantry were reported to be in frontline bunkers, but the bulk of both sides' armor and artillery were held back in their cantonments. Across from the Lahore sector, the Indians had moved toward the border two infantry divisions, which were spread out into small unit formations, lending credence to the Indian claim that forces in Punjab were charged with a defensive, counter-infiltration mission.[35] Complicating military planning along the Punjab border was a 375-mile-long wall erected by India along the border, stretching from the Chenab River north of Jammu city in Kashmir to Fort Abbas, across from the Indian state of Rajasthan. The wall was actually two twelve-foot-high fences of barbed wire, set about twenty feet apart. Intermingled with the barbed wire in the fence facing Pakistan was electrified wire. The space between the fences was filled with concertina wire. Powerful searchlights, watch towers, and machine-gun nests lined the wall at intervals of 100–200 yards. According to Lieutenant General Alam Jan Mahsud, commander of the Pakistan Army's 4th Corps, the Indians had sealed the Punjab border so tightly that "not even a rabbit can slip through it."[36]

In Rajasthan, across from southern Punjab province in Pakistan, was a three-division Indian Army strike force, including one armored division. These forces were opposed by a Pakistani corps based in Multan, whose armored division remained in its cantonment. In all three regions, only one of the four armored divisions fielded by the two countries (two Indian and two Pakistani) was in an unusual position.

---

34. Subhash Chakravarti and Amit Roy, "Militants Fan War Fever Over Kashmir," *Sunday Times* (London), April 15, 1990; Clad and Ali, "Will Words Lead to War?"; James Clad, "Valley of Violence," *Far Eastern Economic Review*, May 24, 1990, p. 22; Zahid Hussain, "Protest Flag Becomes Focus of Kashmir Border Strife," *The Times* (London), April 24, 1990; Ahmed Rashid, "Kashmir Talks Too Far Off to Ease Rising Tensions," *The Independent* (London), April 16, 1990; and Jose Katigbak, "Indo-Pakistan Border Violations on the Rise, Says U.N.," *Reuter Library Report*, April 23, 1990.

35. Rashid, "Rising Tensions"; Christopher Lockwood, *Daily Telegraph* (London), April 20, 1990; and Salamat Ali, "Avoiding Action," *Far Eastern Economic Review*, May 3, 1990, p. 26.

36. Lockwood, *Daily Telegraph*; Mark Fineman, "Nervous Pakistanis Watch 'the Wall' and Indian Troops," *Los Angeles Times*, April 20, 1990; and Ali, "Avoiding Action," p. 26.

This was the Indian division that had been left behind in Mahajan after the February exercises. The other Indian and Pakistani armored divisions remained in their cantonments. Only the Indian division in Rajasthan was anywhere near the border, and none of the four divisions was moving, intact, toward the frontier. At the time, diplomats in New Delhi and Islamabad said they had detected "no troop movements that could be construed as anything more than logical precautions given the war of words between the two capitals."[37] As the Stimson Center's account of the crisis concludes, "the Indian military leadership deliberately refrained from moving armor associated with its strike forces out of peacetime cantonments," and Pakistan "deliberately refrained from moving its two strike corps to the front."[38]

MUTUAL PERCEPTIONS. The two countries' main concerns can be easily identified.[39] Decision-makers in both India and Pakistan were most concerned about the possibility of invasion at traditionally weak points in their respective defenses. For India, this vulnerability is the road connecting Jammu city in Kashmir with Pathankot in Punjab, which is a section of the only major ground link between the Vale of Kashmir and India proper; Pakistan had attempted to sever this link during the 1965 war. It will also be recalled from Chapter 3 that in 1947, India was forced to fly reinforcements and supplies to Srinagar, an operation it could certainly repeat, but not without substantial effort, in an environment where Indian cargo planes would be easy prey for sophisticated Pakistani interceptors. At a lower level of concern but a higher level of probability, analysts in New Delhi expected that Islamabad would continue its efforts to foment violence on the Indian side of the LAC. Pakistan could, at low cost, keep Indian blood spilling and Indian rupees hemorrhaging from the exchequer; it was also thought possible, though highly unlikely, that Kashmiri insurgents would succeed in their efforts to overturn Indian control of the state, which would allow Pakistan some role in the ultimate settlement of Kashmir's status.

Pakistan's perceived weak point was the area directly across from Indian Rajasthan state, particularly the Sukkur Barrage in Sindh. Islamabad's nightmare was a massive Indian armored thrust that

---

37. Malcolm Davidson, "Pakistani General Says More Indian Troops Deployed Near Border," *Reuter Library Report*, April 19, 1990.

38. Krepon and Faruqee, *1990 Crisis*, p. v.

39. This account is based on numerous interviews with senior Indian, Pakistani, and U.S. officials.

would have severed the vital road, rail, and communications links connecting the northern and southern parts of the country. Anti-government militancy had raged in Sindh since 1983, and the possibility of a Sindhi insurgency developing into a quest for statehood if Indian forces severed the province was not unthinkable to Pakistani leaders. Bangladesh provided a compelling precedent, and Brasstacks offered seeming evidence as to Indian intentions: why would the Indian military focus so intently on desert exercises if it were not poised to launch a conventional thrust into Pakistan from Rajasthan? Islamabad also had a secondary fear, which was that India would carry out more limited raids against militant strongholds in Azad Kashmir, forcing the Pakistani government into a response in order to appease public opinion at home.

INTERNATIONAL CONCERN AND THE GATES MISSION TO SOUTH ASIA

In April 1990, the United States and the Soviet Union began to exhibit alarm over developments on the subcontinent. Washington suggested a U.S.-Soviet appeal for restraint, but Moscow demurred. Instead, the two sides separately encouraged a tension-reducing dialogue between New Delhi and Islamabad. On April 18, Washington made its first senior-level public statement regarding the Indo-Pakistani troop buildup. Robert M. Kimmitt, the third-ranking official in the State Department, warned that "there is a growing risk of miscalculation which could lead events to spin dangerously out of control." Kimmitt urged the two sides to "take immediate steps to reduce the level of tension by lowering rhetoric and avoiding provocative troop deployments." U.S. alarm over events in South Asia crystalized in the middle of May with a visit to the region by Deputy National Security Adviser Robert Gates. The Gates mission's publicly stated objective was "to help both sides avoid a conflict over Kashmir, which would entail great loss of life, and damage to both countries, and to begin the sort of political dialogue which would not only reduce tension but could lead to a peaceful and permanent resolution of the Kashmir problem, as called for under the Simla agreement."[40] According to a former senior Bush administration official, though, the mission was actually intended to avert the immediate possibility of inadvertent escalation to war, not the longer term political problems besetting the Indo-Pakistani relationship.[41]

---

40. Al Kamen, "U.S. Voices Concern Over Kashmir," *Washington Post*, April 19, 1990; and "Regional Issues in the Upcoming U.S.-Soviet Summit," *White House Background Briefing*, Federal News Service, May 24, 1990.

41. Interview with former senior Bush administration official.

GATES IN ISLAMABAD. With Bhutto on a tour of the Middle East to solicit Arab support for Pakistan, Gates and Ambassador Oakley met with President Ghulam Ishaq Khan and COAS Mirza Aslam Beg on May 20. According to several accounts of the meeting, the main points made by the Americans were: Washington had thoroughly war-gamed a potential Indo-Pakistani military conflict, and Pakistan was the loser in every scenario; in the event of a war, Islamabad could expect no assistance from Washington; and Pakistan must refrain from supporting terrorism in Indian Kashmir, avoid military deployments that New Delhi could interpret as threatening, and tone down the war rhetoric. The Pakistani leadership responded defensively, claiming that India was using terrorist tactics in Kashmir, that Pakistani public statements had been moderate, and that Pakistani military movements had been less menacing than India's. Gates was assured, however, that Pakistani training camps for the Kashmiri militants would be shut down.[42]

GATES IN NEW DELHI. In India, Gates met with Prime Minister V. P. Singh, Foreign Minister I.K. Gujral, COAS V.N. Sharma, and Minister of State for Defense Raja Ramanna. In these meetings, his message was essentially the same one he had given the Pakistanis: avoid provocation that could spiral out of control. Gates relayed the Pakistani promise to shut down the training camps for Kashmiri insurgents and urged New Delhi to stop its own meddling in Pakistan's Sindh province. Gates also told the Indians that the United States was "prepared to offer its services in ensuring that the troops of the two countries were pulled back from the borders, and remained pulled back. He offered to share the information obtained by American spy satellites, which by keeping both sides fully and accurately informed could avert the danger that either would try to steal a march on the other."[43]

In sum, the gist of the Gates message was that it would be to neither side's advantage to go to war. India would win, but even if it did, the long-term costs would greatly exceed any short-term benefits.[44] Within two weeks of the Gates mission to South Asia, the crisis had

42. Seymour M. Hersh, "On the Nuclear Edge," New Yorker, March 29, 1993, pp. 67–68; comments of Robert Oakley and William Clark, in Krepon and Faruqee, 1990 Crisis, pp. 4, 8–9; and John F. Burns, "U.S. Urges Pakistan to Settle Feud With India Over Kashmir," New York Times, May 21, 1990. Pakistani officials later denied that they had agreed to shut down any training camps.

43. Hersh, "On the Nuclear Edge," p. 68, Krepon and Faruqee, 1990 Crisis, p. 4; and "The Killing of Hopes for Peace in Kashmir," The Economist, May 26, 1990.

44. Interview with former senior Bush administration official.

passed. In early June, India announced that the armor it had sent to the Mahajan range in February would return to its normal station. Pakistan responded cautiously at first, but grew more enthusiastic as it became clear that the Indians were, in fact, pulling back their forces. Analysts speculated that the withdrawal may have stemmed more from the searing summer heat in the Rajasthan desert than Indian magnanimity, but all agreed that moving armor away from the area where Pakistan considered itself most vulnerable was an important step in the right direction. New Delhi also put forward a package of confidence-building measures, which became a topic for discussion between the two countries' diplomats and contributed to the easing of the crisis atmosphere.

Analysis: Nuclear Dimensions of the Crisis

How did Indian and Pakistani nuclear weapon capabilities influence the 1990 Kashmir crisis? Three possibilities arise. First, the logic of nonproliferation suggests that nuclear weapons should exacerbate crises between their possessors, mainly by promoting preemptive instability. According to this reasoning, examined in Chapter 1, states with small, crude nuclear forces may fear losing those weapons in a crippling first strike by the adversary. This fear breeds a use-them-or-lose-them mentality in which absorbing a first strike is the worst possible outcome, while launching a first strike is the second-worst (and thus preferable) choice. The conventional wisdom on the consequences of nuclear proliferation strongly expects that the next time nuclear weapons are fired—either in anger or inadvertently—it will be the result of a crisis between two Third World states with small nuclear forces.

In contrast, the logic of nuclear deterrence posits a fundamentally different dynamic. According to this heterodox line of thought, also examined in Chapter 1, the main impact of nuclear weapon capabilities during crises is to deter war. Because of their obvious, awesome destructive power, even small nuclear forces provide robust deterrence. Analysts persuaded by this logic find it impossible to imagine realistic scenarios in which the leaders of a nuclear weapon state would choose to launch a nuclear first strike with no assurance of destroying all of the adversary's weapons, and thus with a real possibility of suffering utter devastation in return. Moreover, in addition to deterring nuclear strikes, nuclear weapon capabilities can be expected to deter conventional military attacks across established borders. For the logic of nuclear deterrence, the only military hostilities that are impervious to the effects of deterrence are unconventional operations, which often occur on territory that is disputed or remote from the adversaries' heartlands. (For a longer discussion of this point, see Chapter 2.)

A third possibility is that the effects of nuclear weapons on the outcome of the 1990 Kashmir crisis were negligible, i.e., that nuclear capabilities neither exacerbated nor dampened the crisis. For this to have been the case, however, leaders in New Delhi and Islamabad would have to have been ignorant of each other's capabilities, or would have to have perceived them to be insufficiently developed to constitute a threat. Given the nonproliferation community's unremitting efforts to publicize aspiring proliferants' nuclear transgressions, it is difficult to imagine bitter adversaries like India and Pakistan remaining unaware of each other's nuclear strides; indeed, as noted in Chapter 2, the natural tendency is to be vigilant lest the adversary achieve a technological breakthrough that would threaten one's own national security. It is possible, though, that leaders on either or both sides were aware of their rival's ongoing nuclear research and development efforts, but judged the fruition of those efforts to lie in the future. It will be recalled that this was the situation with Indian leaders during the Brasstacks crisis. In December 1986 and January 1987, Indian decision-makers like army chief K. Sundarji perceived Pakistan to be an aspiring, not an actual, nuclear power. However, as Chapter 5 and Sundarji's comment earlier in this chapter have demonstrated, this was no longer their perception by the spring of 1990. The intervening three years had established beyond a doubt that Pakistan was in fact nuclear weapon–capable. That being the case, the effects of nuclear weapons on the 1990 crisis could hardly have been negligible.

Thus we are left with two possibilities that closely parallel the debate in Chapter 1 between the logic of nonproliferation and the logic of nuclear deterrence. Two nascent nuclear powers, divided by a long border, a history of wars, and continuing animosity, made preparations for war over competing claims to a territory that had already caused two of the wars between them. The weaker of these two states, Pakistan, feared an invasion that might well have detached yet another chunk of its territory, for which the Bangladesh war of 1971 provided a precedent. The stakes could hardly have been higher than they were for Pakistan in 1990. Furthermore, both India and Pakistan had small, crude nuclear capabilities, which the logic of nonproliferation suggests should lead to pressures for the preemptive use of nuclear weapons. The analysis below demonstrates that, of the two perspectives, the logic of nuclear deterrence is better supported by the evidence from this case.

THE CONVENTIONAL INTERPRETATION: SOUTH ASIA'S NEAR-NUCLEAR WAR
Several accounts of the crisis have suggested that India and Pakistan were on the brink of a nuclear war in 1990, and that the timely intervention of the United States averted a catastrophe. The most prominent of these stories, by journalist Seymour Hersh, appeared in the *New Yorker* in March 1993. In text accompanying his story, the magazine claimed that "in the spring of 1990, Pakistan and India faced off in the most dangerous confrontation of the postwar era." Hersh himself wrote that "the Bush Administration became convinced that the world was on the edge of a nuclear exchange between Pakistan and India." He continued: "In the view of American intelligence, the weak governments in place in Pakistan and India in May of 1990 were willing to run any risk— including nuclear war—to avoid a disastrous military, and thus political, defeat in Kashmir." Hersh quotes CIA deputy director Richard J. Kerr as calling the crisis "the most dangerous nuclear situation we have ever faced since I've been in the U.S. government. It may be as close as we've come to a nuclear exchange. It was far more frightening than the Cuban missile crisis." Kerr added, according to Hersh, that "there's no question in my mind that we were right on the edge. This period was very tense. The intelligence community believed that without some intervention the two parties could miscalculate—and miscalculation could lead to a nuclear exchange." As Gates told Hersh, "there was the view that both sides were blundering toward a war" and "I was convinced that if a war started, it would be nuclear."[45]

THE HERSH THESIS. Hersh reports that, as the Kashmir crisis intensified, Pakistan, in response to India's build-up of conventional forces in Kashmir and Rajasthan, "openly deployed its main armored tank units along the Indian border and, in secret, placed its nuclear-weapons arsenal on alert." Specifically, he contends that

sometime in the early spring of 1990, intelligence that was described as a hundred per cent reliable—perhaps an NSA intercept—reached Washington with the ominous news that General Beg had authorized the technicians at Kahuta to put together nuclear weapons. Such

---

45. Hersh, "On the Nuclear Edge," pp. 56–57, 62–64, 66–67.

intelligence, of "smoking gun" significance, was too precise to be ignored or shunted aside. The new intelligence also indicated that General Beg was prepared to use the bomb against India if necessary. Precisely what was obtained could not be learned, but one American summarized the information as being, in essence, a warning to India that if "you move up here"—that is, begin a ground invasion into Pakistan—"we're going to take out Delhi."

Washington increased its satellite coverage of South Asia, which "sometime in May" yielded "photographs of what some offficials believed was the evacuation of thousands of workers from Kahuta." One analyst told Hersh that he thought that in the event of an Indian ground thrust into Sindh, Pakistan would "cut it off with a nuke. We thought they'd go for Delhi." The analyst further stated that "we thought the reason for the evacuation of Kahuta was that they expected a retaliatory attack by India." Soon thereafter, U.S. intelligence produced signs of a truck convoy moving from a suspected nuclear storage site to an air force base in the western Pakistani province of Baluchistan. Eventually, the analyst told Hersh, U.S. intelligence indicated that Pakistan "had F-16s pre-positioned and armed for delivery—on full alert, with pilots in the aircraft. I believed that they were ready to launch on command and that the message had been clearly conveyed to the Indians. . . . These guys have done everything that will lead you to believe that they are locked and loaded."[46]

VARIANTS OF THE NEAR-NUCLEAR WAR THESIS. Other journalistic accounts support Hersh's reconstruction of events. William E. Burrows and Robert Windrem claim that in May 1990, the CIA learned that Pakistan had finally converted its highly enriched uranium from gas to metal bomb cores, two of which were machined and "stored near the other components needed to make a complete weapon so the Pakistani bomb . . . could be assembled in as little as three hours." At some point during the crisis, Burrows and Windrem claim, these bombs were prepared for delivery. Although the U.S. national security community was unsure whether Islamabad had succeeded in making its F-16s nuclear-capable, Burrows and Windrem find "solid evidence" that Pakistani C-130 transport aircraft had been "reconfigured to drop an atomic bomb on New Delhi."[47] The *Far Eastern Economic Review* reported in 1992 that "according to

---

46. Ibid., pp. 56, 64, 65.

47. William E. Burrows and Robert Windrem, *Critical Mass: The Dangerous Race for Superweapons in a Fragmenting World* (New York: Simon and Schuster, 1994), pp. 61–62, 82. What this evidence is, the authors do not say.

leaks from the then V.P. Singh government in New Delhi, Gates was told by Pakistan's President Ghulam Ishaq Khan that in the event of a war with India, Pakistan would use nuclear weapons at an early stage. Gates subsequently relayed this to New Delhi."[48] A week after the Gates mission, the London *Sunday Times* reported that "new information in the hands of both superpowers suggests that" India and Pakistan "have been readying their nuclear arsenals." In a twist on the later Hersh story, the *Sunday Times* wrote that "American spy satellites have photographed heavily armed convoys leaving the top-secret Pakistani nuclear weapons complex at Kahuta, near Islamabad, and heading for military airfields. They have also filmed what some analysts said were special racks designed to carry nuclear bombs being fitted to Pakistani F-16 aircraft." Also, according to this report, "the Soviet Union has detected signs that" India's nuclear weapons "are being readied for use."[49]

ASSESSING THE CONVENTIONAL INTERPRETATION

These accounts of the crisis are subject to considerable doubt. Most damaging to their credibility have been the categorical denials by U.S. diplomats and military attachés posted in Islamabad and New Delhi during the spring of 1990. In particular, the U.S. ambassadors involved in the crisis decision-making, Robert Oakley in Islamabad and William Clark in New Delhi, directly contradict the central claims made by Hersh and others. Senior officials—U.S., Indian, and Pakistani—concur that, at a minimum, Hersh and other journalists exaggerated the nuclear dimension of the crisis. Hersh and others also have their defenders, though, who say that the dangers they described were real, and that those who disagree with their assessment are guilty of what one senior U.S. intelligence analyst calls "historical revisionism."[50]

PAKISTANI NUCLEAR ACTIVITY. There is little doubt that the Pakistani nuclear weapon program crossed an important threshold sometime during the early spring of 1990, although exactly when is uncertain. Oakley confirms that "the freeze on the Pakistan nuclear program was . . . removed. And the program began to move forward

48. Hamish McDonald, "Destroyer of Worlds," *Far Eastern Economic Review*, April 30, 1992, p. 24.

49. James Adams, "Pakistan 'Nuclear War Threat'," *Sunday Times* (London), May 27, 1990.

50. Interview with senior U.S. intelligence analyst.

again." By the time the Gates mission reached South Asia, Oakley remembers, "we had ascertained beyond a shadow of a doubt that the promises that Mrs. Bhutto had made and kept during 1989, and that the Chief of Army staff had made and kept during 1989, had been broken and the nuclear program had been reactivated." According to offficial U.S. sources, Islamabad had resumed enriching uranium at Kahuta as tension built with India.[51]

   Although Pakistan had apparently crossed the line drawn by the United States for compliance with the Pressler Amendment, Hersh's allegations about Pakistani nuclear delivery preparations have been disputed by the ranking U.S. diplomats in Islamabad and New Delhi in 1990. Summing up the nuclear dimension of the crisis, Clark remembers: "There was a little bit of nuclear tension: 'don't threaten me with yours because I've got mine.' I don't think it went beyond that. Nobody was loading weapons, and I'm not convinced they have weapons they can load."[52] Oakley and Clark also deny any knowledge of the possible NSA intercept that Hersh claims may have indicated that the Pakistani leadership had authorized the assembly of nuclear weapons. Oakley contends that the issue of Pakistan violating the Pressler Amendment "had nothing to do . . . at least so far as we knew, with the preparation or deployment of nuclear weapons. It had to do with other factors, which were required for certification." On the supposed evacuation of Pakistan's main uranium enrichment facility, Oakley says, flatly: "We know nothing about any evacuation of Kahuta." He further maintains that "so far as I can recall, we never had any credible evidence that the F-16s were fitted out to deliver a nuclear device; that Pakistan had a nuclear device that could be delivered by an F-16. . . . Nor did we know anything about any nuclear devices being moved from point 'x' to point 'y,' if there were any." Colonel Don Jones, who was the U.S. air force attaché in Islamabad at the time, is even more strident in his denial of Hersh's claims, particularly those relating to F-16s on strip alert, which he calls "the silliest allegation I read in the article, and there were a lot of silly things in the article. . . . some of the things he said were just on the face of it, ridiculous. It's not true." Jones adds: "The Pakistan Air Force F-16s were . . . all in sheltered revetments. You'd have to have a camera capable of seeing through three feet of concrete to

51. Krepon and Faruqee, *1990 Crisis*, pp. 7, 40; and R. Jeffrey Smith, "U.S. Stiffens Policy on Nuclear Arms, Pakistan Aid," *Washington Post*, November 20, 1990.

52. Interview with Clark.

know what was underneath. They did not leave their alert birds out in the open. . . . So from any aspect that you care to look at it, that particular statement simply . . . does not hold water. It's so silly that it . . . found its way into print astounds me." The moderator of the Stimson Center meeting, Michael Krepon, had the participants reiterate their recollections: "As I hear the answer to [the] question, at least with respect to the evacuation of Kahuta and this truck convoy with nuclear material in Baluchistan, and F16s armed or equipped to carry nuclear weapons, we have categorical 'No's'." Both Jones and Oakley responded, "so far as I know."[53]

WHY THE GATES MISSION? Hersh claims that the Gates mission was a direct outcome of signs picked up by U.S. intelligence that Pakistan was making nuclear delivery preparations. In fact, the embassies' concern was different: they believed that without timely intervention, Indo-Pakistani tension would develop an inexorable momentum toward war. As Oakley says: "Let me make this very clear. I tried to make it clear to Mr. Hersh and he diddled with it. But at least from Islamabad, we never believed, in part because of what we did see and in part because of the very good information which Bill [Clark] was getting from the Indian Army, that there was going to be an explosion in the spring of 1990." Rather, Oakley recounts, "we feared that if the momentum of this ratcheting up were not stopped by the fall, the prime fighting season, the two armies might be face-to-face again, as they had been at the time of Brasstacks, and the momentum would be so strong that it couldn't be stopped. So we wanted intervention in the spring in order to preempt something we feared might happen in the fall." Oakley elaborates on the nuclear element of the equation: "Despite what Hersh says—at least in Islamabad, we were not worried about a conflict becoming nuclear. There's always that potential, but there was nothing at that time to indicate that this was the case." Clark agrees, adding that "my views were not as apocalyptic" as Hersh's. "My comments really didn't fit his thesis, and so you will not find me in the article anywhere . . . He . . . chose not to use what I said."[54]

U.S. intelligence estimated at the time that there was a fifty-fifty chance of war.[55] As one former senior Bush administration official says, the U.S. view was that "there was a considerable chance of war. That said, no one could map out exactly what it meant. How serious

53. Krepon and Faruqee, *1990 Crisis*, pp. 20–22, 44–46.

54. Ibid., pp. 2, 4, 8, 39.

55. Interview with senior U.S. intelligence analyst.

it would go, how it might escalate, whether it would become a major conventional war, or something else; nobody knew exactly whether it would take place, much less how it might evolve." This official further recalls that the Indians and Pakistanis "were not acting with sufficient sobriety. There was a little bit of recklessness in the air. There was a little bit of blindness or forgetfulness about how destructive wars can be." Furthermore,

I think for most of us who were involved, nuclear weapons formed the backdrop for the crisis. . . . the concern was not that a nuclear exchange was imminent; the concern was that this thing was beginning to spin out of control and that would lead to clashes, potentially conventional warfare. Most of our analysis suggested that India would fare better than Pakistan, and that very early on, as a result, Pakistan might want to consider threatening . . . a nuclear action. Or, that India, thinking about that, would escalate conventionally very early on, to eradicate it.

According to this official, the Hersh article "exaggerated considerably the sense that there was kind of a situation where the nuclear trigger was cocked or something."[56]

Senior Indian and Pakistani decision-makers have also rebutted the Hersh thesis. General Beg, who Hersh claims authorized the assembly of nuclear weapons, "has staunchly denied" Hersh's version of events. According to one account, "he claimed that Pakistan did not possess a usable nuclear device at that time. Therefore his country could not have been poised to use such a weapon against India. Moreover, in his opinion, such readiness was unnecessary because Pakistan had not faced a critical or desperate situation. Furthermore, 'There was a solid fear of massive retaliation from India,' he recalled, 'as they [the Indians] have a stockpile of more than a dozen warheads'."[57] Beg's Indian counterpart, General Sharma, also scoffs at the notion of the Pakistanis preparing for nuclear war: "There is a lot of bluff and bluster from Pakistan. It is different to talk about something and totally different to do something. In return it is bluff and bluster from India that we would do this and that. In hard military terms your capability is not judged by the bluff and bluster, but by what you have in your pocket and what you can do with it."[58]

---

56. Interview with former senior Bush administration official.

57. Pervez Hoodbhoy, *Nuclear Issues Between India and Pakistan: Myths and Realities,* Occasional Paper No. 18 (Washington, D.C.: Henry L. Stimson Center, 1994), pp. 2–3.

58. "Bluff and Bluster."

The evidence presented in the Stimson transcript is devastating to the thesis that Pakistan was preparing in the spring of 1990 to launch nuclear weapons against India. Much of Hersh's analysis of the crisis, including his allegations about the evacuation of Kahuta, the movement of the truck convoy, and the F-16s on strip alert, come from an anonymous U.S. analyst whose interpretation of the intelligence data seems not to have been corroborated by anyone else. The evidence against Hersh's characterization of events comes from on-the-record discussions with multiple senior policymakers—U.S., Indian, and Pakistani—who were privy to the most highly classified intelligence information their governments could generate. The truth is further obscured by the fact that there were honest disagreements within the U.S. government over exactly what the Pakistani leadership was doing with its nuclear capabilities. As Oakley says, "ISI was putting out all sorts of messages." At least one intelligence analyst in Washington found these messages to be more credible than the diplomats in the field, which illustrates an institutional rift within the government. As a U.S. "nuclear-intelligence expert" reportedly told Hersh: "It's a warning situation, but they want smoking guns for everything."[59] A senior U.S. diplomat, now retired, responds that intelligence analysts often "worst-case" their judgments, piecing together fragments of information into an alarming "big picture" that may not correspond with reality.[60]

PAKISTANI NUCLEAR BLUFFING? It is also possible that Pakistani actions suggestive of nuclear delivery preparations were a colossal bluff. Without corroboration from Pakistani leaders, only a circumstantial case can be made for the claim that Islamabad devised a clever hoax to achieve its objectives in 1990. That evidence is compelling nonetheless. Pakistan certainly had the motive: it interpreted Indian deployments in Rajasthan as possible preparation for a massive conventional assault that could have severed the strife-ridden Sindh province from northern Pakistan. As tensions rose, Pakistani officials may have believed it necessary to do something dramatic to signal their deterrent resolve. Faking nuclear delivery preparations would have spurred the United States into action; Washington would intervene to ease the tension, or at least pass along its observations to Indian leaders, who would be deterred from any aggression they

---

59. Krepon and Faruqee, *1990 Crisis*, p. 18; and Hersh, "On the Nuclear Edge," pp. 65, 66.

60. Interview with former senior U.S. diplomat.

might be contemplating. Hersh's anonymous source said of the Pakistani truck convoy, "their big mistake was putting on more security than they needed." A contrary interpretation is that the Pakistanis put on just the right amount of security: enough to set off alarm bells in Washington. Burrows and Windrem note that the idea of a Pakistani bluff "was later given credence in some intelligence circles," especially considering that "the data collected by U.S. intelligence systems, far from being ambiguous, were almost unbelievably explicit."[61] To make an analogy to a court case, Pakistan had the motive and the means, and was at the scene of the crime. Missing is an eyewitness account of precisely what happened and a confession from the defendant.

THE IMPACT OF THE GATES MISSION. The Hersh article and the Burrows and Windrem book characterize the Gates mission as an unbridled success. In fact, early reports generally characterized the U.S. intervention as unsuccessful, while retrospective accounts support the notion that the mission achieved its aims. On May 24, three days after Gates met with Indian and Pakistani leaders, a senior administration official told reporters that the situation in South Asia "is deteriorating very rapidly and ominously."[62] With time, however, reviews of the U.S. peacemaking effort have grown more favorable. They range from positive (Gates helped to defuse the crisis) to neutral (the crisis was winding down anyway), with few informed people suggesting that the mission was a failure. The prevailing view among U.S. officials is that Islamabad and New Delhi publicly resisted the Gates message for domestic political reasons, but quietly used the intervention as an excuse to de-escalate the crisis. As Clark says: "At the end of the day, I think you could say that both Delhi and Islamabad used Bob Gates and his mission as an excuse, if you will, to back off of positions they had been taking."[63]

This judgment is not limited to U.S. decision-makers, who, after all, recommended the Gates mission and thus had a stake in its success. South Asian officials also view the U.S. intervention positively. As Abdul Sattar says: "I think that what is important is not what was happening in the months of January and February, but the projection of what might happen if the trends in motion were not arrested. And I think it is here that the American diplomacy deserves credit....

---

61. Hersh, "On the Nuclear Edge," p. 65; and Burrows and Windrem, *Critical Mass*, p. 85.

62. "Regional Issues in the Upcoming U.S.-Soviet Summit."

63. Krepon and Faruqee, *1990 Crisis*, p. 4.

What happened in the spring of 1990 is an illustration of good, useful preventive diplomacy." Clark reports that Indian officials, too, appreciated the chance to ease the tension: "I did have several senior people, including the Prime Minister, tell me afterwards that it had been a useful visit, it had allowed a way to back off for both sides, without one having to back down to the other."[64] In sum, few knowledgeable people would likely quibble with the views of a former senior Bush administration official:

At worst, you could say what we did was unnecessary. . . . I think that at the risk of sounding self-serving, it was a success. . . . my instincts are we slowed it down, we forced people to face up to the consequences. . . . What matters is sometimes that when you leave town, the internal debates that took place on either side were affected by what it was we said. . . . And my hunch is again we may have stabilized it by simply what we said. . . . we certainly didn't make the situation worse, and my guess is we made it better. The facts speak for themselves. If one looks at what South Asia was like, say June 15th, it looked a lot better than it looked May 15th.[65]

NUCLEAR WEAPONS AND THE GATES MISSION. As noted above, the *Far Eastern Economic Review* reported in 1992 that Gates relayed a nuclear deterrent threat from Pakistani to Indian leaders. Its essence was said to be that in the event of an Indian invasion of Pakistan, Islamabad would launch a nuclear strike against India. This story has gained credence due to its repetition by others, such as Burrows and Windrem in *Critical Mass*. It enjoys particularly wide currency in Pakistan, where it has become part of the country's nuclear lore. As one Pakistani analyst crowed: "Robert Gates told the Indians that we were mad enough to use the bomb and they believed him."[66] In turn, influential Indians deny that Islamabad sent any such signal. Says one: "Whatever Mr. Gates may have discussed with Pakistanis, no policymaker in India recalls his raising the issue of nuclear confrontation.[67] These contradictory positions are unsurprising, since the story implies a militarily stronger India buckling under pressure from a tenacious, nuclear-armed Pakistan, an image attractive to Pakistanis and abhorrent to Indians.

---

64. Ibid., pp. 20, 30–33.

65. Interview with former senior Bush administration official.

66. Charles Smith, "Atomic Absurdity," *Far Eastern Economic Review*, April 30, 1992, p. 25.

67. K. Subrahmanyam, "Down Memory Lane," *Economic Times* (Bombay), March 24, 1993.

Is the story true? Oakley and Clark both deny that Gates transmitted any nuclear deterrent message from Islamabad to New Delhi. Oakley says: "Certainly, it was not part of our dialogue." According to Oakley, Pakistan's crossing the line by converting highly enriched uranium from gas to metal "was a matter of discussion between Gates, myself, and the President and the Chief of Army staff, but not in the context of the Kashmir tension. It was a totally separate part of the conversation." Clark adds that the question of nuclear weapon use "was not an element that Bob Gates was using to frighten someone. How do you frighten someone with something he already knows, to start with? But no, it wasn't used in that context."[68] Those who repeat the *Far Eastern Economic Review* story fail to explain why Pakistani President Ghulam Ishaq Khan would make such a brazen statement to Gates, given the pressure Islamabad was under to conform to U.S. nonproliferation laws. The termination of U.S. economic and military aid would have meant the loss of $564 million annually for fiscal years 1990 and 1991.[69]

AN ALTERNATIVE INTERPRETATION: EXISTENTIAL DETERRENCE
PREVENTS WAR

A strong case can be made that India and Pakistan were deterred from war in 1990 by the existence of nuclear weapon capabilities on both sides and the chance that, no matter what Indian and Pakistani decision-makers said or did, any direct military clash could ultimately escalate to the nuclear level. The case for existential deterrence is admittedly circumstantial; as with all deterrence theory, tracing the causality of non-events is practically impossible. In this instance, one would have to get authoritative Indian and Pakistani officials to admit that they were planning to go to war, but were dissuaded from doing so by the possibility that conventional conflict might have escalated to a nuclear exchange. For two reasons, no leader would do this. First, such an admission would reveal that his country was actually planning to start a war, which would make it look bad internationally; second, backing down from such plans would imply national weakness. Having acknowledged the difficulty of "proving" that India and Pakistan were deterred from war in 1990 by the shadow of nuclear destruction hanging over them, what evidence suggests the plausibility of this interpretation?

68. Krepon and Faruqee, *1990 Crisis*, p. 40; and interview with Clark.
69. Susumu Awanohara and Salamat Ali, "Devalued Ally," *Far Eastern Economic Review*, February 14, 1991, p. 10.

CAPABILITIES, RESOLVE, AND SIGNALLING. India and Pakistan were objectively judged to be nuclear weapon–capable by 1990. New Delhi exploded a nuclear device in 1974; despite its subsequent nuclear restraint, statements by senior Indian officials throughout the 1980s left no doubt that India would reserve the right to deploy nuclear weapons if its security predicament demanded such a course. After the Brasstacks crisis, India increased its nuclear preparedness by stockpiling plutonium and by making qualitative improvements in weapon design and delivery capabilities. Beginning in the mid-1980s, Islamabad had been judged nuclear weapon–capable by the United States and the rest of the nonproliferation community in increasingly explicit terms. By warning of Islamabad's nuclear strides and exhorting Pakistan to refrain from developing nuclear weapons, Washington inadvertently gave credibility to a Pakistani nuclear deterrent where it mattered most—in New Delhi. Increasing evidence of India's and Pakistan's growing nuclear prowess in the 1980s raised mutual concerns that a fourth Indo-Pakistani war would be fought in the shadow of nuclear weapons.

Furthermore, the available evidence indicates that Indian and Pakistani leaders were acutely familiar with, and believed, these extra-regional assessments of each other's capabilities. In their military planning at the turn of the decade, both New Delhi and Islamabad operated on the assumption that the other side could quickly deploy nuclear weapons early in a war; and public statements by leaders in each country fueled profound concern in the other. As discussed in Chapter 5, senior Pakistani officials, including President Zia, had used the Brasstacks crisis to convey to India a sense of Islamabad's nuclear muscle. Between 1987 and 1990, notwithstanding their denials that Pakistan was a nuclear weapon state, Pakistani leaders at the highest levels often referred to a prevailing situation of mutual nuclear deterrence on the subcontinent. Indian statements were less pointed, but their net effect was the same. In sum, the evidence suggested that both sides were nuclear weapon–capable, while mutual mistrust meant that the opponent's capabilities loomed even larger than objective circumstances would warrant. In the area of intentions, public statements emanating from New Delhi and Islamabad during the late 1980s could leave no doubt that the two sides would be at least prepared to consider using nuclear weapons in the event of a future war.

There is also ample evidence that nuclear signals were both sent and received during the 1990 crisis. At the height of the war of words in April, Indian Prime Minister V.P. Singh took to the floor of the Indian parliament and warned Pakistan not to underestimate India's nuclear capabilities. His message was reiterated by former COAS K. Sundarji, one of India's leading nuclear strategists and a man whose public utterances were taken very seriously across the border. Clark remembers, too, that the Pakistanis made "slightly veiled threats" to the effect that "'we have something that will make you very sorry'." The Indians replied that "'if something happens, we will respond in the appropriate manner'." Clark says, "I know how to read that: 'we've got one too'."[70] Pakistan may also have signalled its resolve to deter a conventional invasion by making certain "visible" nuclear preparations or by insinuating such preparations. Until the relevant documents are declassified, we will not know the exact nature of Pakistani nuclear activities in 1990.

THE LOGIC OF NONPROLIFERATION UNREALIZED. Perhaps the strongest circumstantial evidence that existential deterrence "worked" in 1990 is that despite nearly every element of the logic of nonproliferation being in place, war did not break out. The 1990 crisis was a severe political conflict between two nascent nuclear weapon states. The struggle over Kashmir directly threatened each state's *raison d'être*. India and Pakistan were consumed by fundamental differences and plagued by weak leaderships and an uncertain international environment. Their command and control sophistication was limited, which that the logic of nonproliferation predicts should have led to intense pressures for preemptive nuclear strikes, either intended or inadvertent. In Pakistan, the military controlled the nuclear decisionmaking process, a circumstance that the logic of nonproliferation suggests should lead to at least the contemplation of offensive nuclear options. A shrill cross-border war of words created an overriding impression of impending conflict. Yet war did not erupt. Why? In an opaque nuclear competition, there is simply no way that Indian or Pakistani planners could have had confidence in launching an entirely successful nuclear first strike. Even at the height of the crisis, U.S. analysts were deeply divided over the precise nature of Pakistan's nuclear capabilities. As one said: "The intelligence community is divided as to whether this is a real threat or just bluff. Some people in the CIA believe Pakistan has nuclear weapons already, others believe they could put a bomb together in two weeks. A third faction thinks they may be as much as six months away from going

---

70. Interview with Clark.

nuclear."[71] Given this uncertainty, how could Indian leaders, with their lesser intelligence capabilities, possibly plan an effective pre-emptive strike?

THE LOGIC OF EXISTENTIAL DETERRENCE IN 1990. Unlike the Brasstacks episode, the 1990 crisis was driven by a serious political dispute that had already thrust India and Pakistan into two wars. India had the option of mounting offensive operations like air strikes against militant sanctuaries or supply routes, as many in India were urging. Alternatively, it could have launched a ground incursion across the LAC, with the aim of creating a defensive buffer zone. Existential nuclear deterrence provides the most compelling explanation of why New Delhi refrained from these actions. Indian leaders perceived Pakistan to be an aspiring nuclear weapon state in 1987, but an actual nuclear weapon state in 1990. Any lingering ambiguity about Pakistan's nuclear status had been erased by both the available evidence, provided by the nonproliferation community, and the public statements of Pakistani leaders, who signalled at every turn their country's capability to deploy nuclear weapons in a future conflict. Another way to look at this issue is to ask whether India would have refrained from attacking the Kashmiri militants' sanctuaries and supply routes in Azad Kashmir since 1990, absent the small but not negligible chance that such a course might escalate to the use of nuclear weapons. Given the carnage in Kashmir, the pinning down of hundreds of thousands of Indian soldiers, and the battering that India's human rights reputation has taken, the answer is probably not. In a nonnuclear South Asia, India would most likely have chosen to punish Pakistan for its transgressions in Kashmir, as it did in 1965. However, in the context of opaque nuclear capabilities and the existential deterrent effect they create, India was forced to limit its military operations to Indian-held Kashmir. In short, existential nuclear deterrence inhibited escalation from unconventional conflict to conventional or nuclear war.

NUCLEAR DETERRENCE EMBRACED IN RETROSPECT. As was noted in Chapter 5, senior Pakistani officials began talking about nuclear deterrence in South Asia as early as 1988. Before 1990, Indian commentary on the regional nuclear balance was more restrained: few analysts publicly accepted the thesis that nuclear weapon capabilities deter war between India and Pakistan. The Kashmir crisis brought about a pronounced shift in India's nuclear discourse. Although serving

---

71. Adams, "Pakistan 'Nuclear War Threat'."

officials still do not discuss nuclear deterrence in South Asia, other members of India's strategic elite now do. A quasi-official community, composed mainly of retired civil servants and military officers, has in the last few years closely examined the implications of regional nuclear capabilities for Indian security. For the most part, India's strategic thinkers now embrace the idea that nuclear deterrence dampens tendencies toward war between India and Pakistan, and that this phenomenon was especially apparent in 1990.

India's two most prominent nuclear strategists (along with two coauthors) observe that, unlike its predecessor nuclear weapon states, "India has been content to demonstrate capability, put basic infrastructure in place, and leave deterrence implicit and somewhat ambiguous. . . . It appears that atomic capabilities on both sides in the Indo-Pakistani conflict have so far led to a moderation in actions between the two states."[72] K. Subrahmanyam writes elsewhere:

The awareness on both sides of a nuclear capability that can enable either country to assemble nuclear weapons at short notice induces mutual caution. This caution is already evident on the part of India. In 1965 when Pakistan carried out its "Operation Gibraltar" and sent in infiltrators, India sent its army across the cease-fire line to destroy the assembly points of the infiltrators. That escalated into a full-scale war. In 1990 when Pakistan once again carried out a massive infiltration of terrorists trained in Pakistan, India tried to deal with the problem on Indian territory and did not send its army into Pakistan-occupied Kashmir.[73]

K. Sundarji concurs: "The chances of a conventional war between India and Pakistan have gone down considerably." He argues that "if you could go back to 1947 as a method of replaying events once again, but with the added change of a nuclear capability of this nature as a backdrop, I rather suspect that many of those three wars wouldn't have happened." While leaders on both sides once viewed war as a means to achieve certain policy objectives, "today I don't think the same calculus can apply." Sundarji adds that, because of nuclear deterrence, the menu of Indian responses to Pakistani provocation in Indian-held Kashmir no longer includes launching a bold

---

72. M. Granger Morgan, K. Subrahmanyam, K. Sundarji, and Robert M. White, "India and the United States," *Washington Quarterly*, Vol. 18, No. 2 (Spring 1995), p. 164.

73. K. Subrahmanyam, "Capping, Managing, or Eliminating Nuclear Weapons?" in Kanti P. Bajpai and Stephen P. Cohen, eds., *South Asia After the Cold War* (Boulder, Colo.: Westview, 1993), p. 184.

offensive thrust across the Punjab border. Of Indian leaders, he says: "The reason why they've hesitated to take recourse to their stated, avowed strategy of reacting in the plains conventionally is because of the nuclear equation. . . . I've got no doubt in my mind at all."[74] As a senior Indian general reportedly remarked, "what the nuclear capability does is to make sure the old scenarios of Indian armour crossing the Sukkur barrage over the Indus and slicing Pakistan in two are a thing of the past."[75]

As would be expected, faith in nuclear deterrence is even stronger in Pakistan. Abdul Sattar notes the "indispensable contribution" Pakistan's "nascent nuclear capability has made to deterrence of aggression and maintenance of peace."[76] Now retired, former President Ghulam Ishaq Khan and former COAS Mirza Aslam Beg have stated their belief that Islamabad's nuclear posture has prevented India from attacking Pakistan. As Beg says: "Far from talk of nuclear war, there is no danger of even a conventional war between India and Pakistan. . . . As compared to previous years, there is no possibility of an India-Pakistan war now."[77] Beg's comments also illustrate the usefulness of ambiguity: "The very fact that the people believe that we have the nuclear capability serves as deterrence. They keep repeating that we have the nuclear capability and we assert that we do not have it, and it is this state of uncertainty and ambiguity which serves as a meaningful deterrent."[78] Islamabad's perspective was best captured by Prime Minister Benazir Bhutto during her April 1995 visit to Washington: "Our nuclear program is peaceful. But if the existence of our technology and perceived capability has served as a deterrent to India—as a deterrent to a proven nuclear power that has gone to war against us three times in the last 48 years—I certainly have no apologies to make, not in Islamabad, not in New Delhi and not in Washington."[79] In sum, for many South Asians, it is now an article of

---

74. Interview with Sundarji.

75. Abdul Sattar, "Reducing Nuclear Dangers in South Asia," *Regional Studies* (Islamabad), Vol. 8, No. 1 (Winter 1994–95), p. 20.

76. Ibid., p. 3.

77. See "Ex-President Discusses Nuclear Program, Politics," *Foreign Broadcast Information Service (FBIS), Daily Report, Near East and South Asia,* July 26, 1993, pp. 69–71; and "General Beg Claims Country Conducted 'Cold' Nuclear Test," *FBIS, Daily Report, Near East and South Asia,* August 3, 1993, p. 56.

78. "General Mirza Aslam Beg's Major Presentations," *Defence Journal* (Karachi), June–July 1991, p. 41.

79. Thomas W. Lippman and R. Jeffrey Smith, "Bhutto: Deliver F-16s or Return Payment," *Washington Post,* April 11, 1995.

faith that nuclear weapon capabilities deter war between India and Pakistan. When it comes to nuclear deterrence, believing is seeing.

THE WEAKNESSES OF ALTERNATIVE EXPLANATIONS. The existential deterrence interpretation is also supported by the relative weaknesses of alternative explanations for South Asia's non-war of 1990. Explanations rooted in theories of learning and conventional deterrence are flawed for the same reasons discussed in Chapter 4. Another possible explanation for conflict resolution in 1990 is that both India and Pakistan were democracies, which, according to some international relations scholars, rarely fight one another.[80] This explanation, too, is easily discounted. In the first place, Pakistan was nominally a democracy in 1990, but as was noted in this chapter's introduction, Islamabad's most sensitive national security decisions were made not by Prime Minister Bhutto, but by the army and a civilian president with close ties to the army. Ghulam Ishaq and Beg simply were not subject to the pressures of public opinion, parliamentary oversight, and the like, which scholars suggest are the mechanisms by which democracies refrain from fighting one another. Equally important, there was no perception in New Delhi that it was dealing in 1990 with a like democracy, whose shared principles would compel the two sides to resolve their disputes on a peaceful basis. Indian officials had grown cautiously optimistic that Bhutto's election would herald new democratic momentum in Pakistan, but they had no illusions about the army's influence in Pakistani politics.

The available evidence suggests that in both countries, public opinion, a centerpiece of the "democratic peace" thesis, actually exacerbated rather than dampened tendencies toward conflict. Benazir Bhutto's initial instincts on the Kashmir crisis were dovish. It was only after sustained pressure from conservative opposition parties that her rhetoric on Kashmir grew more bellicose. Political pressure caused her to threaten war in Kashmir and to actively court support from the wider international Islamic community. In India, the V.P. Singh government faced relentless pressure from the newly influential BJP and the recently ousted Congress to take a tough stand against Pakistani transgressions in Kashmir. The BJP stridently advocated striking out at insurgent sanctuaries and supply routes in Pakistani Kashmir. Former prime minister Rajiv Gandhi also chided the government for its alleged weakness in addressing the Kashmir problem. It was in response to these provocations that Singh grew

---

80. Brown, Lynn-Jones, and Miller, *Debating the Democratic Peace.*

more hawkish and began warning Indians to prepare for war. Clearly, then, this explanation also fails to capture the essence of conflict resolution in 1990.

All in all, the case for existential deterrence is strong, albeit ultimately unprovable. Although no single cause can explain complex decisions involving war and peace, existential deterrence seems most powerfully to explain how the 1990 crisis was resolved without war. The alternatives are deficient, for the reasons I have described. If the 1986–87 Brasstacks crisis marked Pakistan's debut as a perceived nuclear weapon state, the 1990 Kashmir crisis institutionalized existential nuclear deterrence as the chief foundation for peace in South Asia. Chapter 7 assesses how well the subcontinent's nuclear history—examined in Chapters 3 through 6—matches the theoretical expectations generated in Chapters 1 and 2.

Chapter 7

Lessons and Implications

The goal of this study has been to examine the consequences of nuclear proliferation in South Asia. I have tried to assess the impact of maturing nuclear weapon capabilities on Indo-Pakistani relations, especially during a critical period from December 1986 to May 1990, when two crises brought Islamabad and New Delhi to the brink of a fourth war. Chapter 1 surveyed and analyzed the ongoing debate over the effects of proliferation, in order to provide a conceptual framework for the subsequent empirical analysis. I divided this debate's opposing arguments into two composite logics, each of which yielded a set of expectations about the dynamics of the Indo-Pakistani nuclear arms competition. Broadly, my theoretical analysis suggested that nuclear weapon capabilities should deter war in South Asia, but that the dangers of loose nukes are a distinct and more worrisome question. In Chapter 2, I explored the logic of opaque nuclear proliferation and then developed a theory of existential deterrence under conditions of opacity. I argued that deterrence in this situation is achieved via tacit bargaining between the proliferants themselves and inadvertent transparency-building by the international nonproliferation community.

In Chapter 3, I provided a brief historical overview of the Indo-Pakistani security rivalry and the early years of the South Asian nuclear arms competition. Chapter 4 contained a case study of the 1986–87 Brasstacks crisis, in which a series of large Indian military exercises evolved into an intense competitive mobilization—and nearly a war—between New Delhi and Islamabad. My interpretation was that the nascent Indian and Pakistani nuclear weapon capabilities had little discernible influence on the outcome of the crisis, which was resolved peacefully because there was no compelling political dispute driving either side to a decision for war. However, Brasstacks had a profound impact on subsequent South Asian nuclear developments by fueling weaponization momentum in both India and Pakistan. In a process I described in Chapter 5, Islamabad intensified its efforts to achieve a deliverable nuclear weapon capability and loudly projected itself as a nuclear power; meanwhile, New Delhi enhanced its own nuclear preparedness and signalled that it would never put its military forces at a nuclear disadvantage *vis-à-vis* Pakistan. By 1990, each side viewed the other as an actual—not aspiring—nuclear weapon state. Chapter 6 contained a case study of the 1990 Kashmir crisis, which was resolved without war mainly because of the pacifying effects of existential nuclear deterrence. Unlike in 1986–87, a severe political dispute created strong incentives to resort to military force; these were countered, though, by even more powerful disincentives: unambiguous Indian and Pakistani nuclear capabilities and the possibility that any military hostilities could ultimately lead to a nuclear exchange.

In this chapter, I examine what lessons we can draw from the South Asian nuclear experience. The following section is a brief overview of regional nuclear developments from 1990 to 1997. Then I revisit the Chapter 1 debate about the consequences of nuclear proliferation. For each element of the debate, I ask which logic is better supported by evidence from the Indo-Pakistani nuclear arms competition. Overall, my analysis suggests that the Indo-Pakistani nuclear experience more closely matches the expectations of the logic of nuclear deterrence than the logic of nonproliferation, which goes against the conventional wisdom. Next, I examine the wider implications of this conclusion for proliferation scholarship, nuclear deterrence theory, and security studies in general. I then revisit the subject of Chapter 2 by refining the small literature on opaque nuclear proliferation, based on new evidence from the South Asia case. The concluding section of this study analyzes the prospects for subcontinental strategic stability and nuclear arms control.

South Asian Nuclear Developments, 1990–97

In October 1990, George Bush refused to certify that Pakistan did not possess a nuclear explosive device, thereby terminating all U.S. economic and security assistance to Islamabad. The aid cutoff was a direct result of Pakistani decisions during that spring's Kashmir crisis. As discussed in Chapter 6, Islamabad had resumed enriching uranium, machined nuclear bomb cores, and undertaken activities that some U.S. intelligence analysts interpreted as preparations to deliver nuclear weapons against India. Also, with the Soviet Union having vacated Afghanistan in 1989, the United States no longer felt compelled to give Pakistani protestations of nuclear innocence the benefit of the doubt. Islamabad's first official admission that it maintains unassembled nuclear weapons came in February 1992, when Foreign Secretary Shahryar Khan told the *Washington Post* that "the capability is there." Pakistan, he continued, possesses "elements which, if put together, would become a device." The Pakistani diplomat also said that Islamabad had in 1991 frozen its production of highly enriched uranium and bomb cores, but would not destroy its existing cores unless India reciprocated.[1] Islamabad's ambassador to the United States, Syeda Abida Hussain, reiterated her government's position a few days later, when she told a group at George Washington University: "We have achieved the ability and we have imposed a restraint. We do not roll back; we do not advance."[2]

The timing of these February 1992 declarations by senior Pakistani diplomats was suggestive. Subcontinental tension had risen dramatically due to a planned march by thousands of supporters of the Jammu and Kashmir Liberation Front (JKLF), a group of Islamic militants who championed Kashmiri independence from both India and Pakistan. The marchers were to cross from Pakistan-controlled to Indian-controlled Kashmir, where they planned to step up their insurgency against New Delhi. Before they could do so, though, the militants were attacked by a Pakistani government that was demonstrably nervous about losing control of the situation in Kashmir. Pakistani police opened fire on the marchers and dynamited avalanches of boulders and trees to block the roads leading to the Line of Actual Control (LAC). At least 12 JKLF supporters were reportedly killed, with another 150 injured.[3] The idea of a government in Islamabad killing Muslims in the disputed territory of

---

1. R. Jeffrey Smith, "Pakistan Can Build One Nuclear Device, Foreign Official Says," *Washington Post*, February 7, 1992. U.S. intelligence analysts reportedly confirmed that Pakistan had frozen its production of fissile material. See Emily MacFarquhar, "Breaking a Chain Reaction," *U.S. News and World Report*, March 9, 1992, p. 42.

2. "Pakistan Stands Firm on Nuclear Threshold," *Washington Times*, February 11, 1992.

3. "'Suicide March' in Kashmir Leaves 12 Dead," *Toronto Star*, February 13, 1992.

Kashmir lends powerful support to the conclusion that India and Pakistan are much more alarmed by the possibility of war than they were in South Asia's pre-nuclear era; so does the fact that Indian and Pakistani leaders worked together to defuse the 1992 crisis by communicating over their military hotline. The Indian Army even praised Pakistani officials for "taking proper steps to prevent the JKLF activists from crossing" the LAC.[4] At a news conference after the march had been halted, Pakistani Prime Minister Nawaz Sharif was terse about his motivations in ordering the police attacks: "We've had three wars with India. We don't want to have a fourth war."[5]

U.S. POLICY UNDER PRESIDENT CLINTON

Since coming to office in January 1993, the Clinton administration has pursued an ostensibly new approach to the South Asian nuclear arms competition. Its overall policy seeks "to first cap, then reduce, and eventually eliminate" Indian and Pakistani "capabilities to produce nuclear weapons and ballistic missiles."[6] In essence, this policy aims at freezing the subcontinent's nuclear equation short of an overt arms race. The administration's main initiative concerns the 1989 U.S. sale of F-16s to Pakistan, discussed in Chapter 5. Although Islamabad paid $650 million for twenty-eight of the aircraft, Washington held up their delivery as part of the 1990 Pressler Amendment aid cutoff. After a January 1995 visit to South Asia, Defense Secretary William J. Perry said that the suspension of U.S. aid to Pakistan has "not brought about the policy goals of the amendment's supporters. In fact, the weakening of Pakistan's conventional forces which resulted from this amendment has led Pakistan's leaders to conclude that the nuclear capability is even more important to maintaining security in their country." He continued: "This amendment is a blunt instrument. I saw no evidence that it has increased our influence or leverage with Pakistan. To the contrary, I saw ample

---

4. Mushahid Hussain, "South Asia: Back from the Brink of War in Kashmir," *Inter Press Service*, February 14, 1992.

5. "Pakistan Fires on Kashmiri Marchers; 12 Die," *Chicago Tribune*, February 13, 1992. Out of office two years later, Sharif said he could "confirm that Pakistan possesses the atomic bomb." According to Sharif, his admission was meant to "preempt Indian aggression against Azad Kashmir," which he warned could lead to a "nuclear holocaust." See "Pakistani is Rebuked on A-Bomb Remark," *New York Times*, August 25, 1994; and Ahmed Rashid, "Nuclear Gambit," *Far Eastern Economic Review*, September 8, 1994, p. 21.

6. Office of the Secretary of Defense, *Proliferation: Threat and Response* (Washington, D.C.: U.S. Government Printing Office, 1996), p. 35.

evidence that it has undermined the influence that we formerly had there."[7] Then, during an April 1995 visit to Washington, Prime Minister Benazir Bhutto urged U.S. leaders either to deliver the F-16s or return Islamabad's money. Her lobbying bore partial fruit that October, when Congress approved the transfer of $368 million in military equipment and spare parts purchased by Islamabad but not yet delivered due to the 1990 aid cutoff. Conspicuously absent from this one-time waiver of the Pressler Amendment (known as the Brown Amendment after its sponsor, Senator Hank Brown of Colorado) were Islamabad's F-16s, but the United States promised to search for a new buyer so that Pakistan's money could be returned. All in all, the Clinton administration's policy is remarkably similar to that pursued by the Reagan administration throughout the 1980s: its main goal is to provide sufficient security reassurance to Pakistan that Islamabad will not be tempted to move in the direction of overt nuclear weapon deployments.[8]

SOUTH ASIAN NUCLEAR AND DELIVERY CAPABILITIES
The Pentagon estimated in 1996 that India has a "stockpile of fissile material sufficient for fabricating several nuclear weapons and could probably assemble at least some of these weapons within a short time." Pakistan "possesses all the components necessary for producing a nuclear device, and it probably has sufficient fissile material now to assemble a few nuclear weapons." According to this assessment, both New Delhi and Islamabad "have aircraft capable of delivering" nuclear weapons, with the "most likely platforms" being the Indian Mirage 2000, MiG-27, MiG-29, and Jaguar, and the Pakistani F-16 and Mirage III.[9] Regarding other potential nuclear delivery systems, India has completed testing and begun production of the *Prithvi*-150, a mobile ballistic missile capable of delivering a 2,200 pound warhead ninety miles. Seventy-five *Prithvi*-150s are said to be in service. New Delhi is also developing more advanced missiles, including the *Agni*, which can carry a 2,200-pound warhead to a range of 1,550 miles. Pakistan is believed to have purchased thirty

---

7. Secretary of Defense William J. Perry, Address to the Foreign Policy Association, New York, January 31, 1995.

8. For a longer discussion and critique of the first Clinton administration's nuclear policies in South Asia, see Devin T. Hagerty, "South Asia's Nuclear Balance," *Current History*, April 1996, pp. 165–170.

9. Secretary of Defense, *Proliferation*, pp. 36–41.

M-11 ballistic missiles from China. The M-11, which may be operational, can deliver an 1,100-pound warhead roughly 190 miles. Open sources do not reveal whether either New Delhi or Islamabad has successfully miniaturized nuclear warheads for delivery by missiles, and the precise operational status of the Indian *Prithvi*-150 and Pakistani M-11 is uncertain.[10]

INDIAN AND PAKISTANI NUCLEAR POLICIES

While refining their nuclear weapon capabilities and keeping their deployment options open, New Delhi and Islamabad also remained aloof from two significant developments in the nonproliferation regime. Despite strong pressure, neither country signed the Nuclear Non-Proliferation Treaty (NPT) during the intense diplomatic activity preceding the treaty's indefinite extension in May 1995.[11] Their longstanding positions on the NPT remain intact: India regards the treaty as a fundamentally discriminatory document, which separates the world into legitimate and illegitimate nuclear weapon states, solely on the basis of when countries first acquired a nuclear explosive capability. Indian policymakers understandably view as unjust the fact that China's 1964 nuclear test gained Beijing membership in the nuclear club, while India's 1974 test branded it a nuclear outlaw. For its part, Islamabad continues to claim that it will sign the NPT if and when New Delhi does, but not a moment sooner.

THE COMPREHENSIVE TEST BAN TREATY. New Delhi and Islamabad also bucked international momentum toward a complete cessation of nuclear explosive testing. Late 1995 brought a flurry of media reports suggesting that India was preparing for a second nuclear test in the Rajasthan desert.[12] A subsequent U.S. government analysis

10. *India-Pakistan Nuclear and Missile Proliferation: Background, Status, and Issues for U.S. Policy* (Washington, D.C.: Congressional Research Service, December 16, 1996), pp. 12–18. New Delhi's intentions for the *Agni* missile are uncertain. In December 1996, the Indian defense ministry announced that it had no plans to deploy the *Agni*. See "India Shelves Agni IRBM Program," *Arms Control Today*, January/February 1997, p. 27. However, Indian Prime Minister Deve Gowda told parliament in March 1997 that his government would give "full support to the scientists working on this programme." *Times of India News Service*, March 5, 1997.

11. For a concise discussion of the treaty extension process and related issues, see Lewis A. Dunn, "High Noon for the NPT," *Arms Control Today*, July/August 1995, pp. 3–9.

12. Tim Weiner, "India Suspected of Preparing for A-bomb Test," *New York Times*, December 15, 1995; and R. Jeffrey Smith, "Possible Nuclear Arms Test by India Concerns U.S.," *Washington Post*, December 16, 1995.

determined that activity at India's Khetolai military range was indeed "consistent with nuclear test preparations, planned *Prithvi* field testing, or a combination of both."[13] As it became apparent in 1996 that the declared nuclear powers would soon agree to a Comprehensive Test Ban Treaty (CTBT), Indian opposition to such a pact intensified. New Delhi argued that the anticipated CTBT would solidify the division of countries into nuclear haves and have-nots. Continuing to resist such "nuclear apartheid," India instead championed a firm timetable for total nuclear disarmament, an initiative that the five acknowledged nuclear weapon states resolutely opposed. The CTBT's entry into force was made contingent on the adherence of the "threshold" nuclear states, i.e., India, Israel, and Pakistan. New Delhi succeeded in blocking passage of the treaty at the United Nations Conference on Disarmament, but the CTBT was then adopted overwhelmingly by the UN General Assembly. Washington, Moscow, Beijing, London, Paris, and Jerusalem have since signed the pact. Islamabad voted for the CTBT in the General Assembly, but has refused to sign the treaty until India does.[14]

The Consequences of Nuclear Proliferation in South Asia: Implications for Theory

Twenty-five years have now passed since the last Indo-Pakistani war. During that period, both New Delhi and Islamabad have moved steadily down the path of opaque nuclear weaponization. South Asia's long transition to nuclear weapons has seen two crises and several additional instances of serious tension between India and Pakistan. A quarter-century of peaks and valleys in one of the contemporary world's most volatile relationships is enough time to begin drawing some meaningful conclusions about the effects of nuclear proliferation in South Asia, and about how well this empirical evidence matches the two logics that I surveyed and analyzed in Chapter 1.

As I noted in this chapter's introduction, the Indo-Pakistani experience with nuclear weapon capabilities lends more support to the

---

13. Vipin Gupta and Frank Pabian, "Investigating the Allegations of Indian Nuclear Test Preparations in the Rajasthan Desert: A CTB Verification Exercise Using Commercial Satellite Imagery," *Science and Global Security*, Vol. 6 (1996), p. 144.

14. *India-Pakistan Nuclear and Missile Proliferation*, p. 24; and "The Signing of the Comprehensive Test Ban Treaty," *Arms Control Today*, September 1996, pp. 8–14.

logic of nuclear deterrence than to its competitor, the logic of non-proliferation. All but a handful of proliferation analysts would expect that South Asia's small, crude nuclear forces; intense, high-stakes political conflicts; history of warfare; and possibly irrational decision-making should add up to a formula for nuclear disaster on the subcontinent. Indeed, for those analysts persuaded by the logic of nonproliferation, the Indo-Pakistani nuclear-security competition could serve as a paradigm for every conceivable calamity that might ensue from the spread of nuclear weapons to Third World countries. However, contrary to these grim expectations, nuclear weapons evidently deter war in South Asia, much as they did between the United States, the Soviet Union, and China during the Cold War. As in the U.S.-Soviet, Sino-U.S., and Sino-Soviet cases, preventive nuclear strikes were early on considered and rejected, first-strike uncertainty has dampened the "reciprocal fear of surprise attack," and loose nukes fears have gone unrealized. Furthermore, Indian and Pakistani decision-makers appear to be no less deterrable than their U.S., Russian, and Chinese counterparts. These two-and-a-half decades of subcontinental peace stand in stark contrast to the first twenty-five years of Indo-Pakistani relations, which saw war erupt on three different occasions, including twice over Kashmir.

THE TWO LOGICS: EXPECTATIONS AND OUTCOMES

In Chapter 1, for each element in the debate over proliferation's effects, the logic of nonproliferation and the logic of nuclear deterrence yielded competing expectations. In this section, I will briefly reiterate those arguments and ask two key questions: does the evidence from South Asia's nuclear rivalry support the logic of nonproliferation or the logic of nuclear deterrence? Alternatively, is the evidence available at this time too skimpy to be conclusive one way or the other?

THE QUANTITATIVE ARGUMENT. The logic of nonproliferation holds that any increase in the number of nuclear powers inevitably increases the risks of nuclear weapon use, either intended or inadvertent. Each new nuclear pair will be subject to nuclear instability, cumulatively raising the chances of a nuclear war over time. To the contrary, the logic of nuclear deterrence posits that each new pair of nuclear weapon states will generate a deterrent relationship similar to the one that existed between the United States and the Soviet Union during the Cold War.

Obviously the addition of two South Asian nuclear decision centers to the global mix has not resulted in the dire outcomes predicted by the logic of nonproliferation. Indeed, the fact that New Delhi and Islamabad can now threaten each other with nuclear devastation may be the chief reason for the relatively peaceful Indo-Pakistani relationship over the last twenty-five years.[15] However, despite the fact that the South Asian experience seems to support the logic of nuclear deterrence, I categorically reject the idea that we can specify with any quantitative sophistication what the consequences would be if additional states were to develop nuclear weapons; the effects of proliferation in any particular region will depend to a great extent on that region's distinctive history, geography, political dynamics, and other variables. I will return to this theme below.

THE GEOPOLITICAL ARGUMENT. Supporters of the logic of nonproliferation believe that the geopolitical conditions that characterize most Third World regions make nuclear weapon use more likely in those regions than it was in the superpower balance. Not only will political conflicts, crises, and wars be more frequent, but the stakes in these altercations will be so high that they might simply overwhelm any nuclear deterrent restraint. Proponents of the logic of nuclear deterrence counter that the deterrent power of nuclear weapons is so strong that it will be impervious to such considerations. Within this argument, though, lies one area of convergence between the two logics: proliferation analysts of both persuasions worry that new proliferants may have so little time to adjust to being nuclear weapon–capable before conflict erupts that the ultimate result may be nuclear war between "immature" nuclear states.

---

15. A secondary factor has been the more lopsided balance of power between the two countries since the 1971 Bangladesh war, especially in that war's immediate aftermath. This power asymmetry between India and the rump Pakistan was so pronounced throughout the 1970s and early 1980s that Pakistan had no desire to challenge India, and India felt no threat from Pakistan. This raises an interesting question: did Pakistan's achievement of a nuclear weapon capability in the late 1980s embolden Islamabad to take advantage of the unrest in Indian-controlled Kashmir in 1990 and thereafter? This argument is logically and circumstantially plausible, but I have discovered no evidence to support it. As with the broader issue of proving that deterrence has worked in a given case, no Pakistani leader would admit publicly that his government is being more aggressive in Kashmir due to the deterrent insurance provided by Pakistani nuclear capabilities. I have attempted to resolve this question in my own mind, but the methodological hurdles have seemed too high. For more intrepid scholars, the place to begin is Glenn Snyder's discussion of the "stability-instability" paradox in the U.S.-Soviet nuclear relationship. See his "The Balance of Power and the Balance of Terror," in Paul Seabury, ed., *The Balance of Power* (San Francisco: Chandler, 1965), pp. 184–201.

Here the South Asian experience supports a stronger version of the logic of nuclear deterrence than even its supporters are willing to expound. India and Pakistan have for fifty years now been embroiled in a tense security rivalry, which has often erupted in crises and wars. The Kashmir dispute and other cross-border tensions have made the stakes extremely high for decision-makers in New Delhi and Islamabad. Within this broad historical context, the months from late 1986 to early 1990 saw two crises break out during the very period when India and Pakistan were in that opaque netherworld somewhere between nuclear and nonnuclear status. Despite these circumstances, the two sides have fought no wars since the beginning of South Asia's nuclear era in 1972.

Furthermore, at no time since 1990 has the intensity of the Kashmir insurgency—in which New Delhi and Islamabad have supported opposing combatants for more than eight years—overwhelmed the countervailing effects of nuclear deterrence by escalating into conventional or nuclear war. This was especially evident during the 1990 crisis itself, when India had every reason to go on the offensive in response to Pakistani meddling in Indian-controlled Kashmir, but refrained from doing so. Also, the fact that the 1990 crisis was in significant ways a repeat of the events preceding the 1965 war— that the ultimate outcome was very different in South Asia's nuclear era— lends convincing empirical support to the logic of nuclear deterrence.

THE COMMAND AND CONTROL ARGUMENT. The logic of nonproliferation maintains that the crude command and control arrangements that are likely to govern small Third World nuclear forces will be subject to intense preemptive pressures during international crises, and to accidental or unauthorized nuclear use during domestic unrest. In contrast, analysts persuaded by the logic of nuclear deterrence argue that the powerful deterrent effect of nuclear weapons will dampen preemptive tendencies during crises, and that loose nukes are a less daunting challenge than proliferation pessimists believe.

The evidence from South Asia strongly rebuts the notion that there is any inevitability to preemptive nuclear escalation during crises between states with small, crude nuclear capabilities. Here, too, both the Brasstacks and Kashmir crises are instructive. Although we know now that India and Pakistan had not yet weaponized their nuclear capabilities by early 1987, decision-makers during the Brasstacks crisis had no way of knowing that for sure. The February 1986 comments of Indian army chief General K. Sundarji bear repeating, because they exemplify this uncertainty: "There are enough indicators to suggest that Pakistan *has achieved or is close to achieving* a nuclear weapons capability."[16] Given the logic of nonproliferation's fear that new proliferants may first assemble their nuclear weapons in the heat of battle (see Chapter 1, footnote 30), India and Pakistan should have been subject to enormous pressures first to assemble, and then to "use or lose" their valuable nuclear weapons. Alternatively, if the two countries were at that time incapable of delivering nuclear weapons, the imperatives to launch conventional preemptive strikes against the opponent's nuclear installations should have been equally strong. Subsequently, during the 1990 Kashmir crisis—when India and Pakistan judged each other to be actual, rather than aspiring, nuclear weapon states—the logic of nonproliferation would again suggest that their leaders had every reason to move preemptively against one another during the rapid escalation of tensions. Based on what is known now, there is no sign whatsoever that Indian and Pakistani decision-makers were thinking along these lines during either crisis.

On the loose nukes question, the South Asian experience is inconclusive. I have unearthed no evidence to suggest that either the Indian or Pakistani nuclear program has ever suffered major accidents or security lapses, but neither country has seen serious domestic strife in areas where important nuclear facilities are located.

THE "UNDETERRABLES" ARGUMENT. According to the logic of nonproliferation, the spread of nuclear weapons increases the likelihood that they will one day fall into the hands of leaders whose insanity or radical political agendas will make them immune to any constraints on using the weapons. The logic of nuclear deterrence rebuts this viewpoint, arguing instead that even allegedly irrational rulers will be subject to the powerful influence of the nuclear shadow.

The Indo-Pakistani nuclear arms competition provides no confirmation at all of the logic of nonproliferation's worst fears in this area. South Asian leaders seem to be no less rational in their decisionmaking than their nuclear predecessors. In fact, if the subcontinental approach to nuclear deterrence is any guide, Indian and Pakistani leaders have accepted the fundamental principles of the nuclear revolution more readily—and thus more rationally—than did U.S. and Soviet leaders during the Cold War. The superpower competition generated an intense arms race, in which Washington and Moscow

---

16. Inderjit Badhwar, "The Thinking Man's General," *India Today*, February 15, 1986, p. 78 (emphasis added).

strove to develop technologies and doctrines that would somehow make nuclear weapons militarily usable. According to some accounts, the ultimate outcome of this competition was that two sophisticated, tightly coupled nuclear command and control systems brought the United States and the Soviet Union closer to unintended nuclear war than most people suspected at the time.[17] Indian and Pakistani officials are more respectful of the notion that nuclear weapons have great political, but hardly any military, utility. As George Perkovich writes, "wisdom may lie beneath the surface of casual nuclear discussions in South Asia. By intuition, calculation, or penury, military specialists in India and Pakistan appear to reject the hyper-elaborate intellectual and technical apparatus of the U.S.-Soviet nuclear competition." As one Pakistani general said regarding the "requirements" for survivable second-strike nuclear forces, "this is not our issue. It is your concern."[18]

THE PREVENTIVE WAR ARGUMENT. Analysts persuaded by the logic of nonproliferation worry that Third World states will be subject to preventive strikes either conventional or nuclear—during their precarious transition to nuclear weapons. Those convinced by the logic of nuclear deterrence believe that preventive strikes, especially nuclear ones, will be a highly unlikely feature of new nuclear rivalries. Here again, the South Asian experience provides compelling support for the logic of nuclear deterrence. Throughout the early 1980s, media reports suggested that India was seriously considering launching a preventive attack against Pakistan's nascent uranium enrichment plant at Kahuta. Short flight times would have made such an operation fairly easy, especially before the delivery of U.S. F-16s to Pakistan in 1983. Still, Indian leaders refrained from ordering preventive strikes for the reasons described in Chapter 3, the most important of which was the ease with which Islamabad could have retaliated against India's own nuclear installations. Later, in 1986–87, New Delhi could well have used the Brasstacks crisis as an excuse to destroy Kahuta and other Pakistani nuclear facilities; again, though, India chose no such course. All in all, then, the subcontinent's nuclear history buttresses the logic of nuclear deterrence in the area of preventive imperatives.

---

17. See, for example, Bruce G. Blair, *The Logic of Accidental Nuclear War* (Washington, D.C.: Brookings, 1994).

18. George Perkovich, "A Nuclear Third Way in South Asia," *Foreign Policy*, No. 91 (Summer 1993), pp. 88, 89.

SUMMARY OF FINDINGS. Table 3 juxtaposes this theoretical debate with evidence from the Indo-Pakistani case. Each row of the table depicts one of the six theoretical arguments reiterated above. I have split the command and control argument into its international (preemption) and domestic (loose nukes) consequences. Each column represents a possible conclusion about the match between theory and the South Asian experience. There are five alternatives: strong (S) support for the logic of nonproliferation (LNP), moderate (M) support for the logic of nonproliferation, inconclusive (INC), moderate support for the logic of nuclear deterrence (LND), and strong support for the logic of nuclear deterrence.

Table 3. The Consequences of Nuclear Proliferation: Theory and South Asian Evidence.					
	LNP			LND	
Argument	S	M	INC	M	S
Quantitative				*	
Geopolitical					*
Preemption					*
Loose Nukes			*		
Prevention					*
Undeterrables					*

In four of the areas—geopolitical, preemption, prevention, and undeterrables—the Indo-Pakistani nuclear arms competition lends strong support to the logic of nuclear deterrence. It does not do so in two other areas. Regarding quantitative arguments, I cannot accept the notion that stability or instability can be predicted solely on the basis of the number of nuclear powers. However, the subcontinental nuclear pair still provides support for a moderate version of the logic of nuclear deterrence's stance in the quantitative argument. Moreover, as mentioned above, the South Asian evidence regarding loose nukes questions is insufficient to be conclusive. To summarize my findings, in not one of these central areas of the debate does the Indo-Pakistani experience with nuclear weapon capabilities support the conventional wisdom about nuclear proliferation's effects.

IMPLICATIONS FOR PROLIFERATION SCHOLARSHIP, DETERRENCE
THEORY, AND SECURITY STUDIES

What are the wider implications of my research for proliferation
scholarship, deterrence theory, and security studies in general? Most
important, Indo-Pakistani nuclear dynamics lend further support to
our cumulative evidence that the chief impact of nuclear weapons is
to deter war between their possessors. There is no more ironclad law
in international relations theory than this: nuclear weapon states do
not fight wars with one another.[19] Although the number of such
states constitutes a small sample from which to derive such a sweeping generalization, the law's power is enhanced by the fact that it has
encompassed a wide variety of countries. Several of the most embit-
tered international relationships in the postwar era—between the
United States and the Soviet Union, the United States and China, the
Soviet Union and China, China and India, and India and Pakistan—
have now fallen under its rubric. Together, these states represent five
of the seven or eight major civilizations whose differences Samuel
Huntington predicts will be the "key issues on the international
agenda" in the post–Cold War world.[20] Also, the political nature of
these states spans a continuum from totalitarian (the Soviet Union
and China) to authoritarian (Pakistan) to liberal (the United States
and India). For years, scholars who are relatively sanguine about the
consequences of proliferation have been admonished not to read too
much into the circumstantial evidence that nuclear deterrence prevented war between the Soviet Union and the United States during
the Cold War. We now have evidence from a strikingly dissimilar
political, cultural, and geographical milieu that adds to our confidence in the logic of nuclear deterrence.

BLINDED BY ELEGANCE? The South Asia case calls into question the
conceptual utility of Thomas Schelling's "reciprocal fear of surprise
attack." The idea that nuclear weapon states in crises will inevitably
face strong, perhaps irresistible, pressures to preemptively strike
their opponent's nuclear forces is deductively appealing but empiri-
cally unsupported. Five decades of the nuclear age have witnessed
nuclear powers enduring several serious crises without succumbing
to the supposedly inherent logic of preemption. A less elegant but
apparently more accurate representation of nuclear reality is

---

19. I suspect that this law receives less attention than the democratic peace thesis
because of its disconcerting normative implications.

20. Samuel P. Huntington, *The Clash of Civilizations and the Remaking of World Order*
(New York: Simon and Schuster, 1996), p. 29.

McGeorge Bundy's notion of existential deterrence. Contrary to what we would expect to see if the reciprocal fear of surprise attack were the fundamental dynamic between nuclear powers in conflict, nuclear weapons seem to deter war by virtue of their very existence. In superpower crises over Berlin, Cuba, and the Middle East, the Sino-Soviet crisis of 1969, and the Kashmir crisis of 1990, the main impact of nuclear weapons on the disputants was to slow escalation to war. Rather than operationalizing the nuclear doctrines devised by their military planners, leaders have chosen instead to focus on how not to use the nuclear weapons they command. In the realm of pre-emptive imperatives, the historical record yields 100 percent correspondence with the expectations of the logic of nuclear deterrence and zero correspondence with the logic of nonproliferation, a curious fact considering the reciprocal fear of surprise attack's conceptual hold on U.S. strategists.

AREA STUDIES ARE STILL IMPORTANT. Notwithstanding these observations, the South Asia case also suggests the need to separate the general effects of nuclear weapons from the particular consequences of proliferation in specific regions. Nuclear weapons deter war, but patterns of proliferation and modes of deterrence will vary across strategic environments. For this reason, it would be fatuous simply to transfer lessons from the subcontinent to the Korean peninsula or the Middle East. Effectively analyzing the prospects for nuclear stability in these regions would require a delicate blending of sound strategic concepts, insights carefully derived from other nuclear arms competitions—including South Asia's—and an in-depth knowledge of regional history, cultures, geography, and politics.

WESTERN STRATEGIC THOUGHT: BREAK THE MOLD IF NECESSARY. These points have further implications for security studies in general. In the post–Cold War era, prudent analysts will judiciously merge useful strategic concepts from the social sciences with their extensive knowledge of different regions of the world. The decades-old debate about the efficacy of social science methodologies versus area studies expertise is pointless; it stands to reason that selectively fusing the two is the most useful way to analyze security (or any other social) issues. Unfortunately, many U.S. strategic analysts continue to view the rest of the world through the prism of U.S.-Soviet relations, which raises the possibility that we may profoundly misunderstand regional security dynamics. Instead, U.S. analysts should be prepared to question, modify, or even jettison the strategic concepts they have inherited from their Cold War predecessors.

As one illustration, many U.S. scholars would likely agree with Steve Fetter's assertion that "military organizations are more likely to favor offensive operations such as preventive and preemptive attacks."[21] In a Western political-military context, this may be a useful assumption, but in other contexts it may not be. In South Asia, none of the three Indo-Pakistani wars was instigated by military leaders whose enthusiasm for the offensive exceeded that of their civilian colleagues. In 1947–48, India's and Pakistan's senior military leadership was still composed of British officers whose main concern was to keep the two new states out of war. Blame for the 1965 conflict can be placed squarely on the shoulders of Pakistani Foreign Minister Zulfikar Ali Bhutto, a civilian, who goaded President Ayub Khan into a reckless preventive war against India. Similarly, responsibility for the 1971 Bangladesh war belongs mainly to three civilians—Bhutto, Indian Prime Minister Indira Gandhi, and Bengali nationalist Sheikh Mujibur Rahman.

To extend this example, Pakistan was far less disposed to challenge India under the leadership of General Zia ul-Haq from 1977 to 1988, in part because he had been a firsthand witness to defeat at the hands of superior Indian forces and realized that provoking India into war was good for neither the Pakistan Army nor the country at large. Indeed, many Indian leaders have quietly admitted that dealing with Pakistan under Zia's firm control was less vexing than managing relations with their neighbor's unpredictable civilian rulers. In short, civil-military relations may have very different dynamics in less developed countries than in industrialized, liberal democracies. In many Third World states, military officers are the best and the brightest, and the army is the most developed institution in the entire polity. Under such circumstances, it is not unusual to discover the populace hoping that the military will keep the civilian politicians in line, rather than vice-versa. Thus, even if it were true that "civilian control over the military is likely to be weaker in proliferant countries" (another common U.S. assumption that is belied by the Indian and Israeli cases), this will not necessarily "tend to increase the risk of nuclear use."[22]

When repeated time and again without sufficient scrutiny, theoretical assumptions become dogma. Like concepts, models,

---

21. Steve Fetter, "Correspondence: Nuclear Deterrence and the 1990 Indo-Pakistani Crisis," *International Security*, Vol. 21, No. 1 (Summer 1996), p. 180.
22. Ibid.

hypotheses, laws, and theories themselves, assumptions are tools meant to help us apply scientific or near-scientific standards to the analysis of social life. When they instead assume the status of theological tenets, their value is diminished. Simply put, some of the old assumptions about nuclear dynamics need to be converted into hypotheses and tested.

SOUTH ASIAN NUCLEAR DYNAMICS AND THE CONCEPT OF OPACITY
What does the South Asian nuclear experience tell us about the concept of opacity? This is an important question in a world where opacity has fundamentally supplanted overt nuclearization as the dominant mode of proliferation. Or has it?

OPACITY AND THE END OF THE COLD WAR. Benjamin Frankel, who invented the concept of opacity, argues that the Cold War's end "may make opaque proliferation a thing of the past." During the Cold War, India, Israel, and Pakistan enjoyed a measure of superpower protection, expressed a variety of treaties, agreements, and informal understandings. In a world without superpower patrons and thus with strengthened self-help imperatives, Frankel believes that "opacity would lose its usefulness, as the benefits associated with keeping one's nuclear capabilities opaque will diminish, while the rewards of an open nuclear stance will increase."[23]

But the concept's inventor may have underestimated its longevity. It could just as convincingly be argued that the end of the Cold War strengthens the imperatives of opacity. In the new international order, the great powers have fewer incentives to give other foreign policy goals priority over stemming proliferation. They can therefore bring more effective pressure to bear against nuclear proliferants. As discussed in Chapters 3 through 6, the United States during the 1980s placed a higher priority on defeating the Soviet Red Army in Afghanistan, with Pakistan's help, than on preventing Pakistan from attaining a nuclear weapon capability. Once the Soviets withdrew from Afghanistan in 1989, U.S. policy changed. After years of deeming Pakistan nuclear weapon–free, as a statutory condition for U.S. aid to Islamabad, the U.S. government refused for the first time in 1990 to make such a judgment. Since then, Islamabad has vigorously pursued the restoration of its ties with Washington, a policy that has dictated continued opacity, not nuclear openness.

---

23. Benjamin Frankel, "An Anxious Decade: Nuclear Proliferation in the 1990s," *Journal of Strategic Studies*, Vol. 13, No. 3 (September 1990), p. 2.

Furthermore, as Third World countries like India and Pakistan pursue policies of economic liberalization, they will rely more heavily than ever before on foreign benefactors, multinational investors, and international financial institutions. The post–Cold War great powers have used their influence, individually and within these institutions, to tie economic assistance to recipient-country restraint in developing weapons of mass destruction. This gives opaque proliferants another reason to keep their nuclear programs out of sight. Decision-makers in Islamabad and New Delhi know that if they test nuclear explosive devices, the economic penalties would be severe. New nuclear proliferants' diminished leverage over the great powers might make nuclear opacity as much an economic necessity as a defense policy choice. There is no manifestly superior logic to suggest that second-generation proliferants will abandon their opaque nuclear postures in the years ahead. Predictions are hazardous, but this analysis suggests that all future proliferants will nuclearize in an opaque fashion.

THE RESILIENCE OF SOUTH ASIAN OPACITY. This argument is supported by the most recent developments in the Indian and Pakistani nuclear weapon programs, as discussed above. For example, few policymakers on either side of the Indo-Pakistani border know the exact operational status of the other state's ballistic missiles. Nor do these officials know conclusively whether their adversary can miniaturize nuclear warheads for delivery by those missiles, if in fact the missiles are deployed in such a way as to be used quickly. Further, neither government has any idea how many nuclear explosive devices the other side has, or whether it even stockpiles assembled devices. In sum, the fundamental dynamic of nuclear opacity in South Asia is intact: both India and Pakistan require the security reassurance provided by existential nuclear deterrence, but prevailing global norms prevent them from seeking it openly.

OPACITY AND ARMS CONTROL

In Chapter 2, I discussed the importance of thresholds in Thomas Schelling's theory of tacit bargaining. The South Asian nuclear experience indicates that India and Pakistan have reached a stabilizing threshold: an unspoken taboo on the overt deployment of nuclear weapons. If one or the other country took the step of overt nuclear deployments, the genie would be out of the bottle and the other side would almost certainly respond in kind. The result would likely be a less restrained nuclear arms race. The threshold provided by non-deployments or non-open deployments of nuclear weapons thus gives opaque nuclear balances a firebreak against unfettered arms racing. This taboo against open nuclear deployments is itself an arms control measure, one negotiated not formally through detailed agreements, but informally through tacit communication.

Opacity is also an arms control measure in the sense that it allows the leaders of these states the flexibility not to indulge in arms racing in the first place. Islamabad's freeze on the enrichment of uranium to weapons-grade falls into this category of self-restraint, as does the slowing of India's *Agni* ballistic missile program. It should be noted, too, that nuclear-related confidence-building measures between opaque proliferants are not impossible to negotiate. As discussed in Chapters 3 and 5, India and Pakistan agreed not to attack each other's nuclear facilities, without compromising their cherished opacity. On the other hand, if two countries in a regional nuclear arms competition are believed to have already deployed nuclear weapons, opacity can hinder more formal arms control agreements. Opaque proliferants see advantages to projecting ambiguity about their exact capabilities that would be compromised by making public to adversaries the details of their force postures, a prerequisite for formal arms control. Table 4 depicts this analysis.

Table 4. The Impact of Opacity.		
Proliferation Concern	Opaque Proliferation	Transparent Proliferation
Arms Racing	Tacit Threshold, Flexibility for Self-Restraint	Incentives to Race
Arms Control	Formal Agreements Less Likely	Formal Agreements More Likely
Preemptive Stability	Extremely Stable	Stable
Loose Nukes	Partially Secure	Potentially Insecure

Table 4 also summarizes two other implications of opaque nuclear postures, based on the theoretical analysis in Chapter 2 and the South Asian evidence from subsequent chapters. As discussed in Chapter 2, opaque proliferants should logically be more resistant to preemptive nuclear escalation than overt proliferants. Think of an Indian military planner trying to convince the prime minister that a nuclear first strike would definitely destroy all of Pakistan's potential second-strike capabilities. The military planner would have to account for all of Pakistan's assembled nuclear warheads, not to mention components, which are stored separately but which could be assembled within a few days. Alternatively, the military planner could try to target all of Pakistan's nuclear-capable aircraft, i.e., every F-16, Mirage III, and, for that matter, C-130 transport aircraft. But what about Pakistan's roughly thirty M-11 ballistic missiles, which may or may not be operational and which may or may not be fitted with nuclear warheads? Under these uncertain circumstances, what general officer would recommend going ahead with a preemptive first strike?

In addition, as I argued in Chapter 2, opacity may actually diminish the prospects for loose nukes problems. An opaque nuclear establishment's limited decision-making circle, obsessive secrecy, and small, perhaps unassembled, nuclear capabilities should logically reduce the likelihood of the accidental or unauthorized use of nuclear weapons. It bears reiterating, though, that I have found insufficient South Asian evidence concerning loose nukes challenges to add any empirical heft to this argument.

To summarize, opaque proliferation is arguably the best of all possible worlds except for the outright prevention of proliferation, a policy stance the international community has been unable, and often unwilling, to impose on aspiring nuclear weapon states. This suggests that, contrary to the analyses of Shai Feldman and Susan Burns mentioned in Chapter 2, in regions where adversaries are determined to develop nuclear deterrent strategies, the international community should prefer opaque nuclear postures to transparent ones.

The Stability of Nuclear Deterrence in South Asia

Several types of nuclear deterrence act as a firebreak between peace and war in South Asia. First, nuclear weapons cast an existential deterrent shadow over Indo-Pakistani relations: both sides are dissuaded from fighting by the simple fact that their nuclear capabilities exist, and thus that war between them could escalate to a nuclear exchange. Another concern is that either country's nuclear first strike could redound to its disadvantage, given the short distances separating Indian and Pakistani targets, the vagaries of prevailing winds, and the consequent chance that radioactive fallout could drift back over the attacker's own territory. New Delhi and Islamabad are also dissuaded from aggression by the fear that any outbreak of hostilities might lead the opponent to attack one's own nuclear facilities with advanced conventional weapons, thereby raising the possibility of widespread radiation poisoning. This concern was illustrated by India's restraint in launching preventive strikes against Pakistan's nascent nuclear installations in the 1980s, a course of action that was apparently considered but ultimately rejected.

COULD DETERRENCE FAIL? While nuclear weapons have a deterrent impact on decision-making in South Asia, as they do elsewhere, no deterrent balance is impervious to breakdown. Deterrence of war is always a question of probability, not certainty. Where would India and Pakistan lie on a crisis stability continuum with war at one end and deterrence at the other? The outcome with the lowest probability is a premeditated attack by either side. At the nuclear level, the window of opportunity for an Indian preventive strike against Pakistani nuclear facilities has passed. Islamabad's nuclear program is too advanced for New Delhi to have sufficient confidence that it could disable Pakistan's retaliatory capability without suffering a devastating response. Preemptive nuclear strikes are also extremely unlikely, due to the deterrent power of first-strike uncertainty, or the existence of a kernel of doubt in the minds of the potential attacker's leaders about whether they could destroy all of the opponent's nuclear weapons preemptively. Also, having weathered the Brasstacks and Kashmir crises, Indian and Pakistani leaders can rest more easily in the knowledge that as tempers flared during these war scares, neither side was tempted into preemptive action.

At the conventional level, either country's full-scale invasion across established borders is also difficult to imagine. Islamabad knows that it would lose any conventional war it started, and while India could surely defeat Pakistan in a ground war, New Delhi would in doing so have to worry about the possibility of suffering a last-resort nuclear reprisal. No political objective would be worth that risk. At the unconventional level, the chance of war is still remote, but less so. India could conceivably launch limited military strikes across the LAC in Kashmir, whether to interdict supplies, destroy militant sanctuaries, or simply to warn Pakistan that India's tolerance has run out, that enough is enough. After all, New Delhi has paid a steep price for its counterinsurgency in Kashmir. The guerilla war is tying down several hundred thousand Indian Army and paramilitary soldiers, and at least 20,000 people have been killed in the fighting. Furthermore, India's international image has taken a severe beating since 1990, as human rights organizations have documented an array of excesses by Indian troops, such as rapes, looting, and torture. Finally, some Indian decision-makers fear that insurgent successes in Kashmir may embolden separatists in other states, ultimately threatening the integrity of the Indian federation.[24]

Balanced against these incentives to lash out at Pakistan is the overriding disincentive posed by Islamabad's nuclear muscle. This deterrent effect is best illustrated by comparing New Delhi's restraint since 1990 with its more aggressive behavior in South Asia's pre-nuclear era. In 1965, Pakistani support for rebellion in Indian-held Kashmir provoked Indian counterattacks on insurgent positions in the Pakistani part of the disputed territory. The result was war. New Delhi has so far refrained from such a strategy in the 1990s, at least in part because of the possibility that any major military engagement could lead to a nuclear war. Still, in the unlikely event that deterrence were to fail in South Asia, the most probable scenario is an Indian attack initially limited to Kashmir.

INADVERTENT WAR. Another possibility is inadvertent war. This is the notion that during a future crisis India and Pakistan might stumble into a conflict neither side actually wants. This fear of inadvertence stems from the supposedly inherent logic of preemption, each side's stated conventional military doctrine of "offensive-defense," and the shaky intelligence estimates of India's Research and Analysis Wing and Pakistan's Inter-Services Intelligence. From this perspective, miscalculation of the adversary's intentions by one or both sides might lead inexorably to a shooting war. As the fighting progresses, either or both sides (but most likely Pakistan) might ready nuclear weapons for last-resort use. At this point, goes this reasoning, all bets are off and a nuclear exchange is a real possibility. While compelling on the surface, this logic does not hold up to sustained scrutiny. None of the three Indo-Pakistani wars began inadvertently; indeed, all of the major international wars since the end of World War II have been premeditated. It is even less likely that two nuclear powers would slide down the slippery slope into war, given the additional margin of caution induced by nuclear weapons.

SOUTH ASIA'S MISSILE AGE. Another pressing issue for South Asian crisis stability concerns the likely strategic impact of nuclear-capable ballistic missiles. Indian and Pakistani missile deployments may have mixed effects. On one hand, nuclear-tipped ballistic missiles

---

24. For a concise update on the insurgency in Kashmir, see Surinder Singh Oberoi, "Kashmir is Bleeding," *Bulletin of the Atomic Scientists*, March/April 1997, pp. 24–32.

would further complicate each side's planning for a crippling first strike, thereby strengthening deterrence. On the other, they might also increase mutual counterforce temptations. As far as is known, today's subcontinental deterrent standoff is a pure, aircraft-borne, countervalue balance of terror: New Delhi and Islamabad implicitly threaten to inflict massive punishment on each other's cities. Absent ballistic missiles, there is little prospect of either side carrying out successful nuclear counterforce attacks. Deploying missiles may increase the likelihood of India and Pakistan adopting counterforce doctrines, mainly because missiles are invulnerable to interception. First-strike uncertainty would still be a daunting deterrent, but counterforce temptations would be stronger in a strategic dyad than in the current equation. All in all, it would be preferable to stay on the countervalue side of this threshold, but missile deployments are unlikely to generate severe instabilities.

LOOSE NUKES REVISITED. A final possibility—and the main nuclear danger in South Asia today—involves nuclear accidents and the unauthorized use of nuclear weapons. Although there is no evidence that loose nukes have posed problems during the region's short nuclear arms competition, neither is there any guarantee that this record will stand indefinitely. If another crisis erupts and war appears imminent, Islamabad might move to assemble nuclear weapons or at least signal such preparations to New Delhi for deterrent purposes. As discussed in Chapter 5, Pakistan may have made some nuclear preparations in 1990; the historical record at this point is incomplete. The main concern in this regard is that, as Gregory Giles writes, "any one of a number of shocks (e.g., fire, unintentional drops, or stray electrical charges) can directly or indirectly detonate the high explosive sphere surrounding a weapon's fissile core. Depending on the weapon's design, this could lead . . . to a full nuclear detonation."[25] If, however, India and Pakistan do not maintain assembled nuclear weapons, this stance constitutes a buffer against nuclear accidents and unauthorized nuclear use.

The Prospects for Nuclear Arms Control in South Asia

Given Indian and Pakistani recalcitrance regarding the NPT and the CTBT, is there any hope for nuclear arms control in South Asia? It will

---

25. Gregory F. Giles, "Safeguarding the Undeclared Nuclear Arsenals," *Washington Quarterly*, Vol. 16, No. 2 (Spring 1993), p. 173.

be useful here to recall that, contrary to the popular perception, Islamabad and New Delhi have already adopted several significant nuclear arms control measures, some tacit and some explicit. First and foremost, India (since 1974) and Pakistan have refrained from testing nuclear explosive devices. This is a tacit restraint that inhibits a variety of nuclear-related activities, including the miniaturization of nuclear warheads for mating with ballistic missiles and the development of thermonuclear weapons.[26] Second, New Delhi and Islamabad have signed and implemented an agreement not to attack each other's nuclear facilities, an accord unique in the short history of nuclear arms control. Third, Pakistan has evidently capped its production of highly enriched uranium, thereby limiting the number of nuclear weapons it could assemble quickly. Fourth, India has slowed and possibly halted the development of the *Agni* missile, which would arguably be its most effective nuclear delivery system. That these measures are different in form and substance from the various superpower arms control agreements should not blind us to the fact that the subcontinent's nuclear arms competition has been much less of a race than that of the superpowers.

DETERRENCE IS KEY. The key to future Indo-Pakistani nuclear arms control will be the continued robustness of deterrence. Although New Delhi and Islamabad each had its own particular combination of motivations for going nuclear, both share—along with other nuclear powers—the fundamental belief that nuclear weapons deter aggression. In an anarchical international system, where no supreme authority exists to impose stability, countries have two alternatives to nuclear deterrence: conventional deterrence and alliances. Conventional deterrence is likely to be problematic for New Delhi and Islamabad, owing to two pronounced imbalances of conventional power: Pakistan's *vis-à-vis* India and India's *vis-à-vis* China. In addition, external security guarantees are not likely to be forthcoming soon, both because of the continuing fluidity of post–Cold War international politics and the domestic preoccupations of the great powers. It is unrealistic, then, to expect that India and Pakistan will embrace nuclear disarmament in the future.

In all probability, New Delhi and Islamabad will only begin thinking seriously about denuclearization if and when the broader strategic arms reduction process expands to include Beijing, Jerusalem,

---

26. For a more detailed discussion of this issue, see *India-Pakistan Nuclear and Missile Proliferation*, pp. 29–33.

London, and Paris. Although there has been perceptible intellectual momentum in this direction,[27] it has yet to be accompanied by concrete political agreements. Ironically, the South Asian nuclear experience may provide a valuable model for a denuclearizing world.[28] Much of the recent thinking about long-term strategic nuclear arms control emphasizes the need to mitigate the possibility of preemptive, inadvertent, and accidental nuclear war by de-alerting the world's extant nuclear forces. This vision of the nuclear future resembles the status quo on the subcontinent: India and Pakistan probably maintain unassembled (albeit uninspected) nuclear arsenals, which deter aggression while minimizing the likelihood of nuclear accidents and nuclear terrorism. It is hard to dispute the contention that movement toward the Indo-Pakistani model by the other six nuclear powers would enhance global nuclear stability.

What makes this thought counterintuitive is not any objective reality; rather, it is that India and Pakistan have been labeled nuclear outlaws, despite the fact that they have simply been emulating their nuclear predecessors. The only difference is that the door to the nuclear club was slammed before they got inside. We would do well to remember that India and Pakistan are not nuclear criminals; unlike Iraq and North Korea, they did not sign the NPT only to violate its provisions when it became convenient to do so. Rather, they have reserved their right as sovereign nations to acquire—for deterrent purposes—the ultimate weapon. The United States should stop preaching nonproliferation while continuing to rely on nuclear deterrence to meet its own security needs. If a country protected by two vast oceans and a seemingly insurmountable lead in conventional military technologies still requires the insurance provided by nuclear weapons, why should India and Pakistan—with their much more vulnerable geopolitical positions and technological inferiority—be expected to denuclearize first? Paradoxically, it is mainly Washington's attitude, not New Delhi's or Islamabad's, that ensures the continuing legitimacy of nuclear weapons. The United States

---

27. See, for example, Bruce G. Blair, *Global Zero Alert for Nuclear Weapons* (Washington, D.C.: Brookings, 1995); Michael J. Mazarr, "Virtual Nuclear Arsenals," *Survival*, Vol. 37, No. 3 (Autumn 1995), pp. 7–26; *Report of the Canberra Commission on the Elimination of Nuclear Weapons, 1996* (available on the world-wide web home page of the Embassy of Australia, Washington, D.C.); and the remarks of retired U.S. Air Force General Lee Butler, National Press Club, Washington, D.C., December 4, 1996.

28. Perkovich, "Nuclear Third Way," pp. 102–104.

should stop preaching nuclear chastity until it, too, is willing to forswear nuclear weapons. The dictum "do as we say, not as we do" is hypocritical; great powers lead by example, not by empty words.

INDEX

A

Abdullah, Farooq, 137–138
  resignation of, 140
Abdullah, Mohammad, 66, 137
Afghanistan
  Soviet defeat in, 134
  Soviet invasion of, 75–76
  superpowers and, 92–93
  U.S. role in, 92–93
Arms control, 4
  opacity and, 188–190
Asymmetrical situations,
  preventive war scenarios and, 34–36
Atoms for Peace proposal, 73
Azad ("Free") Kashmir, 66

B

Bangladesh War (1971), 70–71
Bargaining. See Tacit bargaining
Beg, General Mirza Aslam, 131,
  135–136, 145
  Hersh thesis and, 154–155, 159
  meeting with Gates, Oakley, and
  Khan, 151
  nuclear deterrence and, 168
  Punjab military exercise and, 142
Bharatiya Janata Party (BJP), 136
  Indian government and, 144–145
Bhutto, Benazir
  briefing in Washington, 129–130
  election of, 135
  Kashmir crisis and, 140–141
  Kashmir militants and, 144
  lobbying for U.S. support (1995), 175
  nuclear deterrence and, 168
  nuclear non-attack agreement and,
  128–129
  U.S. Pakistan deal and, 129–130

Bhutto, Zulfikar Ali, 69, 73–74, 186
Blair, Bruce
  Cold War and, 27
  crisis instability and, 24
Border violations, Kashmir crisis
  (1990) and, 148
Brasstacks crisis, 91
  conventional deterrence and,
  113–114
  existential deterrence and, 112–113
  faux nuclear dimensions of, 110–112
  impact of, 132
  India's intentions and, 105–106
  India's motives and, 106–107
  India's stance on, 101–102
  India's stated objectives and, 96–97
  Indo-Pakistani military
  dynamics in, 99–100
  non-war and, 114–115
  Pakistan's concerns over, 97–99
  Pakistan's military movements
  and, 99
  Pakistan's northward feint, 100–101
  Pakistan's northward feint, India's
  response to, 110
  Pakistan's northward feint
  explained, 109
  Pakistan's perceptions, response to,
  108–109
  political-military dynamics of, 110
  quickened nuclear proliferation
  and, 117
  Sikh insurgency and, 94–95
  U.S. transparency-building and,
  118–120
Brown Amendment, 175
Bueno de Mesquita, Bruce, 15, 19
  on nuclear deterrence, 17
Bundy, McGeorge, 3, 46, 61, 185
Burns, Susan, 57, 59, 190
Burrows, William E., 155–156, 161
Bush, George, 172–173

C

Carnegie Endowment for International Peace, 120

Carter, Jimmy, 74–75

Castro, Fidel, 31, 32

Chernobyl, 30

China, 44

Clark, William, 143, 156–158, 161–162, 163, 165

Clinton, Bill, 174–175

Cohen, Avner, 3, 40–42

Cold War
counterforce targeting strategies and, 27
ending of, repercussions and, 134
existential deterrence and, 47–48
Indo-Pakistani animosity and, 67–68
nuclear weapons and, 11
opacity and the end of, 187–188
Soviet invasion of Afghanistan and, 75–77

Command, control, communications, and intelligence (C³I), 24, 27

Communication, tacit bargaining, opacity and, 53–54

Comprehensive Test Ban Treaty (CTBT), 4, 176–177

Conventional attacks
existential deterrence and, 60–61
troop deployment and, 147–148

Conventional deterrence, Brasstacks crisis and, 113–114

Countervalue doctrines, 27

Cuban Missile Crisis, 31
lessons of, 49–51

D

Democracy, Pakistan, India and, 135

Deterrence, governments versus terrorists and, 29–30

Dunn, Lewis, 11, 24, 33

E

Eisenhower, Dwight, "Atoms for Peace" and, 73

Escalation, fear of, 46

Existential deterrence, 3, 169–170, 184–185
Brasstacks crisis (1986–87) and, 112–113
Cold War and, 47–48
conventional attacks and, 60–61
defined, 46–47
Indo-Pakistani averted war and, 163–164
logic of, 52, 166
logic of nonproliferation unrealized and, 165–166
low-intensity operations and, 61–62
nuclear weapon stability, opaque proliferation and, 62
opacity and, 45, 48–49

F

Feldman, Shai, 56–57, 58–59, 190

Fetter, Steve, 20, 24, 186

Frankel, Benjamin, 2–3, 40–42, 57
Cold War, opacity and, 187

G

Gandhi, Indira, 73, 137
assassination of, 95

Gandhi, Rajiv, 76–77, 84–85, 86–87, 105–106, 138, 144
signed nuclear non-attack agreement, 128–129

Gates, Robert, 150
meeting with Khan, Oakley, and Beg, 151
meeting with Singh, Gujral, Sharma, and Ramanna, 151–152

Gates mission, 150

impact of, 161–162

message of, 151–152

nuclear weapons and, 162–163

Geopolitical arguments, 19–21

logic of nonproliferation and, 21–22, 179–180

logic of nuclear deterrence and, 20–21

Gujral, L.K.

meeting with Gates, Singh, Sharma, and Ramanna, 151–152

Gulf War, 25–26

H

Hersh, Seymour, 154–155

dispute of allegations of, 157

Gates mission, explanation of, 158

Hersh thesis and, 154–155, 159–160

Hersh thesis, 154–155, 159–160

disputed claims of, 159–160

Hinton, Deane, 118–119

Hussain, Mushahid, 131

editorial on A.Q. Khan's statements, 104

resignation of, 104–105

Hussein, Saddam, 32–33, 42

I

Inadvertent transparency-building, 55–56

Inadvertent war, 192

India

Comprehensive Test Ban Treaty and, 176–177

defense spending (1960–65), 69

leaders in, 95–96

nonalignment, leverage with superpowers and, 68

nonproliferation laws and, 74–75

nuclear capabilities (1996), 175–176

nuclear goals of, 53

nuclear policies of, 176

nuclear program evolution in, 72–73

nuclear weapon developments (1980s), 80

Pakistan's nuclear growth and, 84–85

Soviet Union and, 76–77

Indo-Pakistani

nuclear discourse, 123–124

nuclear dynamics (early 1980s), 87–88

nuclear non-attack agreement (1985), 87

nuclear preparedness (1990), 164–165

nuclear status (1986), 88–89

relations (1970s–80s), 137–138

Indo-Pakistani animosity

Bangladesh War (1971) and, 70–71

Cold War and, 67–68

Kashmir crisis, mutual perceptions and, 149–155

Kashmir dispute, genesis of, 65–67

pre-independence period and, 64–65

roots of, 64

South Asian nuclear arms competition and, 71–72

terms of partition and, 66

United Nations role in, 67

U.S preventive war measures in, 85

Indo-Pakistani near-nuclear war. See South Asia's near-nuclear war

Indo-Pakistani security rivalry (1986–87), 92–93

ethnic insurgencies and, 93–94

military scenarios for, 97

Indo-Pakistani War (1965), 69–70

Indo-Soviet peace and friendship treaty (1971), 76

International Atomic Energy Agency (IAEA), 74–75
Inter-Services Intelligence (ISI), 108, 140
Israel
    attack on Osirak nuclear facility, 86
    nuclear testing and, 40–41
    nuclear threats and, 42
    nuclear weapons and, 41–42
    opaque proliferation and, 44
    Osirak strike, 35

J

Jagmohan, 139–140
Jamaat-i-Islami, 140, 141
Jammu and Kashmir Liberation Front, 173–174
Junejo, Mohammad Khan, 96, 98

K

Kahn, Gulham Ishaq, 135–136, 156
    meeting with Gates, Oakley, and Beg, 151
    nuclear deterrence and, 168
Kashmir crisis (1990)
    background of, 134–136
    border violations and, 148
    genesis of, 65–67
    international implications of, 140–141
    military movements in, 142–144
    nuclear deterrence and, 147, 152–154
    nuclear threat and, 152–153
    war of words and, 144–145
Kashmiri Muslim "terrorists", 139
Kennedy, John, Cuban missile crisis and, 47–48
Kerr, Richard, 126, 154

Khan, A.Q., 82
    affair, responses and, 102–104, 120–121
    denial of claims, 104
    interview, faux nuclear implications and, 110–112
    Pakistani nuclear revelations and, 102–103
Khan, Ayub, 69, 186

L

Line of Actual Control (LAC), 137, 173–174
Logic of existential deterrence, 52, 166
Logic of nonproliferation, 1, 9, 11–14
    command, control argument of, 180–181
    existential deterrence and, 165–166
    five main arguments of, 16
    geopolitical arguments and, 179–180
    leaders and, 30–31
    loose nukes and, 28
    preventive war argument and, 182
    quantitative arguments for, 16–17, 178–179
    role in Kashmir crisis, 152–154
    timing and, 22
    undeterrables argument and, 181–182
    See also Nonproliferation
Logic of nuclear deterrence, 1–2, 9, 14–16, 152–154, 179–180
    command, control and, 24–25
    geopolitical arguments and, 20–21
    Kashmir crisis and, 152–154
    loose nukes and, 29
    preventive war and, 34
    "undeterrables" and, 31–32
Logic of nuclear nonproliferation
    irrationality, outcomes and, 32–33

Loose nukes, 193
  logic of nonproliferation and, 28
  logic of nuclear deterrence and, 29
  opacity and, 59
  problem of, 28
  South Asia experience and, 181

M

McNamara, Robert, 16–17
  Cuban missile crisis and, 47–48
Mearsheimer, John, 29, 113–114
Memorandum of Understanding,
  (May 1985), 77
Missile era, South Asia and, 130,
  192–193
Movement for the Restoration of
  Democracy, 93–94
Mutual assured destruction (MAD), 51

N

Nayar, Kuldip, 103–105
  accuracy of article by, 120–121
  interview, faux nuclear
  implications and, 110–112
  Pakistani nuclear revelations and,
  102–103
  release of story by, 103
Nehru, Jawaharlal, 68, 72
Nonproliferation
  command, control argument of,
  180–181
  command and control of small
  nuclear forces and, 23
  five main arguments of, 16
  geopolitical arguments and, 21–22
  intellectual lineage of the logic of,
  11–14
  irrationality, outcomes and, 32–33
  leaders and, 30–31
  logic of, 1, 9, 11

  preventive war argument and, 182
  preventive war imperatives and, 33
  quantitative arguments of, 16–17,
  178–179
  undeterrables argument and,
  181–182
  See also Logic of nonproliferation
NPT. See Nuclear Non-Proliferation
  Treaty (NPT)
"*n*th country problem", 12
  nuclear nonproliferation, quantitative arguments of and, 16–17
Nuclear arms control
  deterrence and, 194–196
  in South Asia, 193–194
Nuclear bluffing, 160–161
Nuclear danger, 3–4
  in South Asia, 5–6
Nuclear debates, 42
Nuclear deterrence, 179–180
  command, control and, 24–25
  existential deterrence and, 61–62
  failure potential and, 191–192
  geopolitical arguments and, 20–21
  logic of, 1–2, 9, 14–16, 152–154
  preventive war and, 34
  role in Kashmir crisis of, 152–154
  security studies and, 184
  South Asia and, 130–131, 168–169,
  190–192, 194–196
  stability of Third World versus
  superpowers and, 13
  Subrahmanyam, K. and, 167
  Sundarji, K. and, 167–168
  "undeterrables" and, 31–32
Nuclear developments, South Asia
  Brasstacks impact on, 118
  capabilities, resolve, signalling,
  164–165
Nuclear explosive device, defined,
  129

Nuclear Nonproliferation Act of 1978, 74

Nuclear Non-Proliferation Treaty (NPT), 2, 4, 176
  opaque proliferation and, 44
  results of, 2–3

Nuclear powers, interdependent interactions of, 25

Nuclear proliferation
  Brasstacks crisis and, 117–118
  debate over, 9–11
  quantitative arguments and, 17
  in South Asia, 1, 164–165, 171, 177–178
  summary of findings on, 183
  theoretical issues in, 1–2

Nuclear taboo, 6, 23, 55
  post-1945, 10

Nuclear weapons
  concerns about, 6
  denials about, 41–42
  deployment of, 42–43
  ethnocentric arguments about, 10–11
  Gates mission and, 162–163
  maturing of, 5–6
  opacity and, 56
  opaque proliferation, existential deterrence and stability of, 62
  soothing effects of, 6
  testing of, 40–41

O

Oakley, Robert, 138, 140, 156–158, 163
  Gates mission, explanation of, 158
  meeting with Gates, Khan, and Beg, 151

Opacity
  arms control and, 188–189
  Cold War and, 187

crisis stability and, 56–57
  impact of, 189
  loose nukes and, 59
  nuclear weapon stability and, 56
  Pakistan, U.S. pressure and, 81
  South Asian nuclear dynamics and, 187
  South Asian resilience and, 188
  tacit bargaining and, 53–54
  unknown risks, capabilities and, 58–59

Opaque proliferation, 2–3, 39–40, 187
  as an ideal type, 40–43
  communication spectrum in, 53–54
  defined, 40
  denial of nuclear weapons and, 41–42
  deployed nuclear weapons and, 42–43
  domestic imperatives for, 44–45
  existential deterrence and, 46, 48–49
  inadvertent transparency-building and, 55–56
  nuclear debates, doctrines and, 42
  Nuclear Non-Proliferation Treaty (NPT) and, 44
  nuclear program insulation and, 43
  nuclear threats and, 42
  nuclear weapon stability, existential deterrence and, 62
  reasons for, 43–44

P

Pakistan
  Comprehensive Test Ban Treaty and, 176–177
  inclusionary doctrine of, 68
  krytron affair and, 83–84
  leaders in, 95–96
  nonproliferation laws and, 74–75
  nuclear activity, (1983–85), 81–82

nuclear activity (1990), 156–157
nuclear activity (1996), 175–176
nuclear bluffing and, 160–161
nuclear goals of, 53
nuclear program evolution in, 73–74
nuclear signalling and, 82, 126
nuclear testing and, 40–41
nuclear weapon–free status of, 119–120
nuclear weapons and, 41–42
Pressler Amendment and, 83, 119, 174–175
Punjab military exercise and, 142–143
Soviet invasion of Afghanistan and, 75–77
U.S. aid to Pakistan, (1980–83), logic of, 79–80
U.S. pressure, opacity and, 81
U.S. strategic planning (1950s) and, 68
Peace, nuclear weapons and, 11
Political instability, 19–20
Political kidnapping, 139
Poonch rebels, 66
Potter, William, 13–14
Preemptive pressures, developing countries and, 23–24
Pressler Amendment, 83, 174, 175
definition of possession under the, 122–123
Pakistan's nuclear weapon–free status and, 119–120
Pakistan's violation of, questions about, 157
Preventive war argument, nonprolif-eration and, 182
Preventive war imperatives
logic of nuclear deterrence and, 34
nonproliferation and, 33
scenarios of, 34–36

Proliferation studies
(1940s–50s), 11–12
(1950s–60s), 12
(1970s–80s), 13
shift from central balance to Third World and, 13
Punjab border, 148

Q

Quantitative arguments
problems with, 17–18
for nonproliferation, 16–17
for nuclear deterrence, 17
nuclear pairs and, 18
stability argument problem and, 18–19

R

Ramanna, Raja, 141
meeting with Gates, Singh, Gujral, and Sharma, 151–152
Reagan, Ronald, 125–126
certification, Pakistan non-nuclear (1988), 128
Reorganized Army Plains Infantry Division (RAPID), 97
Research and Analysis Wing (RAW), 108
Riker, William, 15, 19
on nuclear deterrence, 17
Russett, Bruce, 17
problem of quantitative argument of, 18

S

Saf-e-Shikan, 99
Satellite coverage, 155
Sattar, Abdul, 140–141
Brasstacks and, 108–109

Gates mission and, 161–162
nuclear deterrence and, 168
Sayeed, Mufti Mohammad,
daughter's kidnapping and, 139
Schelling, Thomas, 53–54, 184–185
preemptive pressures and, 23–24
Sharma, V.N., 142–143
Hersh thesis, disputed claims of
and, 159
meeting with Gates, Singh, Gujral,
and Ramanna, 151–152
Sikh insurgency, 94
Simla Agreement, 77, 136–137
UN resolutions and, 137
Singh, V.P., 136, 139, 144–145, 146–147,
165
election of, 135
meeting with Gates, Gujral, Sharma,
and Ramanna, 151–152
nuclear warning to Pakistan of, 145
Sledge Hammer, 99
South Asia
Brasstacks, nuclear development
and, 118
consequences of nuclear
proliferation in, 171, 183
loose nukes and, 181, 193
missile age and, 1, 192–193
nuclear arms competition in, 71–72
nuclear arms control, prospects for,
193–194
nuclear capabilities (1980–86), 78
nuclear capabilities (1988–90),
126–127
nuclear capabilities (1990–97),
172–174
nuclear capabilities (1996), 175–176
nuclear danger in, 5–6
nuclear deterrence and, 130–131,
168–169, 190–191
nuclear proliferation, consequences
of, 177–178

opacity and resilience of, 188
South Asian Association for Regional
Cooperation (SAARC), 98
South Asia's near-nuclear war
aversion interpreted, 154
Hersh thesis and, 154–155, 156
U.S. intelligence regarding, 158–159
Soviet Union
Afghanistan, invasion of, 75–76
Afghanistan, vacating of, 173
appeal for restraint in South Asia to,
150
disintegration of, 4
India and, 76
Spector, Leonard, 124, 127–128, 131,
132
Stimson Center
Kashmir crisis, account of, 149
meeting, 158
Stimson transcript, Hersh thesis and,
160
Sundarji, General K., 88–89, 96–97,
105–106, 131, 147, 165
nonproliferation, command, control
argument of and, 180–181
nuclear deterrence and, 167–168
Superpowers
balance of, 51
nuclear competition of, 26–27
stability of versus Third World
countries, 13
Symington Amendment, 75, 79
extension of, 124–125
U.S. aid to Pakistan and, 122

T

Tacit bargaining
opacity and, 53–54
thresholds and, 54–55
Terrorists, deterrence of, 29–30

Third World
  civil-military relations in, 186
  economic liberalization and, 188
  nonproliferation, command, control of and, 23
  stability of versus superpowers, 13
Three Mile Island, 30
Trachtenberg, Marc, 46
  Cuban missile crisis and, 47–48
Transparency-building, 55–56
  Pakistan aid deliberations and, 122–123
  U.S., Islamabad's nuclear activities and, 124–126
  U.S. (1988–89), 127–128

U

United Nations, 67, 137
United States
  aid to Afghanistan and, 78
  aid to Pakistan, cutting of and, 124
  aid to Pakistan (1980–83), 78, 79–80
  aid to Pakistan (1980s), 75–77
  appeal for restraint in South Asia, 150
  "Atoms for Peace" and, 73
  Bhutto visit and, 129–130
  Carter administration and, 74–75, 78–79
  Clinton administration and, 174–175
  Cuban missile crisis and, 47–48
  Johnson administration and, 15
  preventive war measures, Indo-Pakistani animosity and, 85
  Reagan administration and, 75, 124–126
  South Asian nuclear arms race and, 82–83

  South Asian nuclear development and, 118
  South Asia's near-nuclear war and, 154
  Soviet invasion of Afghanistan and, 75–76
  Soviet relations, strategic views and, 185–186
  strategic planning and Pakistan and, 68
  transparency-building, Brasstacks and, 118–119

W

Waltz, Kenneth, 34
  command, control, nuclear deterrence and, 23
  geopolitical arguments and, 20–21
  loose nukes and, 29
  nonproliferation, Third World and, 23
  nuclear deterrence theory and, 15, 16
War
  inadvertent, 192
  preventative scenarios and, 34–36
  timely warning to prevent, 147
Weltman, John, 21, 31–32
Wentz, Walter, 14–15
Windrem, Robert, 155–156, 161

Y

Yom Kippur War, 22

Z

Zia, President, 131
  concerns regarding Brasstacks and, 108
  "cricket diplomacy" and, 102

The Robert and Renée Belfer Center for Science and International Affairs

Graham T. Allison, Director
John F. Kennedy School of Government
Harvard University
79 JFK Street, Cambridge, MA 02138
(617) 495-1400

The Belfer Center for Science and International Affairs (BCSIA) is the hub of research, teaching, and training in international security affairs, environmental and resource issues, and science and technology policy at Harvard's John F. Kennedy School of Government. The Center's mission is to provide leadership in advancing policy-relevant knowledge about the most important challenges of international security and other critical issues where science, technology, and international affairs intersect.

BCSIA's leadership begins with the recognition of science and technology as driving forces transforming international affairs. The Center integrates insights of social scientists, natural scientists, technologists and practitioners with experience in government, diplomacy, the military, and business to address these challenges. The Center pursues its mission in four complementary research programs:

- The International Security Program (ISP) addresses the most pressing threats to U.S. national interests and international security.

- The Environment and Natural Resources Program (ENRP) is the locus of Harvard's interdisciplinary research on resource and environmental problems and policy responses.

- The Science, Technology, and Public Policy (STPP) program analyzes ways in which science and technology policy influence international security, resources, environment, and development, and such cross-cutting issues as technological innovation and information infrastructure.

- The Strengthening Democratic Institutions (SDI) project catalyzes support for three great transformations in Russia, Ukraine, and the other republics of the former Soviet Union—to sustainable democracies, free market economies, and cooperative international relations.

The heart of the Center is its resident research community of more than one hundred scholars: Harvard faculty, analysts, practitioners, and each year a new, interdisciplinary group of research fellows. BCSIA sponsors frequent seminars, workshops, and conferences, many open to the public; maintains a substantial specialized library; and publishes books, monographs, and discussion papers. The Center's International Security Program, directed by Steven E. Miller, publishes the BCSIA Studies in International Security, and sponsors and edits the quarterly journal *International Security*.

The Center is supported by an endowment established with funds from Robert and Renée Belfer, the Ford Foundation, and Harvard University, by foundation grants, by individual gifts, and by occasional government contracts.